Enlightenment's Wake

'Gray is one of our best social and political theorists. . . . This powerful and radical work opens as many doors as it closes.'

New Statesman

'Gray is a clever and energetic political theorist in the analytical mode. He is also dauntingly well-read and up to date.'

Guardian

D1533990

Routledge Classics contains the very best of Routledge publishing over the past century or so, books that have, by popular consent, become established as classics in their field. Drawing on a fantastic heritage of innovative writing published by Routledge and its associated imprints, this series makes available in attractive, affordable form some of the most important works of modern times.

For a complete list of titles visit
www.routledge.com/classics

John
Gray

Enlightenment's Wake

Politics and culture at the close of the modern age

with an introduction by the author

London and New York

First published 1995 by Routledge

First published in Routledge Classics 2007
by Routledge
2 Park Square, Milton Park, Abingdon, Oxon OX14 4RN

Simultaneously published in the USA and Canada
by Routledge
270 Madison Ave, New York, NY 10016

Reprinted 2008

Routledge is an imprint of the Taylor & Francis Group, an informa business

© 1995 John Gray

Introduction to the Routledge Classics edition © 2007 John Gray

Typeset in Joanna by RefineCatch Limited, Bungay, Suffolk
Printed and bound in Great Britain by
The Cromwell Press, Trowbridge, Wiltshire

All rights reserved. No part of this book may be reprinted
or reproduced or utilized in any form or by any electronic,
mechanical, or other means, now known or hereafter
invented, including photocopying and recording, or in
any information storage or retrieval system, without
permission in writing from the publishers.

British Library Cataloguing in Publication Data
A catalogue record for this book is available from the British Library

Library of Congress Cataloging in Publication Data
A catalog record for this book has been requested

ISBN10: 0–415–42404–6
ISBN13: 978–0–415–42404–2

Contents

PREFACE

In this book a train of thought developed in my earlier books, *Liberalisms: Essays in Political Philosophy, Post-liberalism: Studies in Political Thought* and *Beyond the New Right: Markets, Government and the Common Environment*, is brought to a conclusion. In *Liberalisms*, I considered the search for foundations within liberal thought, examined the various strategies of argument in which that search had been embodied, and concluded that all of them – including those I had myself pursued – ended in failure. *Liberalisms* concluded on a sceptical note, in that it suggested that all foundationalist versions of liberalism were bound to fail, but said little as to what then became of liberalism, or how liberal practice was best to be conceived. In *Post-liberalism*, I tried to remedy this defect, arguing more positively for an historicist understanding of liberal practice in which the central institutions of liberal civil society were theorized as being generally appropriate vehicles for the protection and enhancement of human well-being in the circumstances of the late modern period, but the universalist claims of doctrinal liberalism were firmly rejected. The subject matter of *Beyond the New Right* was the capture of Western conservatism by a species of paleo-liberalism whose intellectual credentials were slight, and which in political practice was likely to prove self-defeating. In that book, I attacked the political thought of the New Right for its fundamentalist conception of market institutions and its hubristic neglect of the human need for common life. My argument in that book ended with a defence of traditional conservatism, qualified by concerns about environmental stability and integrity suggested by Green thought. The argument of *Beyond the New Right* was a development of that of *Post-liberalism*, in that it suggested that the historic inheritance of liberal institutions and practice was endangered, not as hitherto by left-liberal policy and ideology, but by the market fundamentalism sponsored by the New Right.

In *Enlightenment's Wake* a decade's thinking about liberalism, its grounds, scope and limits, is completed. Against the position adopted at the end of *Beyond the New Right*, I argue here, most comprehensively and systematically in Chapter 7, that the hegemony within conservative thought and policy of neo-liberal ideology is so complete that there is now no historical possibility – political or intellectual – of a return to traditional conservatism. Western conservatism everywhere, but especially in the United States, is now merely a variety of the Enlightenment project of universal emancipation and a universal civilization. Further, contrary to the view I adopted at the close of *Post-liberalism*, the historicist argument for liberal institutions – that they are nearly universally mandated as conditions of human well-being in the late modern period – neglects the variety of institutions within which a *modus vivendi* can be achieved in our time, and unduly privileges variations on Western models. In several sections of the book, but particularly in Chapter 5 on the post-communist countries, I argue that Western liberal institutions not only have no universal claim in theory but also are often flawed in practice; except where their underlying cultural and political traditions are themselves European, the post-communist countries have good reason to seek to develop new, non-Western institutions of their own. The thesis that the institutions of Western civil society are functionally indispensable to the success of a modern economy, though at first sight plausible, is theoretically and historically groundless. Accordingly, I move forward from the position set out in *Post-liberalism* to defend a pluralist perspective, in which no privileges are accorded to liberal practice, and the animating project is that of framing terms of harmonious coexistence among different cultures and traditions. This position is developed in Chapters 8 and 9, against the background of my criticisms of the dominant schools of Anglo-American liberal fundamentalism, which are set out in Chapter 1.

In the last and longest chapter, which has been written for this volume, I argue that all schools of contemporary political thought are variations on the Enlightenment project, and that that project, though irreversible in its cultural effects, was self-undermining and is now exhausted. Fresh thought is needed on the dilemmas of the late modern age which does not simply run the changes on intellectual traditions whose matrix is that of the Enlightenment. This is so, in part, because some of our dilemmas issue from aspects of the Enlightenment itself – in particular its assault on cultural difference, its embodiment of Western cultural imperialism as the project of a universal civilization, and its humanist conception of humankind's relations with the natural world. This last element of the Enlightenment has been transmitted even to cultures which have modernized without Westernizing, and constitutes the West's only truly universal inheritance to humankind, which is nihilism. Because this condition has its roots in ancient and even primordial Western traditions, there can be no question of curing the disorders of modernity by a return to tradition. Nor does the stance of post-modernism, in which the emancipatory project of the Enlightenment is asserted incongruously from within the perspective of a critique of its cultural ground in the modern world-view, begin to plumb the depth of our condition. I try to open up a new path of thinking on these questions in the last chapter of this book.

I am grateful to the directors and staff of the Social Philosophy and Policy Center, Bowling Green, Ohio, where part of the work on some of the chapters that make up this book was done, for their support. I am indebted to the Principal and Fellows of my College for periods of sabbatical leave in which I was able to pursue the thoughts about which I have written here.

John Gray
Jesus College, Oxford
September 1994

ACKNOWLEDGEMENTS

Chapter 1 was published as 'Against the New Liberalism', *Times Literary Supplement*, 3 July 1992; Chapter 2 was published as 'Why the Owl Flies Late: The Inadequacies of Academic Liberalism', *Times Literary Supplement*, 15 October 1993; Chapter 3 was published as 'The Failings of Neutrality', *The Responsive Community*, vol. 3, no. 2, Spring 1993; Chapter 4 was published as the concluding chapter of my monograph, *The Strange Death of Perestroika: Causes and Consequences of the Soviet Coup*, by the Institute for European Defence and Strategic Studies, London, September 1991; Chapter 5 was published as *The Post-Communist Societies in Transition: A Social Market Perspective* by the Social Market Foundation, London, February 1994; Chapter 6 was published as 'Agonistic Liberalism', *Social Philosophy and Policy*, vol. 12, no. 1, Winter 1995; Chapter 7 was published as *The Undoing of Conservatism* by the Social Market Foundation, London, June 1994; Chapter 8 was published as 'After the New Liberalism', *Social Research*, vol. 61, Fall 1994, special issue on *Liberalism*; Chapter 9 was published as 'From Post-liberalism to Pluralism', in Ian Shapiro (ed.) *Nomos XXXVIII*,

Political Order, New York: New York University Press, 1995; Chapter 10 is published for the first time in this volume.

INTRODUCTION TO THE ROUTLEDGE CLASSICS EDITION

When *Enlightenment's Wake* first appeared twelve years ago the idea that we inhabit a post-Enlightenment world was received with some scepticism. The claim that we are living in 'an age distinguished by the collapse of the Enlightenment project on a world-historical scale', 'dominated by renascent particularisms, militant religions and resurgent ethnicities' – as I put it at the start of the book's first chapter – seemed to be at odds with the dominant forces of the time. Communism had collapsed, democracy was spreading and globalization was advancing rapidly. Western governments and international institutions framed their policies on the assumption that these trends were irreversible. In the academy liberal political theorists dutifully reproduced the consensus: the process might not be strictly inevitable, but there could be no reasonable doubt that, sooner or later, all of humankind would join the West in accepting Enlightenment values.

Not much more than a decade later this certainty has crumbled into dust. Enlightenment values are now seen as mortally threatened, while the faith in progress that was affirmed so adamantly just a few years ago has been replaced by a sense of being locked in an apocalyptic struggle with the forces of darkness. A major factor in this shift of mood has been Islamist terrorism – a genuine threat, but far less serious than those of Nazism and communism that were overcome in the last century. Others are the development of a new type of authoritarianism in post-communist Russia, which is using its natural resources to reassert itself as a great power, and the dawning realization that with the emergence of China the global hegemony of Western political values is finally at an end. Again, the revival of religion has shaken the belief that society is bound to become more secular as science advances. If the Enlightenment myth of progress in ethics and politics continues to have a powerful hold, it is more from fear of the consequences of giving it up than from genuine conviction.

The shift of mood from a sense of triumph to moral panic was predictable. One of Enlightenment's Wake's themes is that the collapse of communism was a world-historic defeat for the Enlightenment project. Communism was not a type of oriental despotism, as generations of Western scholars maintained. It was an authentic continuation of a Western revolutionary tradition, and its downfall – after tens of millions of deaths were inflicted in the pursuit of its utopian goals – signalled the start of a process of de-Westernization. Liberal economists may have imagined that in rejecting central planning Russia and China would embrace the free market; but in holding to this reductive faith they showed themselves to be the last Marxists. Having shaken off communism these countries have not adopted another, neo-liberal Western ideology. They have resumed their long-term histories, with Russia ambiguously positioned between Europe and Asia, and China borrowing freely from Western countries while standing definitely outside 'the West'. Again, there is nothing surprising in the onward march of fundamentalism in

America, the Middle East and other parts of the world. It is an Enlightenment dogma that the advance of science advances human rationality; but there has never been much to support this article of humanist faith. The fall of communism was the death of an Enlightenment utopia. Its demise was to be welcomed; but it did no more than return us to the normal pattern of human conflict. The growth of knowledge increases human power, otherwise it leaves humans as they have always been – weak, savage and in thrall to every kind of fantasy and delusion.[1]

As in the last century, so at present there are powerful currents of thought that claim to reject the Enlightenment. A spurious kind of Counter-Enlightenment can be found in many areas of religion, politics and the arts; but in nearly all cases it will be found that Enlightenment thinking continues to exercise a formative influence. Fundamentalist religion is not the radical rejection of modernity it imagines itself to be: like Nazism, it is a peculiarly modern phenomenon.[2] Radical Islam sees itself as the enemy of the Enlightenment; but Islamist thought has been deeply shaped by modern Western radical ideologies – such as Jacobinism and Leninism – that seek to realize Enlightenment hopes by the methodical use of violence. Christian fundamentalists may believe they reject the modern world. Yet their flirtation with pseudo-sciences such as Creationism and Intelligent Design shows that they submit to the power of modern science, and like followers of the Enlightenment believe human salvation can be found in an increase of knowledge. Though they reject the Enlightenment, they are unable to escape its spell.

For most of its disciples the appeal of the Enlightenment has always been that of an *ersatz* religion. The Enlightenment was another version of Christian myth more than it was a critique of Christianity, and the evangelical atheism that has staged an anachronistic revival in recent years is significant chiefly as a sign of the unreality of secularization. Yet within the Enlightenment there are thinkers in whom we can find a genuine critique of transcendental and secular faith. Spinoza's philosophy understands humans as integral parts of the natural world[3] – a view of things developed by Freud, perhaps the twentieth century's greatest Enlightenment thinker. In another Enlightenment tradition the writings of Hobbes and Hume contain an incisive criticism of later conceptions of progress. Yet again Schopenhauer – a more than usually sceptical disciple of Kant, the supreme Enlightenment philosopher – shows how critical thinking pursued to the end subverts Enlightenment humanism. One way or another these are all Enlightenment thinkers. The fact that we can still learn from them shows that we cannot simply reject our Enlightenment inheritance – any more than we can simply reject the religious inheritance of which the Enlightenment was a late and oblique expression.

The Enlightenment is a part of the way we live and think. The point is not to accept or reject it but to understand it. This requires that we view it not as partisans or enemies but from a distance, as if we were excavating a lost religion. In fact, even more than when this book was first published, commentators and politicians are invoking 'Enlightenment values' as an antidote for contemporary ills. If only we return to these pristine verities, they assure us, freedom will be secure and toleration will thrive. Yet Enlightenment values have very often been illiberal, racist or totalitarian. 'Scientific racism' – a spin-off from nineteenth-century Positivism – was used in the twentieth century as a rationale for genocide, and there can be no doubt about the Enlightenment pedigree of Leninism. Just as religious fundamentalists present a severely simplified version of the faith to which they want to return, Enlightenment fundamentalists present a sanitized copy of the tradition they seek to revive. In so doing, they block understanding of the Enlightenment's role in our present difficulties.

Enlightenment thinkers believed they served the cause of civilization. But when the political movements they spawned adopted terror as an instrument of social engineering – as happened in revolutionary France and communist Russia and China – it was barbarism that ensued, and a similar process is underway today. In a curious turn the world's pre-eminent Enlightenment regime has responded to terrorism by relaxing the prohibition on torture that was one of the Enlightenment's true achievements. Neo-conservatism – which is still, despite its ruinous record, the predominant political tendency in a number of Western countries – may be the last of the Enlightenment ideologies; but it too is ready to use terror to realize its utopian goals. It cannot be long before liberal theory, faithfully following in the track of power, contains theories of justice in which the right to torture is officially recognized.[4] Liberal theorists are less likely to follow the neo-conservative shift towards a chiliastic view of history, if only because the academy – now as in the past obsessively secular – has a blind spot in regard to religion. In America Christian and Enlightenment fundamentalists have joined forces, with the result that belief in progress has been supplanted by a chiliastic view of history. In the US as in Iran, the apocalyptic myths of Western religion, which fuelled the totalitarian movements of the past century, have re-emerged as forces in global conflict. Whereas Enlightenment thinkers believed religion would in future wither away or become politically marginal, at the start of the twenty-first century religion is at the heart of politics and war.[5]

The clamour for a return to the Enlightenment should not distract us from the fact that it has ceased to be a living body of thought. It would be useful to accept that we live in a post-Enlightenment time and do what we can to cope with its dangers. Instead the wake continues, while those who have not been invited to the party turn to other faiths.

NOTES

1   I explore contemporary humanism in *Straw Dogs: Thoughts on Humans and Other Animals*, Granta Books, 2nd edn, 2003.

2   The role of Enlightenment thinking in Nazism and radical Islam is examined in my *Al Qaeda and What It Means To Be Modern*, Faber and Faber, 2nd edn, 2007.

3   I discuss the power of Spinoza's philosophy in my 'Reply to Critics' in John Horton and Glen Newey (eds), *The Political Theory of John Gray*, Routledge, 2007.

4   I present a Swiftian liberal defence of torture in *Heresies: Against Progress and Other Illusions*, Granta Books, 2004, Chapter 15, 'Torture; a modest proposal', pp. 132–8.

5   For the influence of Christian myth on Enlightenment thinking and the re-emergence of apocalyptic beliefs in politics see my book *Black Mass: Apocalyptic Religion and the Death of Utopia*, Penguin Books, 2007.

1

AGAINST THE NEW LIBERALISM

It is a commonplace that political philosophy was reborn in 1971. In the interwar period, and then again for a quarter of a century after the Second World War, we are told, scepticism about the subject itself had inhibited any treatment of its fundamental questions that was systematic and comprehensive and, above all, that issued in rationally compelling principles for the evaluation of political institutions and the guidance of political conduct. The climate of opinion in general philosophy – as expressed in positivist accounts of meaning, emotivism in moral theory and the broader influence of the ordinary language philosophies – seemed to have rendered hopeless the projects of political philosophers working in an older and grander tradition that encompassed Aristotle and John Stuart Mill. It seemed to suggest that the most that could reasonably be hoped for was a succession of exercises in 'the analysis of concepts' – that is to say, armchair investigations of recent and local uses of words which derived whatever interest or authority they possessed from an appeal to the linguistic and moral intuitions, not of the words' users, but of philosophers in their armchairs – of the sort undertaken in 1965 in Brian Barry's *Political Argument*.[1]

Whatever else may be questionable in the conventional wisdom, it is sound in its judgement that we were spared the dismal prospect of political philosophy coming under the influence of an anachronistic methodology of conceptual analysis by the publication in 1971 of John Rawls's *A Theory of Justice*,[2] in which the classical enterprise of the subject was resumed in an uncompromising and architectonic fashion. Nor can it sensibly be denied that political philosophy since the early 1970s has been – at least in the English-speaking world – in very substantial part a commentary on Rawls's work. It remains very doubtful that Rawls's work has revived the enterprise of political philosophy in anything resembling its traditional forms. Indeed, it is arguable that the tradition of liberal theorizing it inaugurated has done little more than articulate the prejudices of an Anglo-American academic class that lacks any understanding of political life in our age – an age distinguished by the collapse of the Enlightenment project on a world-historical scale. Because political philosophy in the Anglo-American mode remains for the most part animated by the hopes of the Enlightenment, above all by the hope that human beings will shed their traditional allegiances and their local identities and unite in a universal civilization grounded in generic humanity and a rational morality, it cannot even begin to grapple with the political dilemmas of an age in which political life is dominated by renascent particularisms, militant religions and resurgent ethnicities. As a result, the main current in political philosophy, which remains wedded to the Enlightenment project in the particularly uncompelling form of a species of eviscerated Kantian liberalism, has condemned itself to political nullity and intellectual sterility. Political philosophy may have been reborn in 1971, but it was a stillbirth.

The common tale of the recent death and miraculous rebirth of political philosophy is in truth a piece of academic folklore. The 1950s and 1960s witnessed a number of seminal contributions to the subject – Berlin on liberty, Hart on law, Hayek on the constitution of a liberal state and Oakeshott on rationalism in politics, to mention only the most distinguished of them. Moreover, what is not often noticed is the peculiar, and for that matter parochial character of the species of political philosophy that Rawls's work exemplifies, and whose hegemony within political philosophy Rawls's work has assured. For Rawls, as for those who follow him in the most essential aspects of his project, such as Ronald Dworkin and Bruce Ackerman, political philosophy is the application to the constitution of the state of the moral point of view, where this is conceived as the impartial or the impersonal point of view. The enterprise of the political philosopher is that of propounding and grounding a political morality – one that is agent-neutral in that it does not rest on particularistic loyalties or conceptions of the good but instead has its foundation in universal principles of justice or rights. For these writers political philosophy is not, as it was for Aristotle and for John Stuart Mill, say, an inquiry into the human good that has as its precondition a theory of human nature. It is an inquiry into the right whose agenda is justice and whose content is given, not by any investigation of human beings as we find them in the world, with their diverse histories and communities, but by an abstract conception of the person that has been voided of any definite cultural identity or specific historical inheritance. It is obvious that this project – the project of deriving principles of justice or right from the nature of the person – is a Kantian project. The oddity of this project, as it is pursued in Rawls and his followers, is that it is conducted without reference to the metaphysical doctrines – about noumenal selfhood, for example – that are the matrix of all of Kant's ethics and political thought.

The Kantian liberalism sponsored by Rawls, which has secured a dominant place for itself in Anglo-American political philosophy, has the dubious distinction of lacking anything like a philosophical anthropology, or any other sort of metaphysical commitment. It takes its bearings, not from an account of human nature or of the more permanent features of the human circumstance, but from a conception of the person that is, avowedly in the work of the later Rawls, a distillation of the conventional wisdom of liberal democratic regimes. In the later Rawls the conventional wisdom is unmistakably that of the liberal establishment in North American universities – which perhaps justifies the description of his project as Kantianism in one country; certainly, it limits the interest of his project for those who do not share the unexamined intuitions of the US academic *nomenklatura*. This new liberalism prides itself in remaining on the surface, philosophically speaking, and in having as its *telos* a practical goal – that of securing agreement on principles of justice that allow for peaceful coexistence in a constitutional democracy of persons having divergent and sometimes incommensurable conceptions of the good life and views of the world. The oddity, and indeed the absurdity, of this new Kantian liberalism – one that has cut itself loose from the traditional concerns of philosophy so as to pursue the political objective of practical agreement – is that it is at the same time elaborated at a vast distance from political life in the real world. The theorists of the new Kantian liberalism speak for no political interest or constituency, even in the liberal democracies to which their reflections are directed; few members of the political classes in their respective countries know what these theorists are thinking, and none cares. Accordingly, the thoughts of the new liberals evoke no political echo in any of the liberal democracies: the project of securing practical agreement on principles of justice among metaphysically and historically neutered Kantian selves arouses little interest, inexplicably, among the political classes, or the voters, of the Western world, or anywhere else.

For the most part, in consequence, contemporary political philosophers of the presently dominant school are reduced to talking with each other, and to no one else, about topics of interest to no one else, least of all in the liberal democracies they are supposed to be addressing. In part, no doubt, the manifest political irrelevance of contemporary political philosophy, exquisitely ironic in view of the declared practical goals of its dominant school, is merely an aspect of the political marginality of the Anglo-American academic class itself. Its self-appointed role as the intellectual voice of an alienated counter-culture, hostile to its own society and enamoured of various exotic regimes – of which it knows, in fact, nothing – has acquired a Monty Pythonish character, as the peoples and even the rulers of these regimes have exposed their failings to a pitiless scrutiny in which the pretensions of their ruling ideologies have been devastatingly deflated. (That the absurdist aspect of contemporary Western academic discourse about economic systems is lost on its practitioners is convincingly confirmed by a 1992 issue of the journal, *Ethics*, in which a motley crew of Western academics gravely discusses various aspects of market socialism – a conception exposed to universal derision in the transitional societies of the post-communist world where it originated decades ago. The contributors to *Ethics* might have done better to discuss the prospects of the restoration of monarchy in Russia – far less of an exercise in anachronism, and just conceivably a topic of some interest to those whose fates it might affect.) The collapse of any political model for the Anglo-American oppositional intelligentsia has done little for its political credibility, already negligible in domestic terms. The political vacuity of much recent political philosophy, especially that of the new Kantian liberalism, may, however, have causes other than, and deeper than, the political risibility of its practitioners. It may be explicable by reference to central features of recent political philosophy, and in particular to the continued hegemony within it of an

Enlightenment project that history has passed by and which is now significant only as the modernist ideology of the liberal academic nomenklatura of Western societies that are themselves in evident decline.

Consider, in this regard, the central category of the intellectual tradition spawned by Rawls's work – the category of the person. In Rawls's work, as in that of his followers, this is a cipher, without history or ethnicity, denuded of the special attachments that in the real human world give us the particular identities we have. Emptied of the contingencies that in truth are essential to our identities, this cipher has in the Rawlsian schema only one concern – a concern for its own good, which is not the good of any actual human being, but the good we are all supposed to have in common, which it pursues subject to constraints of justice that are conceived to be those of impartiality. In this conception, the principles of justice are bound to be the same for all. The appearance of a plurality of ciphers in the Rawlsian original position must be delusive, since, having all of them the same beliefs and motives, they are indistinguishable. So it is that, even in its later version, in which it has suffered a sort of Hegelian or Deweyan mutation, Rawls's project remains a universalist one, in that its results are the same for all those to whom it is meant to apply. The basic liberties – apparently a uniquely determinate and finally fixed set of compossible or dovetailing freedoms – will be, then, the same for all, as will the principles of distribution. It will not matter by whom we are governed, so long as governments satisfy common standards of justice and legitimacy.

Now there is in the recent literature a common objection to this Rawlsian project, made most lucidly and judiciously by Thomas Nagel in his Equality and Partiality,[3] which captures something of its implausibility and strangeness. Like much else in modern moral and political theory that has been influenced by Kant and by utilitarianism, Rawls's theory of justice equates the moral point of view with that of impartiality, and thereby denies moral standing to personal projects and attachments, except in so far as they are compatible with impersonal standards of justice. Nagel argues that this account of the ethical life accords an undue privilege to the standpoint of impartiality, whereas any acceptable view of morality must give full recognition to each, while accepting that their demands will never be wholly reconcilable. This is a refreshing departure from the myopic perspective of impartiality, but it is not a fundamental one, since the personal point of view which Nagel seeks to rehabilitate remains that of the Kantian cipher. In the real world, human beings think of themselves, not as essentially persons having a diversity of contingent relationships and attachments, but as being constituted by their histories and their communities, with all their conflicting demands. It is a fact of fundamental importance that the subjects of the former Soviet Union asserted themselves against its power not as persons, but as peoples. Nor is the disposition of human beings to constitute for themselves particular and exclusive identities, and to link the legitimacy of governments with their recognition, a phenomenon of modern times alone; it is as perennial and universal as the diversity of natural languages, and as distinctively human. It is wholly characteristic of recent liberal theory that, while prepared to acknowledge that political morality cannot be entirely agent-neutral, Nagel refuses to allow that the subject of agent-relative moralities is often collective, not personal: persons may be thwarted if they lack opportunities for expressing the identities they have as members of groups, he tells us,[4] but communities or peoples have no irreducible right to self-determination. The subject matter of justice cannot, except indirectly, be found in the histories of peoples, and their often tragically conflicting claims; it must be always a matter of individual rights. It is obvious that this liberal position cannot address, save as an inconvenient datum of human psychology, the sense of injustice arising from belonging to an oppressed community that, in the shape of nationalism, is the strongest political force of our century. It is not surprising, then, that the truth that human beings individuate themselves as members of historic communities having memories that cross the generations, not as specimens of generic humanity or personhood having a history only by accident, rarely figures in recent work, Stuart Hampshire's *Innocence and Experience* being a noteworthy exception.[5] Nor, given the unreflectively individualist bias of contemporary Anglo-American political philosophy, is it in the least anomalous that there should be only one comprehensive study of the philosophical dilemmas generated by principles of national self-determination, Allen Buchanan's *Secession* – a profound investigation of the subject that is further enriched by its illuminating use of actual historical examples.[6]

The great distance from political life of most political philosophy is partly a result of the abstract individualism by which it is animated. It is far from being confined to works which defend an individualist minimum of government. Individualist assumptions are present, in a wholly unselfcritical fashion, in Robert Nozick's *Anarchy, State and Utopia*,[7] and they are invoked in an incomparably more persuasive, if also ultimately unsuccessful way, in Loren Lomasky's unjustly neglected *Persons, Rights and the Moral Community*.[8] Abstract individualism permeates Ronald Dworkin and Bruce Ackerman's work, where it is harnessed to an egalitarian political morality. It is present (though in a far more reflective and historically self-conscious fashion than in Rawls) in David Gauthier's *Morals by Agreement*.[9] What all these have in common with Rawls's work is the deployment of an unhistorical and abstract individualism in the service of a legalist or jurisprudential paradigm of political philosophy. The task of political philosophy is conceived as one of deriving the ideal constitution – assumed, at least in principle, to be everywhere the same. This is so, whether its upshot be Rawls's basic liberties, Nozick's side-constraints, or Dworkin's rights-as-trumps. The presupposition is always that the bottom line in political morality is the claims of individuals, and that these are to be spelt out in terms of the demands of justice or rights. The consequence is that the diverse claims of historic communities, if they are ever admitted, are always overwhelmed by the supposed rights of individuals. The notion that different communities might legitimately have different legal regimes for abortion or pornography, for example, is hardly considered. Indeed, it becomes difficult to state such a proposition intelligibly, as the discourse of rights increasingly drives out all others from political life. If the theoretical goal of the new liberalism is the supplanting of politics by law, its practical result – especially in the United States, where rights discourse is already the only public discourse that retains any legitimacy – has been the emptying of political life of substantive argument and the political corruption of law. Issues, such as abortion, that in many other countries have been resolved by a legislative settlement that involves compromises and which is known to be politically renegotiable, are in the legalist culture of the United States matters of fundamental rights that are intractably contested and which threaten to become enemies of civil peace. The new liberalism that dominates Anglo-American political philosophy is a faithful image of the political culture that gave it birth.

It is not denied here that recent work contains some trenchant criticisms of the dominant school. In Joel Feinberg's four-volume *The Moral Limits of the Criminal Law*,[10] an older and wiser Millian tradition is revived in which the political philosopher, rather than posing as a constitution-maker, addresses the ideal legislator, who perceives the necessity of trade-offs among conflicting interests and values. A number of communitarian theorists have illuminated the questionable conceptions of the subject and the subject's relations with common forms of life which underpin fashionable liberal ideals of the priority of justice over other political virtues and of the neutrality of justice with regard to rival conceptions of the good. Michael Sandel's *Liberalism and the Limits of Justice*,[11] in which Rawlsian theory is characterized as a theory appropriate to a society of strangers lacking any deep or rich common culture, is usually considered the first of these communitarian critiques. However, in Alasdair MacIntyre's earlier and brilliantly destructive *After Virtue*,[12] the sources of latter-day liberalism in a fragmented moral vocabulary embodying no coherent conception of the human good are exposed, while in his *Whose Justice? Which Rationality?*,[13] a no less interesting, if less successful attempt is made to combine the denial of any conception of rationality that tries to transcend the dependency of all reasoning on the authority of tradition with the thesis that the account of the good found in one tradition – the Thomistic-Aristotelian tradition – nevertheless has a superior claim on reason. A similar argument, focusing on the etiolated conception of the self that suffuses liberal thought, is pursued at instructive length in the work of Charles Taylor. It is in Michael Walzer's *Spheres of Justice*[14] that the most ambitious attempt is made at developing an alternative to the spurious universality of liberal justice – one that forswears the standpoint of externality on our practices affected in Rawls and Dworkin in favour of a method of immanent criticism. Walzer's book is arresting in its insistence that elucidating ideas of justice is a sort of social and historical phenomenology, not the statement of timeless verities; and it is welcome in its pluralist insight that justice is complex not simple, with different distributive principles being applicable to different goods according to the meanings those goods have in various social contexts. This phenomenological approach to justice is helpful, in that it turns us away from the hallucinatory perspectives of Kantian liberalism to the real world of human practices and forms of life – families, schools, workplaces, nation-states, and so on. Like other communitarian thinkers, however, Walzer is reluctant to accept that abandoning the universalist standpoint of doctrinal liberalism leaves liberal practice without privileges, as only one form of life among many. He will not see that the method of immanent criticism he advocates by no means guarantees outcomes congenial to liberal sensibilities – that it may well be subversive of liberal practice. This blindness in Walzer is one he shares with virtually all of the communitarian critics of liberalism, and it has the same root. The community invoked by these writers is not one that anyone has ever lived in, an historic human settlement with its distinctive exclusivities, hierarchies and bigotries, but an ideal community, in its way as much of a cipher as the disembodied Kantian self the communitarians delight in deflating. In our world – the only one we know – the shadow cast by community is enmity, and the boundaries of communities must often be settled by war. This is the lesson of history, including the latest history of the post-communist states. It is typical of recent political philosophy, even in its communitarian variants, that it should be so far removed from the actual practices of common life as it is found everywhere. Communitarian thought still harbours the aspiration expressed in those forms of the Enlightenment project, such as Marxism, that are most critical of liberalism – that of creating a form of communal life from which are absent the practices of exclusion and subordination that are constitutive of every community human beings have ever lived in. There is another irony here – in the fact that, whereas it remains committed to the Enlightenment project in one of its most primitive forms, the main current in recent political philosophy seems to be wholly untouched by the disillusioned sociological vision of Weber and Durkheim, who must be among the Enlightenment's most gifted children.

The most profound and subtle critique of liberalism comes not from a communitarian but from Joseph Raz, in whose *The Morality of Freedom*[15] liberalism itself takes a communitarian turn. Raz's critique is of the utmost importance, partly because it is in considerable measure an immanent criticism of recent liberalism – and all the more devastating for that – and partly because it encompasses a restatement of liberalism in which its dependency on individualism is removed. Raz argues, so far as I can see demonstratively, that no political morality can be rights-based, so that the Kantian project of a purely deontic political morality is broken-backed; that principles of justice and distribution can never be foundational in ethics; that egalitarian and libertarian political principles have no claim on reason; and that utilitarianism, in political morality as elsewhere, runs aground on the reef of incommensurabilities among (and doubtless within) ultimate values. Raz's liberalism seeks to ground rights in their contribution to individual well-being, and affirms that such a derivation of rights will support positive welfare rights as well as the rights that protect the immunities and negative liberties of classical liberalism. Among us, autonomy is a vital condition of well-being, and will support both sorts of rights. Autonomous choice has value, however, only in an environment that is rich in choice-worthy options. Intrinsically valuable forms of common life enter into the value of autonomy itself, accordingly: the life of an autonomous person will have value only if it is lived in a cultural environment containing a decent array of inherently public goods – goods that are constitutive parts of worthwhile forms of life. A liberal state, according to Raz, cannot be a state that is neutral about the good life, if only because liberal freedoms take their value from their contribution to the good life. Its animating virtue will be toleration, not neutrality. Standing solidly within the tradition of analytical philosophy, Raz's book nevertheless diverges from the dominant school in recent political philosophy in three ways that are exemplary. It differs, first, in the conception of philosophical method that informs it. Unlike Rawls's, Raz's liberalism does not harbour the absurdly hubristic aspiration of formulating a definitive list of basic liberties or rights. Instead, it recognizes explicitly that the structure of rights that best promotes autonomy, say, is necessarily indeterminate, and significantly variable. Nor, second, does Raz seek to write our own preoccupation with autonomy into the fabric of human nature. He recognizes that the conditions which make autonomy a vital condition of human well-being do not hold in all human societies, even if they are present in ours. Indeed – and this is, of course, anathema to the parochial dogmas of much liberal theory – Raz denies that an autonomous life is necessarily the best life for human beings: there may be forms of human flourishing, perhaps incommensurable in their value as against our form of life, in which autonomous choice has no part. Lastly, Raz shares with Isaiah Berlin the subversive insight – restated by Berlin in his invaluable *The Crooked Timber of Humanity* [16] – that incommensurabilities among ultimate values set a limit to the ambitions of theory in both ethics and politics. This insight – whose applications in ethics have been best explored in the work of Bernard Williams – has the inestimable value of returning us to the realities of political life, which have to do with balancing competing claims of similar validity, finding a *modus vivendi* among forms of life that are irreconcilable, and mediating conflicts that can never be resolved. This view of political life as being permanently intractable to rational reconstruction strikes a death-blow to one of the central supports of the Enlightenment project. It is, perhaps, because it humbles the ambitions of theoretical reason that the conception of the scope and limits of political philosophy exemplified in the work of Raz and Berlin is at odds with its main current now and in the past.

In a review of Nagel's *Equality and Partiality*, G. A. Cohen makes a comment on the book's blurb that aptly illustrates the limitations of the conventional mainstream of academic political philosophy. [17] He objects to the claim, made in the blurb, that 'Egalitarian communism has clearly failed'. He does not mean to deny that what he calls – with delightfully oxymoronic *naïveté*

– 'Soviet civilisation' has failed. He accepts – as who has not, since we were told it by the Soviets themselves? – that 'Soviet civilisation' failed to create not only a classless, egalitarian society, but even a humanly decent one. And he has noticed that 'Soviet civilisation' has failed in an even more comprehensive sense – that is to say, it has disintegrated, collapsed and disappeared. Despite acknowledging these important truths, Cohen is indignant at the blurb's assumption that the Soviet collapse tells us anything about the feasibility of 'egalitarian communism' as a form of life, and he recommends that we turn to page 28 of Nagel's book, where a more 'nuanced' account of the Soviet collapse is offered. The reader who follows Cohen's advice will be surprised to find only one sentence on the page in question that even mentions the Soviet collapse, in which Nagel tells us that 'twentieth century communism . . . was probably worse than it had to be'. Now this is undoubtedly sage stuff; but where is the nuance – in the 'probably', perhaps?

It is, of course, true enough that the Soviet collapse does not show egalitarian communism to be a logical impossibility of some sort: how could it? The proposition that it tells us nothing as to the achievability of an egalitarian society is none the less a piece of silliness. We know – from the Soviet *glasnost*, from all the countries of Eastern Europe, and from China during its recent period of liberalization – that every twentieth-century communist state has contained inequalities in the basic goods of life – education, housing, medical care, even food – that are vast, and sometimes greater than those found in capitalist countries. We know that socialist central planning of the economy – presumably a feature of a communist form of life in any of its varieties – has in every communist state resulted in catastrophic waste, corrupt malinvestment and popular poverty, and in an almost apocalyptic degradation of the environment, such that basic human needs are everywhere frustrated. We know that these features of communist systems are accounted for, almost invariably, by those who have experienced them, by reference to the destruction of normal incentives that goes with the suppression of a market economy. (And let us not forget the evidence of the indispensable importance of incentives in a modern economy, and of the limits incentives place on egalitarian redistribution, that has come from the collapse of Swedish social democracy.) What more do we need to know to be convinced of the unachievability of egalitarian communism? We even possess theories – such as the Austrian theory, formulated by Mises and Hayek, of the epistemic functions of market institutions and the impossibility of rational economic calculation under socialist institutions – which appear to be corroborated by the revelations of glasnost. What more could anyone – even a contemporary analytical Marxist – want?

There was a time when political philosophers were also political economists, historians and social theorists, concerned – as were Smith, Hume and John Stuart Mill, for example – with what history and theory had to teach us about the comparative performance of different institutions and the constraints of feasibility imposed on human institutions of all sorts by the circumstances of any realistically imaginable world. When these political philosophers of an older tradition were liberals, they were deeply concerned with the cultural and institutional preconditions of liberal civil society, preoccupied with threats to its stability and anxious to understand the deeper significance of the major political developments of their time. The strange death of this older tradition has gone oddly unlamented, as political philosophy has come to be dominated by a school that prides itself on its insulation from other disciplines and whose intellectual agenda is shaped by a variety of liberalism that at no point touches the real dilemmas of liberal society. It is a measure of the distance from human life of the main current in recent political philosophy, of its innocence of history and its ignorance of social-scientific theory, and of its character as a degenerate research programme in political thought, that it is certain to treat the greatest world-historical transformation of our age, the fall of communism, as irrelevant to its concerns and a matter of indifference for the ruling liberal ideal of equality.

2

NOTES TOWARD A DEFINITION OF THE POLITICAL THOUGHT OF TLÖN

In his celebrated fiction, *Tlön, Uqbar, Orbis Tertius*, Jorge Luis Borges tells of the discovery of an encyclopaedia of an illusory world, *The First Encyclopaedia of Tlön*. The fantastic world of Tlön was, he tells us, congenitally Idealist in its philosophy. For the peoples of the planet of Tlön, as for Bishop Berkeley, to be is to be perceived; the world is not a manifold of objects in space, but a series of mental events. In such a world, causal connections are only associations of ideas, and the idea of a continuous universe that exists independently of our momentary states of consciousness is unknown except as a *jeu d'esprit* of metaphysical speculation. The doctrine of materialism has indeed been formulated, but as a paradox or a conceit; however ingenious the arguments in its favour, they do not convince the inhabitants of Tlön. It might be supposed that a world consisting only of successive and irreducible states of mind would be a world without science and philosophy; but this, Borges tells us, would be a mistake. The world of Tlön abounds in sciences, countless in number, as it does in metaphysical systems; all are treated as dialectical games, or branches of fantastic literature, from which is sought not conviction, but astonishment. It is to the description of this illusory world, its languages, religions, numismatics, 'its emperors and its oceans, its architecture and its playing cards', amounting to a complete history of an unknown planet, that *The First Encyclopaedia of Tlön* is devoted.

By an association of ideas that is natural and perhaps inevitable, Borges's elegant story suggests to the reader the idea of a *Companion to Contemporary Political Philosophy* whose subject matter is the political thought of a fictitious world, a world of human beings like ourselves, but having histories and conceptions of themselves very different from those surveyed in Robert Goodin and Philip Pettit's *Companion to Contemporary Political Philosophy*.[1] In this exercise in fantasy, the topics treated encompass nationality and monarchy, ethnicity and political theology; the systems of ideas include legitimism and theocracy, nationalism and Byzantinism. This alternative *Companion* devotes much space, also, to the political philosophy of contemporary Western liberalism. It gives coverage to the question, debated in the notorious *Anti-Sombart*, why in the late twentieth century socialism existed as an intellectual movement only in the United States; to the heroic effort of the foremost contemporary theorist of justice at a transcendental deduction of the British Labour Party as it was in the 1950s; to the ingenious neo-Hegelian interpretation of history, which appears to have governed US foreign policy during the post-communist period in which national or else ethnic allegiances were the only remaining sources of political legitimacy in much of the world, and which affirmed that ethnicity and nationality were spent political forces; to the powerful school of Anglo-American jurisprudence in which all political questions are resolved by appeal to the demands of a single fundamental right, the right to meaning; and cognate topics in contemporary liberal theory. At the same time the fictitious *Companion* does not confine itself to liberal theory, or indeed to Western thought. It treats also the neo-Confucian political ideas of the East Asian peoples, the varieties of Islamic political theory, and the ambiguities of Orthodoxy in recent Russian theorizing. If it deals only in passing with the idea of a secular civil society, focusing principally on the theoretical and political inheritances of Ataturkism, that is because it seeks to understand the thought of countries, such as India, whose emerging political cultures seem to confirm the editors' belief that secularism is in most parts of the world an ephemeral episode. In this imaginary *Companion*, then, Western liberal thought is not neglected; but it is treated as only one trend among many, and not that which has the greatest political resonance in the illusory world it surveys.

Goodin and Pettit's *Companion to Contemporary Political Philosophy* has a coverage and subject matter that are incommensurable with those of its fictitious rival. Nevertheless, particularly if its editors' statement of its intended coverage is taken as authoritative, it is itself best understood as belonging to a sub-*genre* in fantastic literature, by comparison with which the fictitious *Companion* seems a laboured exercise in realism. Their book is divided into three broad parts, with the first treating the contributions of different disciplines – analytical philosophy, sociology, law, economics and so on – to contemporary political philosophy, the second discussing the major ideologies that have figured in the subject, and the third consisting of shorter treatments of a variety of particular topics. In the introduction, the editors give their reasons for treating the ideologies chosen for discussion in the book's second part:

In selecting the ideologies to be covered in the second part, we tried to identify those principled world-views that have a substantial impact in contemporary life as well as an impact on philosophical thinking.

They go on:

> Nationalism – still less racism, sexism or ageism – does not figure, on the grounds that it hardly counts as a principled way of thinking about things . . . Yet other ideologies – like theism, monarchism, fascism – are omitted on the grounds that, whatever impact they once had on public life, they would seem to play only a marginal role in the contemporary world.

These remarks imply that nationalism, easily the most powerful political phenomenon in the contemporary world, not only has no defence in principled thought, but never did; that the reflections of Hegel on the nation-state, and of Herder on national culture, do not count, and presumably never counted, as exercises in principled thought; and they invite the question, if only as a move in a dialectical game: by what standards are these theorists of nationality to be excluded from the canon of principled thinking?

The editors' observation that theism plays only a marginal role in the contemporary world will evoke in many readers – Salman Rushdie, perhaps, or the beleaguered secular intelligentsia of contemporary Egypt – astonishment rather than conviction, at least to begin with. For such readers, whether they be in Algeria or India, Turkey or Pakistan, the claim that theistic ideologies have little impact on contemporary public life may have an air of paradox, if not unreality: their societies may seem to them to be convulsed by a life-or-death struggle between secularism and theocracy. True, with regard to the many parts of their readers' world that are ravaged by conflicts between adherents of different religions – Bosnia, Lebanon, Nagorno-Karabakh, and unnumbered others – the editors might maintain that these countries are sundered by political conflicts whose causes are not found in the religious beliefs of the protagonists, but elsewhere. This hardly justifies the claim – which has an almost fantastic aspect, even in the context of a secular republic such as the United States – that the impact of theism on contemporary public life is marginal; and it leaves members of any contemporary society who believe their lives to be at risk solely because of their religious allegiances with an intriguing conundrum in the logic of social explanation.

Equally, the claim that fascism has only a marginal role in the contemporary world may strike Jews, in France or Germany, say, whose synagogues have been daubed with swastikas, or Hungarian liberals who opposed the triumphal reburial of Admiral Horthy, as unconvincing. The editorial methodology which justifies sections in the book's second part on anarchism and feminism, but not on nationalism or fascism, and in the third section supports briefer discussions of autonomy and democracy, but not of authority or of war, is the Tlönist methodology, according to which only that has reality which is at any particular time perceptible in academic discourse. It is this conventionalist methodology which explains the otherwise anomalous facts that the apocalyptic degradation of the natural and human environments in the former Soviet Union, about which there had long been a mass of evidence from émigré sources which lacked academic and therefore (from a conventionalist perspective) epistemic credentials, surfaced in academic discourse only when the Soviet *glasnost* had given it respectability, while the unreformability of the Soviet system, a commonplace among its subjects, was accepted as a possibility by the Western academic class only after it was informed by trusted nomenklaturist sources that the Soviet Union had, in fact, collapsed. And it is probably the Tlönist methodology of the Western academic class that accounts for the paucity in academic literatures of studies of another world-historical transformation, currently underway – the adoption in China, and in parts of Latin America, such as Mexico and Chile, of market institutions, and the ongoing shift in economic and cultural initiative from Europe and North America to the peoples of East Asia and the Pacific Rim. This latter world-historical shift is as yet barely recognized in academic discourse, and certainly does not feature in Goodin and Pettit's *Companion*. In the life of the academic mind, the owl of Minerva seldom flies as early as dusk.

It must be stressed that the forty-one chapters of this indispensable book contain several that violate Tlönist canons of method by engaging with the real world of human history and experience rather than solely with passages in academic discourse. In the third section on special topics, Allen Buchanan contributes an exemplary section on secession and nationalism, in which the intellectual rigour of analytical philosophy is put to work in a masterly consideration of historical examples. Stephen Macedo gives a consideration of fundamentalism and toleration which is wholly admirable in its comprehensiveness, seriousness and in its historical sense of the multiplicity of challenges that presently confront the old-fashioned liberal ideal of toleration. Chandran Kukathas provides a critical survey of recent thought on liberty which focuses sharply and rightly on the central contributions of Berlin, Cohen, Steiner and Skinner to its philosophical and theoretical analysis while recurrently returning our thought to the institutional and political preconditions and implications of the diverse conceptions of liberty he discusses. John Dunn contributes a fascinating section on trust, which contains (among several other invaluable passages) a distinction between trust as a passion and as policy, an argument for the marginal political contribution, by comparison with economics, of academic philosophy, and a critique of the hollowing-out of the political realm in recent theories of social justice. In the second section, Alan Ryan gives an account of liberalism, and Anthony Quinton of conservatism, which in their treatment of the historical contexts as well as the philosophical contents of these traditions are as nearly definitive as makes no matter. In the long first section on disciplinary contributions to contemporary political philosophy, Geoffrey Brennan discusses the contribution of economics with a degree of sensitivity to the limits of economic explanation that is surpassingly rare among practising economists, and Richard Tuck considers in a marvellously illuminating and balanced piece how the awareness of discontinuous conceptual change promoted by the 'new' history of ideas practised by Quentin Skinner, John Dunn and himself affects the way we theorize our institutions and political life. In these and some other contributions to Goodin and Pettit's *Companion* we see it in its aspect as a compendium of lively essays by first-rate practitioners, which are worth reading in their own right as exemplars of political philosophy when that seeks to reflect the real world of human history.

On the whole, however, the essays collected in this book are to be read as a mirror of the subject as we find it today and not of the world in which we live. It might be argued that Goodin and Pettit's *Companion* can hardly be faulted for being a mirror of the other books that are its subject matter. The questions remain why these other books are such poor mirrors of the world, and why Goodin and Pettit enhance the distorting properties of political thought as an academic subject in their choice of ideologies and topics for inclusion in their book. The answer is not to be found, as might be supposed, in their view of political philosophy as an inherently and centrally normative subject, and in a consequent neglect of feasibility constraints on the attainment of political ideals as these are found in the real world, since Goodin and Pettit need no reminding of the anti-utopian commonplace that politics is the art of the possible. Indeed Goodin makes the suggestion that the main constraint on achieving political ideals is not any one of the more familiar economic, sociological or psychological constraints, but rather the availability of political ideas themselves, a dearth of well-worked-out policy options, of 'technologies to solve ethical problems', and – giving us a clue to the origins of the distorting perspective of contemporary political philosophy – recommends that 'normative theorists ought to shift attention, at least for a while, from values to mechanisms for implementing them'.[2]

From these and other remarks it is apparent that for the editors of this *Companion*, as for the overwhelming majority of practising political philosophers today, there is no doubt as to what are the relevant political ideals; they are the liberal ideals of the European Enlightenment project. These are the ideals – of subjecting all human institutions to a rational criticism and of convergence on a universal civilization whose foundation is autonomous human reason – that are taken as unproblematic, even axiomatic, in virtually all recent Anglo-American political philosophy. Even when, as in communitarian theory, the liberal individualist fiction of the disembodied or unsituated human subject, which has a history only by accident, is criticized as a political residue of the Kantian noumenal self, it is only to advance another fiction, an idea of community – the noumenal community, let us call it – that has none of the particularistic allegiances of every human community that has ever existed. It is plain that Western political philosophers have yet to learn to view the liberal ideals of the Enlightenment project with Nietzsche's 'suspecting glance'. It has not occurred to them to ask what claim these ideals have on human beings, why the Western societies that are identified with them are plagued with anomie and nihilism, nor why they are increasingly repudiated by non-Occidental peoples.

Political philosophy, as it is reflected in the distorting mirror of this *Companion*, is the self-awareness of a Western academic class whose identity is defined by the ephemera of Western liberal opinion. A view of the world as seen through this broken looking-glass occludes perception both of the longer tradition of

Western political thought that is not liberal in any sense and of the non-Western traditions that are being reasserted in many parts of the contemporary world. To say this is not to put in a plea for multiculturalism in political philosophy, since multiculturalism is, after all, a peculiarly, and indeed parochially, Western preoccupation. It is to comment on the oddity, at this point in human history, of an account of contemporary political philosophy that is so Europocentric in its perspective that Confucian ideas, which animate thought and practice in the extraordinary East Asian experiments, underway in Japan, in Singapore, in China and in Korea, of harnessing the dynamism of market institutions to the needs of stable and enduring communities, are not even mentioned in the index. Nor is it to deny liberalism its legitimate place in the Western intellectual tradition. The point is that the virtual hegemony in contemporary political philosophy, and in this Companion to it, of an unhistorical and culturally parochial species of liberal theory disables the understanding when it is confronted by the most powerful political forces of our age. The hegemony of liberal discourse and ideals to which this book attests leaves these forces – of ethnicity and nationalism, for example – in an intellectual limbo, akin to that of sexuality in Victorian times, from which they emerge intermittently as evidences of persisting human irrationality, to be discussed nervously in a strangulated Newspeak of difference and otherness, or else dismissed as barely intelligible departures from principled thought. To pass over in this way, as regrettable atavisms or lapses from theoretical coherence, the ruling forces of the age, does not augur well for contemporary political philosophy, or for liberalism.

Speaking of the heresy of materialism, according to which there is a world of things that persist independently of our consciousness of them, Borges tells us that 'The language of Tlön is by its nature resistant to this paradox; most people do not understand it.' In the Tlönist world, materialism can be only a feat of specious reasoning, or else a play on words, not a compelling view of things. Perhaps, congenitally conventionalist, academic political philosophers will find hard to grasp the proposal that their books should aim to be mirrors of the world before they seek to change it, and will treat it as a mere paradox, even suspecting in it a motive of perversity or of irony. Evidently they cannot accept that a world in which their liberal ideals are constantly mocked does not secretly revere them.

Or it may be that the task of understanding the intractable conflicts of our world does not satisfy the passion for symmetry, the craving for any semblance of order, which finds expression in systems – structuralism, neo-conservatism, critical theory – that at once pacify the intelligence and gratify the moral appetites. If this is so, then perhaps academic political philosophy can be no more than an hermetic activity, whose product is a self-referential text in which the world is mentioned only in inconspicuous and misleading footnotes. It is a measure of how far political philosophy has approached that condition that all but the most perceptive reader of Goodin and Pettit's estimable and useful *Companion* could come from it in ignorance of the Holocaust, of the Gulag, and of every world-historical transformation of our age. Perhaps, given the condition of the subject, the political philosopher is best occupied in the modest exegesis of texts – like Mill's *Liberty*, say – whose charm is in their distance from our world, or any world we are likely to find ourselves in.

3

TOLERATION: A POST-LIBERAL PERSPECTIVE

Toleration has lately fallen on hard times. It is a virtue that has fallen from fashion, because it goes against much in the spirit of the age. Old-fashioned toleration – the toleration defended by Milton, and by the older liberals, such as Locke – sprang from an acceptance of the imperfectibility of human beings, and from a belief in the importance of freedom in the constitution of the good life. Since we cannot be perfect, and since virtue cannot be forced on people but is rather a habit of life they must themselves strive to acquire, we were enjoined to tolerate the shortcomings of others, even as we struggled with our own. On this older view, toleration is a precondition of any stable *modus vivendi* among incorrigibly imperfect beings. If it has become unfashionable in our time, the reason is in part to be found in the resistance of a post-Christian age to the thought that we are flawed creatures whose lives will always contain evils. This is a thought subversive of the shallow optimistic creeds of our age, humanist or Pelagian, for which human evils are problems to be solved rather than sorrows to be coped with or endured. Such pseudo-faiths are perhaps inevitable in those who have abandoned traditional faiths but have not relinquished the need for consolation that traditional theodicy existed to satisfy. The result, however, is a world-view according to which only stupidity and ill will stand between us and universal happiness. Grounded as it is on accepting the imperfectibility of the human lot, toleration is bound to be uncongenial to the ruling illusions of the epoch, all of which cherish the project – which is the Enlightenment project, in all its myriad forms, liberal and otherwise – of instituting a *political providence* in human affairs whereby tragedy and mystery would be banished from them.

Toleration is unfashionable for another, more topical reason. It is unavoidably and inherently judgemental. The objects of toleration are what we judge to be evils. When we tolerate a practice, a belief or a character trait, we let something be that we judge to be undesirable, false or at least inferior; our toleration expresses the conviction that, *despite* its badness, the object of toleration should be left alone. This is in truth the very idea of toleration, as it is practised in things great and small. So it is that in friendship, as we understand it, our tolerance of our friends' vices makes them no less vices in our eyes: rather, our tolerance of them *presupposes* that they are vices. As the Oxford analytical philosophers of yesteryear might have put it, it is the *logic* of toleration that it be practised in respect of evils. So, on a grander scale, we tolerate *ersatz* religions, such as Scientology, not because we think they may after all contain a grain of truth, but because the great good of freedom of belief necessarily encompasses the freedom to believe absurdities. Toleration is not, then, an expression of scepticism, of doubt about our ability to tell the good from the bad; it is evidence of our confidence that we have that ability.

The idea of toleration goes against the grain of the age because the practice of toleration is grounded in strong moral convictions. Such judgements are alien to the dominant conventional wisdom according to which standards of belief and conduct are entirely subjective or relative in character, and one view of things is as good as any other. A tolerant person, or a tolerant society, does not doubt that it knows something about the good and the true; its tolerance expresses that knowledge. Indeed, when a society is tolerant, its tolerance expresses the conception of the good life that it has in common. In so far as a society comes to lack any such common conception – as is at least partly the case in Britain today – it ceases to be capable of toleration as it was traditionally understood. The appropriate response to a situation of moral pluralism, in which our society harbours a diversity of possibly incommensurable conceptions of the good life, and the bearing of such a circumstance on the traditional understanding of toleration, are questions to which I shall return towards the end of these reflections.

Toleration as a political ideal is offensive to the new liberalism – the liberalism of Rawls, Dworkin, Ackerman and suchlike – because it is decidedly non-neutral in respect of the good. For the new liberals, justice – the shibboleth of revisionist liberalism – demands that government, in its institutions and policies, practise *neutrality*, not toleration, in regard to rival conceptions of the good life. Although in the end this idea of neutrality may not prove to be fully coherent, its rough sense seems to be that it is wrong for government to discriminate in favour of, or against, any form of life animated by a definite conception of the good. It is wrong for government so to do, according to the new liberals, because such policy violates an ideal of *equality* demanding equal respect by government for divergent conceptions of the good and the ways of life that embody them. To privilege any form of life in any way over others, or to disfavour in any way any form of life, is unacceptably discriminatory. This is radical stuff, since – unlike the old-fashioned ideal of toleration – it does not simply rule out the coercive imposition of a conception of the good and its associated way of life by legal prohibition of its rivals. It also rules out as wrong or unjust government encouraging or supporting ways of life – by education, subsidy, welfare provision, taxation or legal entrenchment, say – at the expense of others deemed by it, or by the moral common sense of society, to be undesirable or inferior. It rules out, in other words, precisely a policy of toleration – a policy of not attaching a legal prohibition to, or otherwise persecuting, forms of life or conduct that are judged bad but which government tries by a variety of means to discourage. What the neutrality of radical equality mandates is nothing less than the *legal disestablishment of morality*. As a result, morality becomes in theory a private habit of behaviour rather than a common way of life.

In practice things are rather different. The idea of the moral neutrality of the state with respect to different ways of life, considered as a political ideal, faces the problem of what is to count as a *bona fide* way of life. Since there is nothing in the idea of neutrality that addresses this problem, its adherents fall back on the deliverances of the *bien-pensant* opinion of the day. If it has any clear sense at all, the idea of neutrality among different ways of life or conceptions of the good tells us that the way of life of the smoker, the drinker or the person devoted to pleasure even at the expense of health should not by any governmental policy be disprivileged, disfavoured or otherwise discriminated against; but these categories of people have been afforded no protection from the prohibitionist policies of the New Puritanism – the Puritanism that is inspired, not by ideas of right and wrong, but by a weakness for prudence that expresses itself in an obsession with health and longevity. The smoker of unfiltered Turkish cigarettes or the would-be absinthe drinker will get short shrift if they argue that these pleasures are elements in a way of life animated by a definite conception of the good that deserves equal protection along with those of the jogger and the non-smoker. At the level of theory the problem of identifying genuine ways of life is insoluble, since it requires an evaluation of human lives that will inevitably be non-neutral among some ideals of the good. The life of the drinking man may be stigmatized as alcoholism, which is not a way of life but an illness; or the life of a housewife may be characterized as a form of oppression – not an embodiment of any coherent conception of the good. In practice, favoured minorities will obtain legal privileges for themselves while unfashionable minorities will be subject to policies of paternalism and moralistic intervention in their chosen styles of life that earlier generations of liberals – including John Stuart Mill – would at once have rejected as intolerable invasions of personal liberty.

The practical legal and political result of these newer liberal ideas is found in policies of reverse or positive discrimination and in the creation of group or collective rights. For those who have constituted themselves members of a cultural minority group, to be the object of a policy of toleration is to be subject to a form of disrespect, even of contempt or persecution, since they are thereby denied equal standing with mainstream society. More, what is needed to remedy this discrimination, in their view, is not merely parity of treatment, but a form of differential treatment in which their group is accorded privileges over the majority, or over other minority groups. So it is that in the United States – where these practices, predictably, are at their most extreme – there are quotas in universities in favour of some minority groups, and, if rumour is to be believed, there have been quotas against disfavoured groups such as Asians. Some who may not hitherto have considered themselves members of a cultural minority – such as many homosexuals – are encouraged by such practices to constitute themselves as one, thereby transforming a sexual preference into a culture or a way of life that demands protection or privilege along with those of selected ethnic minorities. In all these cases, as with quotas created for women in US universities, it is group membership that now confers rights. Indeed, the rights of groups may well now often trump those of individuals when they come into conflict with each other.

These departures from the old-fashioned ideal of toleration are all too likely to breed more old-fashioned intolerance. The case for toleration appeals in part to the fact that our society contains a diversity of strong and incompatible moral views. Consider the case of homosexuality. There are those, such as some traditional Christian, Jewish and Muslim believers, who hold that homosexuality is immoral in itself; others, such as myself, who regard it merely as a preference, that by itself raises no moral issue of any kind; and yet others who regard it as a form of cultural identity, with its own lifestyle and literature. These are deep differences among us, since they reflect not only divergent judgements on moral questions but also different views as to what is the subject matter and character of morality itself. An attempt to give legal force to any one of these views, in circumstances of deep pluralism of the sort we have now, is likely to further fragment us, and to evoke more intolerance among us. A policy of toleration, in which homosexuals have the same personal and civil liberties as heterosexuals and in which neither bears burdens the other does not, seems the policy most likely to issue in a peaceful *modus vivendi*. (I take for granted here, what is plainly true, that a policy of toleration with regard to homosexuality is incompatible with its criminalization.) Such a policy might involve remedying anomalies and abuses to which homosexuals are still subject. It is evident that the difference in the age of consent for homosexual acts is anomalous; that the pretence that homosexual activity does not occur in prisons is both absurd and – in a time when prophylaxis against AIDS is vitally important – harmful; and that discrimination by insurance companies against homosexuals (and others) who have responsibly had themselves tested for the HIV virus and proved negative is plainly unjustifiable and should be the subject of legislation. These and similar reforms ought to be part and parcel of a policy of toleration.

What a policy of toleration would not mandate is the whole-sale reconstruction of institutional arrangements in Britain such that homosexuals acquire collective rights or are in every context treated precisely as heterosexuals. As matters stand, there is a single form of marriage entrenched in law in Britain. Complete neutrality between heterosexuality and homosexuality would entail the legal recognition of homosexual marriage – just as complete neutrality between Christian and Muslim marriage would presumably entail legal recognition of polygamous marriage. If we go this route, we are not far from the radical, individualist and libertarian *reductio ad absurdum* – the abolition of marriage itself and its replacement by whatever contracts people choose to enter into. This last prospect is one we have reason to avoid, given the value that the legal entrenchment of a single form of marriage possesses in conferring social recognition on the relationships of those who enter into it. (It is often overlooked that marriage has this value even for those who elect simply to live together, since it constitutes a public standard for their relationship they have chosen not to endorse.) This is not to say that the current law of marriage is fixed for all time, any more than the rest of family law, such as the law on adoption, is so fixed. Nor is it to say that future changes in family law, reflecting changes in society at large, may not in time extend full recognition to homosexuals within family law. It is to say that any such changes should be part of a policy of toleration rather than applications of a doctrine of radical equality. Further, it is to say that such extension of legal recognition would not be to homosexuals as a group but to individuals regardless of their sexual orientation.

The creation of group or collective rights is probably the worst form of the legalism that has supplanted the traditional ideal of toleration, and I shall have occasion to return to it in the context of multiculturalism. Founding policy in areas where our society harbours radically divergent conceptions of the good on a legalist model of rights may be injurious to society even when the rights are ascribed to individuals. To make a political issue that is deeply morally contested a matter of basic rights is to make it non-negotiable, since rights – at least as they are understood in the dominant contemporary schools of Anglo-American juris-prudence – are unconditional entitlements, not susceptible to moderation. Because they are peremptory in this way, rights do not allow divisive issues to be settled by a legislative compro-mise: they permit only unconditional victory or surrender. The abortion issue in North America, where it is treated as an issue of constitutional rights rather than of legislation, is the clearest example of a divisive issue rendered yet more dangerous to civil peace by being elevated to an issue in constitutional law and the theory of rights. For such a status precludes stable settlements being reached on the issue of various sorts, at the level of the state legislatures, many of which would no doubt involve compromis-ises – on the term in pregnancy when abortion was no longer permitted, say – which might reflect the views of no one party to the controversy, and yet constitute a settlement most could live with. On the issue of abortion, my own views are those of a liberal, even an ultra-liberal, in that no moral issue of any kind arises in my view, at least early in pregnancy, and the entire controversy is likely to be defused, except in Ireland, Poland and the United States, by the French abortifacient pill. I would not, however, try to impose this opinion of mine on others by repre-senting it as a truth about their basic rights; rather I would attempt to persuade others of its cogency, and in the meantime reconcile myself with whatever settlement achieves a provisional stability. Analogous reasonings apply to the issues of prostitution and pornography. My own views on these issues are again those of an ultra-liberal; unless coercion, the interests of children, or the protection of privacy, say, are at stake, no issue of public policy, no issue of morality even, arises for me. I would not, however, attempt to impose this judgement of mine on a society in which there were many who found it abhorrent, but would argue instead for a policy of toleration. A policy of toleration would not criminalize prostitution and pornography but would contain them by a variety of legal devices – such as the licensing of sex shops, and perhaps of zoning for them – that would itself vary from time to time and place to place, according to changing circumstances. Such flexibility in policy is not possible if, as in rights theorists such as Dworkin, thought about them is done on a legalist and universalist model. Here we have a signal advantage of toleration – that it allows for local variation in policy, according to local circumstances and standards, rather than imposing a Procrustean system of supposed basic rights on all.

It is in the area of multiculturalism that a policy of toleration is most needed, and ideas of radical equality and positive discrimination most unfortunate. We have already noted one disadvantage of policies of affirmative action – that they are applied on the basis of group membership and so entail the collectivization of (at least some) rights. When the groups in question are ethnic groups, policies of affirmative action that include quotas come up against one of the most characteristic facts of pluralism and modernity – the fact that, with many of us, our ethnic inheritance is complex. In modern Western pluralist societies, policies which result in the creation of group rights are inevitably infected with arbitrariness and consequent inequity, since the groups selected for privileging are arbitrary, as is the determination of who belongs to which group. The nemesis of such policies – not far off in the United States – is a sort of reverse apartheid, in which people's opportunities and entitlements are decided by the morally arbitrary fact of ethnic origins rather than by their deserts or needs.

There is a deeper objection to policies of multiculturalism that issue in the creation of group rights. This is that a stable liberal civil society cannot be radically multicultural but depends for its successful renewal across the generations on an undergirding culture that is held in common. This common culture need not encompass a shared religion and it certainly need not presuppose ethnic homogeneity, but it does demand widespread acceptance of certain norms and conventions of behaviour and, in our times, it typically expresses a shared sense of nationality. In the British case, vague but still powerful notions of fair play and give and take, of the necessity of compromise and of not imposing private convictions on others, are elements in what is left of the common culture, and they are essential if a liberal civil society is to survive in Britain. Where multiculturalism and toleration diverge is in the recognition within the ideal of toleration that stable liberty requires more than subscription to legal or constitutional rules – it requires commonality in moral outlook, across a decent range of issues, as well. We can live together in deep disagreement about abortion, but not if we also disagree about the propriety of using force on our opponents. The example of the United States, which at least since the mid-1960s has been founded on the Enlightenment conviction that a common culture is not a necessary precondition of a liberal civil society, shows that the view that civil peace can be secured solely by adherence to abstract rules is merely an illusion. In so far as policy has been animated by it, the result has been further social division, including what amounts to low-intensity civil war between the races. As things stand, the likelihood in the United States is of a slow slide into ungovernability, as the remaining patrimony of a common cultural inheritance is frittered away by the fragmenting forces of multiculturalism.

In Britain things have not yet come to such a pass, but the Rushdie affair suggests that the web of the common culture that undergirds liberal civil society in Britain is far from seamless. This is not to say that all Muslim demands for opportunities for self-expression in Britain are a threat or a danger to civil society. A strong case can be made, indeed, in favour of extending to Islamic schools the state aid that goes to Roman Catholic and some Jewish schools: some such policy may indeed be required by the ideal of toleration. Such state aid should be extended, however, only if Islamic schools, like other schools, conform to the National Curriculum – which includes the requirement that both girls and boys be instructed in basic skills of numeracy and literacy in English. Schools which treat girls and boys differently with regard to these basic skills, or which do not teach literacy in English, the language we hold in common, should not receive state support. Conformity with the National Curriculum in these basic respects is a sign of willingness to adopt the British way of life – a way of life that many British Muslims find in no way incompatible with their faith.

The evidence of the Rushdie affair is that a minority of fundamentalist Muslims are unwilling to accept the norms that govern civil society in Britain. Here a policy of toleration must be willing to be repressive – to arrest and charge those who have made death threats against the writer or those associated with him. Toleration does not mandate turning a blind eye on those who flout the practices of freedom of expression that are among the central defining elements of liberal society in Britain: it mandates their suppression. We may judge that Rushdie's work is worthless, or even pernicious; but that judgement does not deprive the writer of the freedom he rightly enjoys as a subject of the Queen and a citizen of a liberal society. There is, to be sure, an argument that Rushdie's work is a blasphemy on Islam, which does not receive the protection afforded by the blasphemy law to Anglican Christianity; but the blasphemy law looks increasingly anomalous, with abolition rather than its extension being the most reasonable reform. The key point, however, is that even if Rushdie's work had been in breach of an extended blasphemy law – a law that would be objectionable because of its cumbrous indeterminacy and its incursions on free expression – that could in no way sanction the challenge to the rule of law in Britain mounted by the death threats against him. This key point may be put in another way. A great deal of cultural diversity can be contained within the curtilage of a common way of life. Differences of religious belief and of irreligion, of conceptions of the good and of ethnic inheritance may be many and significant, and yet the inhabitants of a country may yet be recognizably practitioners of a shared form of life. The kind of diversity that is incompatible with civil society in Britain is that which rejects the constitutive practices that give it its identity. Central among these are freedom of expression and its precondition, the rule of law. Cultural traditions that repudiate these practices cannot be objects of toleration for liberal civil society in Britain or anywhere else.

Consideration of the Rushdie case brings us back to the vexed question of multiculturalism. An upshot of the foregoing reflections is that a society that is multiracial is likely to enjoy civil peace only if it is *not* at the same time radically multicultural. By contrast, the multiculturalist demand that minority cultures – however these are defined – be afforded rights and privileges denied the mainstream culture in effect delegitimizes the very idea of a common culture. It thereby reinforces the rationalist illusion of the Enlightenment and radical liberalism – an illusion embodied in much current North American practice and inherited from some at least of the early theorists of the American experiment, such as Thomas Paine (but not the authors of the *Federalist Papers*) – that a common allegiance can be sustained by subscription to abstract principles, without the support of a common culture. Indeed, the very idea of a common culture comes to be seen as an emblem of oppression. Accordingly, the often healthy pressures on minority cultures to integrate themselves into the mainstream culture are represented as inevitably the expression of prejudice, racial or otherwise, and so condemnable. (Pressure for the integration of ethnic minorities into the mainstream culture may indeed be unhealthy when, as perhaps in Britain today, the cultural traditions of some ethnic groups embody virtues of community better than the larger society does.) We reach a crux now in the idea and practice of toleration – its bearing on the idea and fact of *prejudice*. The idea of prejudice is, perhaps, not as simple as it looks, but the essence of prejudice as a practice seems to be the discriminatory treatment of people on grounds of their belonging to a group of some sort, where this is not relevant to the matter at issue. Prejudicial law enforcement, or prejudicial hiring policies, would then be practices in which the treatment of people correlated not with relevant facts about them as individuals, but merely with their belonging to a certain group. Now there can be no doubt that prejudice of this sort can be a great evil – witness the long history of Christian anti-Semitism and the differential treatment accorded to members of diverse racial groups by police and judicial institutions under the *apartheid* system in South Africa – and that it is an evil against which there can, and ought to be, legal remedies. It is worth noting again, however, that policies of positive discrimination or affirmative action involving quotas are also condemned by any ideal that condemns prejudice. A consistent rejection of policies based on prejudice would be one that was blind to race, gender and sexual orientation, rather than one that merely reversed earlier or pre-existing prejudicial policies.

There is an even deeper question for the ideal of toleration posed by the reality of prejudice. As it is commonly understood, prejudice connotes not only discriminatory practices, but also, and more generally, conduct and perception based on stereotype or emotion rather than a dispassionate grasp of the facts. Radical liberals have seen in prejudice of this fundamental sort an evil that must be attacked by legislation – by laws against sexist or racist stereotypes in advertising or children's books, for example. For these liberals, prejudice is an evil that issues, in part at least, from a distortion of the cognitive faculties, which is to be remedied by a destruction of the offending stereotypes. What, then, do supporters of the old ideal of toleration say of prejudice of this sort? They will not deny that it is often an evil. No one, I take it, who has been pigeon-holed or marginalized on the basis of offensive group stereotypes can pretend to have enjoyed the experience. There nevertheless remains a question about the radical liberal project of abolishing prejudice. Is the abolition of prejudice desirable, or even possible?

A school of conservative thought, taking its cue from Edmund Burke and Michael Polanyi, finds positive value in prejudice, conceiving it as a repository for tacit or practical knowledge – knowledge embodied in habits and dispositions rather than in theories – we would not otherwise have at our disposal. This view makes an important point in noting that much of our knowledge is possessed and used by us without ever being articulated. It is not entirely convincing as a defence of prejudice, if only because our fund of tacit beliefs contains tacit error as well as tacit knowledge. It was part of the fund of tacit belief of many Russians and Germans, in the last century and in our own, that Jews poison wells and perform ritual sacrifices; and this falsehood made anti-Semitic policies more popular in those countries. As this example shows, tacit error can have serious and sometimes harmful consequences. It does not follow, however, that the project of banishing prejudice from the world is a sensible one. Prejudice does serve a cognitive function that is ineliminable in expressing beliefs that have been acquired unconsciously and that are held unreflectively and unarticulated. The idea that we can do without such beliefs, whatever their dangers, is merely another rationalist illusion. The life of the mind can never be that of pure reason, since it always depends on much that has not been subject to critical scrutiny by our intellect. The project of abolishing prejudice is hubristic in that it supposes that the human mind can become transparent to itself. In truth, such self-transparency is a possibility neither for the mind nor for society. As Hayek has observed:

> The appropriateness of our conduct is not necessarily depend-
> ent on our knowing why it is so. Such understanding is one way
> of making our conduct appropriate, but it is only one way. A
> sterilized world of beliefs, purged of all elements whose value
> could not be positively demonstrated, would probably be not
> less lethal than would be an equivalent state in the biological
> sphere.[1]

The project of abolishing prejudice is in fact closely akin to the Marxian project of rendering social life transparent by transcending alienation. Perhaps they are but versions of the same project of reconstructing social life on a (supposedly) rational model. At any rate, they both involve attempting an epistemological impossibility. A humbler, and more sensible approach – one suggested by the old-fashioned ideal of toleration, with its insight into the imperfectibility of the human mind – would be one that accepts the inevitability of prejudice and acknowledges that it has uses and benefits, while at the same time being prepared to curb its expression when this has demonstrably harmful effects. In general, however, we should guard against the harmful effects of prejudice, not by engaging in the futile attempt to eradicate it, but by trying to ensure that everyone has the same civil and personal liberties. A policy of toleration, in other words, will even be one that tolerates the many false beliefs we have about each other – providing these do not result in the deprivation of important liberties and opportunities. When prejudice does have such an effect, it is usually the liberties and opportunities it threatens that we should aim to protect, rather than the prejudice we should seek to eradicate.

The argument so far, then, is that we will do better if we seek to rub along together, tolerating each other's prejudices, rather than attempting the impossible task of ironing them out from social life. A policy of toleration with regard to all but the most harmful prejudices makes sense for another reason: there is not much agreement among us as to what counts as a prejudice. For some, the idea that heterosexuality is the norm from which homosexuality is a departure is quite unproblematic; for others it embodies unacceptable prejudice. This deep difference of view among us exemplifies a pluralism in our society that is perhaps deeper than ever before in our history. Our society harbours conceptions of the good life and views of the world that, though they may overlap, are sometimes so different as to be incommensurable: they lack common standards whereby they could be assessed. Consider the traditional Christian and the person for whom religion has no importance. The difference between these two may be far greater than that between the traditional Christian and the traditional atheist, such as Bradlaugh, say. For the latter pair had a conception of deity in common and differed only as to its existence, whereas the genuinely post-Christian unbeliever (such as myself) may find the very idea of deity repellent, incoherent or flatly unintelligible. With respect to the religious beliefs of others, the latter sort of unbeliever is in a very different position from the believer in any universalist religion, such as Christianity, Islam or Buddhism. Such universalist faiths can practise toleration with regard to others' beliefs but their universal claims commit them to a policy of proselytizing and conversion. For the post-Christian unbeliever, as for the adherent of particularistic faiths such as Judaism, Hinduism, Bonism, Shinto and Taoism, which make no claim to possess a unique truth authoritative and binding for all people, old-fashioned toleration is irrelevant in respect of the religious beliefs of others. Theirs is a more radical tolerance – that of indifference. An analogous situation holds in moral life. As has already been observed, among us there is disagreement not only about answers to moral questions but also about the subject-matter of morality itself. For some, sexual conduct is at the very heart of morality; for others, it is a matter of taste or preference and acquires a moral dimension only when important human interests – such as those of children – are affected. For those who hold the latter view, such as myself, the appropriate approach to homosexuality, say, is not toleration but the radical tolerance of indifference: I have no more reason to concern myself about the sexual habits of others than I do about their tastes in ethnic cuisine. It is this radical tolerance of indifference that homosexual activists should be aiming at, rather than the divisive project of group or cultural rights, if they remain dissatisfied with old-fashioned toleration.

The radical tolerance of indifference has application wherever there are conceptions of the good that are incommensurable. If there is an ultimate diversity of forms of life, not combinable with one another and not rankable on any scale of value, in which human beings may flourish – an idea defended in our time by Isaiah Berlin[2] – then the adoption of one among them is appropriately a matter of choice or preference. It seems plain that our own society contains such incommensurable conceptions and that the tolerance of indifference is for that reason relevant to us. Several important caveats are worth making nevertheless. First, the claim that there may be, and are present among us, conceptions of the good that are rationally incommensurable is *not* one that supports any of the fashionable varieties of relativism and subjectivism, since it allows, and indeed presupposes, that some conceptions of the good are defective, and some forms of life simply bad. One may assert that the conceptions of the good expressed in the lives of Mother Teresa and Oscar Wilde are incommensurable, and yet confidently assert that the life of a crack addict is a poor one. Second, the radical tolerance of indifference is virtually the opposite of old-fashioned toleration in that its objects are not judged to be evils and may indeed be incommensurable goods. Very different as they undoubtedly are, these two forms of toleration seem no less necessary and appropriate in a pluralistic society such as contemporary Britain. But third, and most importantly, recognition of the value of the radical tolerance of indifference does not mean that we can do without a common stock of norms and conventions or the older virtue of toleration. A common culture – even if one defined thinly in terms of the practices and virtues that make up a liberal civil society – is essential if we are not to drift into American-style chaos; and even such an attenuated common culture will be renewed across the generations only if it is animated by a shared sense of history and nationality. For these reasons, the tolerance of indifference can never be the dominant form of tolerance in a free society; it must always be a variation on the very different, and inescapably judgemental, tolerance I have called old-fashioned toleration.

We return to the thought with which we began. Toleration is a virtue appropriate to people who acknowledge their imperfectibility. Such people will not demand that their preferences be accorded special rights or privileges, or expect that their style of life will receive universal respect. They will be satisfied if they are left alone. Rather than pursuing a delusive utopia in which all ways of life are given equal (and possibly unmerited) respect, they are content if they can manage to rub along together. In this they are recognizing a profound truth, suppressed in the Panglossian liberalisms of the Enlightenment that dominate political thought today – that freedom presupposes peace.

As a neglected political thinker of our time has put it:

> In order to be truly and happily free you must be safe. Liberty requires peace. War would impose the most terrible slavery, and you would never be free if you were always compelled to fight for your freedom. This circumstance is ominous: by it the whole sky of liberty is clouded over. We are drawn away from irresponsible play to a painful study of facts and to the endless labour of coping with probable enemies.[3]

We are most likely to enjoy an enduring liberty if we moderate our demands on each other and learn to put up with our differences. We will then compromise when we cannot agree, and reach a settlement – always provisional, never final – rather than stand on our (in any case imaginary) human rights. Oddly enough, we will find that it is by tolerating our differences that we come to discover how much we have in common. It is in the give and take of politics, rather than the adjudications of the courts, that toleration is practised and the common life renewed.

The virtue of toleration is of universal value because of the universality of human imperfection. It is, nevertheless, of special value for us. With us, the skein of common life is often strained where it is not already broken, and our danger is that of ceasing to recognize one another as members of a common form of life. We will achieve a form of common life that is tolerable and stable, most reliably, if we abandon the inordinacy of radical neutrality and cultural rights and return to the pursuit of a *modus vivendi*, shifting and fragile as it inevitably must be, in the practice of toleration.

4

ENLIGHTENMENT, ILLUSION AND THE FALL OF THE SOVIET STATE

The changes that took place in Eastern Europe and the Soviet Union between October 1989 and August 1991 have significance well beyond the shallow and narrow understandings of conventional Sovietology. The collapse of the East European communist regimes in late 1989 marked not only the bankruptcy of socialist central planning, but also the end of the post-war settlement, negotiated at Yalta, that had divided Germany and Europe in the interests of geopolitical stability. The events of late 1989 signified the unravelling in Europe of the global post-war settlement that had ceded hegemony to two superpowers – the Soviet Union and the United States – and divided Germany for over a generation. It is overwhelmingly likely that in the 1990s we shall see the further undoing of the post-war settlement, with the next major development being the emergence of Japan as a military power in its own right.

The events which occurred in Russia in August 1991 signify a world-historical transformation that is yet deeper in its significance. The fragile and ephemeral settlement of 1919 was animated by Woodrow Wilson's project of imposing a rationalist order conceived in the New World on the intractably quarrelsome nations of Europe. Like Marxism, this rationalist conception had its origins in the French Enlightenment's vision of a universal human civilization in which the claims of ethnicity and religion came long after those of common humanity. It was this vision which inspired the revolution of 1789, and which the events of 1989 and 1991 showed to be an illusion. It is not too much to say that the demise of Soviet communism in late 1991 represents, also, the eclipse of the vision that shapes the post-war world settlement and which inspired the French Revolution. As the Soviet Union vanishes before us, so does the spectre of socialist humanity, which entranced generations of Western *philosophes* and left-liberal nomenklaturists. In the wake of Soviet communism, we find, not *Homo Sovieticus* or any other rationalist abstraction, but men and women whose identities are constituted by particular attachments and histories – Balts, Ukrainians, Uzbeks, Russians and so on. The deepest significance of the Soviet collapse lies in the return it presages to history's most classical terrain of ethnic and religious conflicts, irredentist claims and secret diplomacies. It certainly never heralded the end of history.[1] It is the ancient and primordial passions associated with these ethnic and religious loyalties, rather than any conflict between warring Enlightenment ideologies such as liberalism and Marxism, that will govern the late 1990s and the twenty-first century.

Whereas Soviet communism was destroyed, not by liberalism but by its own inherent flaws, the *coup de grace* was delivered by Russian nationalism. For many reasons, Western opinion is trapped in a knee-jerk reaction of suspicion of Russian nationalism. Any assertion of Russian national sentiment is at once interpreted in the least benign fashion, as a manifestation of the forces which found expression in *Pamyat*, itself a creature of the KGB that never achieved in Russian elections anything proportionately like the votes achieved by Jean-Marie Le Pen's party in France. Such automatic Western hostility to Russian nationalism risks strengthening the parties of the radical Right in post-communist Russia. It has a long history, however, with Soviet communism being perceived by many, in Eastern and Western Europe, as Muscovite tyranny under a new flag, an expression of the inherently despotic culture of the Russians. This banally over-familiar interpretation neglects the structural similarities between communist institutions in Russia and in very different cultures such as those of China, Cuba and Bohemia. In truth, Soviet communism did not emanate from a Russian monastery, steeped in mysticism and piety, nor did it acquire its most distinctively repressive characteristics from Russian cultural traditions. It was a quintessentially Western and European Enlightenment ideology, whose implementation in Russia knocked that people off the trajectory of development it had followed since the abolition of serfdom. To be sure, no people, and certainly not the Russians, can claim innocence of the repressions and cruelties of Soviet communism; all – including the Western powers – are implicated in its evils. At the same time, it will be a fundamental mistake if Western policy sets itself against the emergence of a Russian nation-state. For Russian nationalism, in most of its present forms, is a movement which seeks to make a break with Russia's imperialist past. While cautioning the emergent Russian nation-state against any regression to imperialist relationships with the former subject peoples of the Soviet state, especially in Eastern Europe and the Baltic states, Western policy should acknowledge that it was Russian nationalism that finally ended Soviet communism, and that it will be with Russia as an embryonic nation-state that the West will have to deal in future.

Ironically, but perhaps predictably, it was Western conservatives who were most assiduous in seeking to sustain the collapsing Soviet state. It was they – whose official philosophies are full of the importance of family, nationality and religion as sources of social and political order – who urged support for the greatest rationalist project in human history – the artificial construction of the Soviet state. Thus, former Prime Minister Margaret Thatcher, as late as September 1991, embarked on the absurd and doomed enterprise of recruiting support for the anachronistic figure of Gorbachev. In this she, and her advisers, allowed a shallow and petty *realpolitik* to obscure the genuine reality of the post-Soviet world. This is that it is the preservation of anything resembling the collapsed Soviet state, not amity among its successor states, that is the truly utopian fantasy.

Western policy during the Gorbachev period was one of the uncritical endorsement of the pursuit of a will-o'-the-wisp – the rational reform of communist institutions. The history of that period teaches that Soviet communism could not, as Gorbachev supposed, be reformed, but only abolished; and *perestroika* was, in reality, not a process of renewal of the Soviet state, but the beginning of its revolutionary collapse. The irony of Gorbachev's career is that, in deceiving the West on this fundamental point – no difficult matter, since it wanted to be deceived – he also deceived himself.

No one should imagine that the post-communist world will be all sweetness and light. On the contrary, though we cannot pierce the darkness of the future, it seems likely that the twenty-first century will be characterized by destructive conflicts as the twentieth has been, save that these will be fundamentalist, nationalist and Malthusian convulsions and will not stem from Enlightenment ideologies. In the period of uncertainty in which we find ourselves now, Western policy needs to be at once supremely flexible and unfalteringly resolute, based on the vital perception that the world is an intractably anarchic place in which readiness to use measured military force is a permanent necessity. The irony of the Soviet collapse will be at its bitterest if the West persists in its illusions and does not learn from it the lesson that propping up an unsustainable status quo does not yield peace but merely makes the disorders of transition from a failed Enlightenment regime even less tractable than they need to be. The lesson of the Gorbachev period is that, so powerful was the hold on Western opinion of Enlightenment illusion that it could not perceive that the project of reforming the Soviet system, one of the Enlightenment's most stupendous constructions, was itself only an ephemeral illusion of rationalism.

5

THE POST-COMMUNIST
SOCIETIES IN TRANSITION

Western opinion-formers and policy-makers are virtually unani-
mous in modelling the transition process of the post-communist
states in terms which imply their reconstruction on Western
models and their integration into a coherent international order
based on Western power and institutions. Underlying this virtually universal model are assumptions that are anachronistic
and radically flawed. It assumes that the system of Western-led
institutions which assured global peace and world trade in the
post-war period can survive, substantially unchanged or even
strengthened, the world-wide reverberations of the Soviet collapse; the only issue is how the fledgling post-communist states
are to gain admission into these institutions. This assumption
neglects the dependency of these institutions on the strategic
environment of the Cold War and their unravelling, before our
eyes, as the post-war settlement disintegrates. Both GATT and the
European Union are creatures of the post-war settlement which
rested on the division of Germany and Europe and US hegemony

in Western trade and security policy. It was always foolish to imagine that they could survive unscathed the reunification of Germany and the United States' retreat from global leadership prompted by the disappearance of the Soviet threat. In the event, the after-shock of German reunification has been to derail the movement to European monetary and political union. Whatever form may ultimately be assumed by the European Union, it is unlikely to be that of a federal superstate; and there is at least a real chance that in taking the federal project in Europe off the historical agenda, German reunification has returned us to all the classical dilemmas of an inherently unstable balance of power in Central Europe. It is not unreasonable to hope that these dilemmas can be coped with, on the basis of the many layers of co-operation that have evolved during the last few decades between the nation-states that comprise the European Union, once the mirage of a transnational European state has finally dissolved. At the same time, the weakened strategic commitment of the United States to the European continent has diminished the significance of the successful completion of the Uruguay Round. The final agreement, completed in December 1993, proved far less ambitious than any that was earlier conceived; and the nature and powers of GATT's successor, the World Trade Organization, remain vague and uncertain. The GATT agreement has yet to be ratified by the US Congress: an eventuality that remains likely, but, partly because of earlier Congressional ratification of NAFTA (which in effect created a regional trading bloc), cannot be taken for granted. The prospect of a world of regional blocs has not, in the event, been altogether dispelled by the GATT agreement. Even NATO has suffered a paralysis as to its future role which is far from being resolved and which is only compounded by its indecisive and ineffectual stance in the intractable war in former Yugoslavia.

The strategic consequence of the end of the Cold War has been the return to a pre-1914 world – with this difference, that the pre-1914 world was dominated by a single hegemonic power, Great Britain, whereas the return to nineteenth-century policies and modes of thinking in the United States leaves the world without any hegemonic power. It was to this strategic prospect of a return to a pre-1914 world that I referred, when in December 1989 I wrote:

> The aftermath of totalitarianism will not be a global tranquilliza-
> tion of the sort imagined by American triumphalist theorists of
> liberal democracy. Instead, the end of totalitarianism in most of
> the world is likely to see the resumption of history on decidedly
> traditional lines: not the history invented in the hallucinatory
> perspectives of Marxism and American liberalism, but the
> history of authoritarian regimes, great-power rivalries, secret
> diplomacy, irredentist claims and ethnic and religious conflicts.[1]

The upshot of these developments is that the initial prospect opened up by the events of 1989–90 – the prospect of Western institutions going on unchanged, or even strengthened, by the world-historical collapse of Soviet communism – has proved a complete mirage. On the contrary, the Soviet collapse has trig- gered a meltdown in the post-war world order, and in the domestic institutions of the major Western powers, which has yet to run its course. The fact is that by now there is no system of stable Western institutions into which the post-communist states might conceivably be integrated. The real prospect which looms is rather the reverse – that economic and military chaos in the post-Soviet world might engulf the West. This is the prospect of which we have been warned by George Soros, when he wrote: 'The collapse of the Soviet system threatens to become a defeat for the free world and, instead of being integrated, it is disintegrating. Indeed, what used to be the Soviet Union may become a black hole which may eventually swallow up civilization'.[2]

Soros has argued that the strategic uncertainties produced by the end of the Cold War may strengthen the movement to a closed, Fortress Europe:

> The threat of instability and the influx of refugees are good reasons to band together and build a 'Fortress Europe'. At the same time, the lack of unity in the European Community has the effect of reinforcing the political instability and economic decline in Eastern Europe.[3]

My argument, which goes against that of Soros at several points, will be that there is a real prospect of encompassing the post-communist states of Eastern Europe within an enlarged European Union, only if the project of a federal union in Europe is abandoned. Further, while recognizing the urgency of the problems created by renascent nationalism, and especially the need to protect national minorities, I shall argue that stable democratic institutions, like stable market institutions, must conform with the diverse national cultures in which, in historical practice, they are embedded. The project of a transnational political culture in Europe, animating a supranational polity, is utopian, and ought to be abandoned. We ought to be seeking institutions and policies that temper and contain the passions of nationalism, and render them compatible with the maintenance of a liberal society, rather than pursuing the utopian dream of transcending the nation-state.

The disintegration, or powerlessness and paralysis, of the Western transnational institutions in which the post-war world order was embodied is paralleled by the breakdown in the major Western powers of their domestic post-war political settlements. At present this is occurring very unevenly, with those countries whose post-war political settlement was most subject to exogenous geo-strategic factors, such as Italy and Japan, undergoing the most rapid, profound and irreversible transformations, and others, such as Britain, where the post-war political settlement was largely home-grown, being still in the early stages of its unravelling. Nevertheless, the crisis of Western transnational institutions is complemented by an ongoing meltdown of the various Western models of the nature and limits of market institutions in advanced industrial societies.[4] The alienation of democratic electorates from established political elites is pervasive in Western societies, including the United States.

Even in countries, such as the United States and Britain, where a feeble recovery from recession is occurring, it has the form of jobless growth, with the consequence of the enlargement of the underclass by ever higher levels of long-term unemployment, and, as an unavoidable concomitant, an ever worsening fiscal crisis of the state. Even in New Zealand, where its political prospects seemed brightest, the movement for market reform which dominated the Western political scene in the 1980s has run aground everywhere on the stubborn realities of democratic political life. The bipartisan adoption of neo-liberal policy in New Zealand has had the consequence that the electoral system in that country has been repudiated and a period of considerable political instability entered upon. In the post-communist world, the first post-totalitarian country, Poland, has seen the return to power of reconstituted communist parties, holding between them over two-thirds of the seats in the legislature. The neo-communist political backlash against ill-conceived policies of 'shock therapy', which began in Lithuania and has been strikingly evident in parts of eastern Germany, such as Brandenburg, was not unpredictable; but its lessons have yet to be digested by Western opinion. It is now obvious to all but the most purblind and fundamentalist ideologues of the free market that the post-communist states will not succeed, where all others have failed, in constructing a neo-liberal utopia. Indeed, in one of history's choicest – and cruellest – ironies, a legitimation crisis for Western market institutions, for which neo-Marxist theorists such as Habermas had looked in vain during the decades of

economic prosperity and Cold War, seems now to be underway, in the new historical context in which Soviet enmity has
vanished.

The disappearance of familiar post-war political landmarks has
left Western thought and policy regarding the post-communist
countries rudderless. In so far as there is any coherent Western
policy, it survives as a form of cultural or intellectual lag, intelligible only in an historical context that has now irretrievably
gone. Nor is this a form of intellectual failure without practical
consequences, since, in so far as it promises that a few years
of agonizing economic shock therapy for the post-communist
states will be followed by their speedy integration into a stable
Western economic order, it is setting up a scenario for devastating disillusionment with the West, particularly in Russia,
as it becomes unequivocally clear that the Western countries
are in deep disarray and are in no position to honour such
promises. The electoral success, in December 1993, of Vladimir
Zhirinovsky's radical nationalist, or neo-fascist, Liberal Democratic Party is an ominous portent of the political whirlwinds to
be reaped from the Western endorsement of neo-liberal policy
in the post-communist states. It has evidently eluded the grasp of
most defenders of such policies that their huge social costs are
bound to fuel anti-Western sentiment, especially in Russia. They
are in any case attended by huge political risks. To expect Russia
to converge smoothly and peacefully on any Western model is to
betray an ignorance of its history that is staggering; yet such
expectations are the basis of all Western policy to date, and they
are reinforced by the history-blind perspectives of neo-liberal
theory.

Policy-making on the basis of such expectations is not
only intellectually indefensible, but also politically frivolous,
and dangerous, in the highest degree. As with Yugoslavia, where
Western policy expressed the confusion – common enough
among diplomats and members of international bureaucracies[5]

– of familiarity with stability, and was committed to shoring up a status quo whose foundations had already been eaten away, Western policy toward the post-communist states will be impotent, or self-defeating, to the extent that it is based on the transplantation of Western models that are themselves unstable and in varying degrees of crisis in their countries of origin. Further, and most decisively, Western policy in regard to the post-communist states which encourages them to emulate a favoured Western exemplar – post-war Germany, Bolivia in the mid-1980s, or, most absurdly, Anglo-American capitalism during the brief and abortive episode of Thatcherite and Reaganite neo-liberalism – rests on a fundamental conceptual and methodological error. It presupposes that the development of market institutions in the post-communist countries can track or mirror that in Western countries despite the fact that its point of departure is an inheritance of central planning – an inheritance that is both material and cultural in composition – which no Western market economy has ever had to confront and which is, in truth, unique in human history. The very same intellectual error is expressed in strategies for post-communist transition that model themselves on policies – both of stabilization and of privatization – that have worked in the context of Western market economies, such as Bolivia, which possess the full legal and institutional infrastructure of the market, and whose economies in any case are already overwhelmingly in private ownership. When such policies are implemented in the post-communist countries, they are applied to economies which not only are burdened by the ruinous inheritances of central planning but also in most cases wholly lack the legal and institutional infrastructure of the market. Such policies are bound to end in failure and political upheaval.

It will be one of the central themes of this chapter that the transplantation of Western exemplars of market institutions is neither feasible nor desirable in the historical circumstances of most of the post-communist countries. Indeed the very idea of an exemplar or model for all, or even for any one, of the post-communist states is, or should be, highly suspect. It should be rejected, because it neglects the disastrous inheritance, unprecedented in history, of communist institutions which they all have in common, and also because it disregards the immense diversity of the cultural and political traditions to which the peoples of the post-communist states are now returning. It will also be argued, however, that the intellectual tradition of the social market thinkers, flexibly and resourcefully applied, provides an illuminating theoretical perspective from which the dilemmas of the diverse post-communist states can be understood and, so far as this is possible, resolved. This theoretical perspective has its origins in the Ordoliberalismus of the German Freiburg School of Eucken and his disciples: but I shall argue that, though the Eucken School animated the reforms that inaugurated the postwar German economic miracle, the social market perspective is not to be identified with the German or Rhine model, despite its massive achievements, or with any other model. On the contrary, the insight of the social market theorists that the cultural matrices of market institutions are as important, and no less diverse, than their legal frameworks, should make us sceptical of the claims of any model for market institutions, and of any mode of policy which is based on the tacit assumption that there is a single ideal-typical form of market institutions to which all economies will, should, or can, approximate. It would be wholly mistaken, for example, to suppose that the application of the social market perspective in Britain involves a transplantation into Britain of the practices and institutions of the Rhine model. Such a transplantation is precluded by Britain's historic inheritance of liberal individualist cultural forms, by the many divergences between British and German circumstances, and by the revisions presently underway in the Rhine model itself. In Britain, as elsewhere, the social market perspective dictates conformity with underlying cultural traditions. The primacy of cultural tradition in political life is a truth forgotten, or repressed, by all those who think there is, or that there could be, a Western exemplar for the post-communist states.

In order to set out, more extensively and systematically, the distinctive features of the social market perspective, however, we need first to consider the principal Western exemplars that have been advanced for the post-communist economies, including the example of authoritarian Chile, and understand the reasons for their inapplicability in most of these states. We need also to examine non-Western models of economic development, especially those of Japan and China, which have outperformed (and continue to outpace) all Western models on every relevant measure, so as to consider what may be learned from them about the nature and prospects of market institutions in the post-communist states, especially in Russia, Central Asia and other parts of the former Soviet Union, and how they bear on the social market perspective.

The chief exemplar of Western market institutions invoked for the post-communist states is, of course, the Anglo-American exemplar – or, as Fukuyama terms it with innocent parochialism, 'democratic capitalism'.[6] We may for our present purposes set aside the large differences which undoubtedly exist between the English and the US varieties of market institutions and focus instead on the reasons why neither embodies a model that is exportable to the post-communist lands. The first point to be made is that English market institutions are the result of a very long period of unplanned evolution, in which the common law was centrally important, and – despite the disruptions occasioned by the Civil War – during which England enjoyed a measure of political stability unknown in continental Europe. Indeed, there is a persuasive historical case that England was always an exception in Europe, with the successful industrialization that occurred in the eighteenth and nineteenth centuries being preceded by many centuries of agrarian capitalism and possessive individualism, and facilitated by the form of parliamentary sovereignty which had been established in England by the early eighteenth century. A Great Transformation from feudal to market-based economic institutions, of the sort to which writers such as Engels and Karl Polanyi refer, may have taken place in other European countries, such as France; there is little historical evidence that it occurred in England, where economic individualism is immemorial.[7] This English path of development to market institutions, so far from being in any sense typical or paradigmatic, is in every sense a special and limiting case. Contrary to Hayek,[8] who generalizes from the English experience to put forward a grandiose theory of the spontaneous emergence of market institutions that is reminiscent in its unhistorical generality of Herbert Spencer and Karl Marx at their most incautious, the English example is a singularity, not an exemplar of any long-run historical trend. The English experience is *sui generis*, not a paradigm for the development of market institutions, because the unique combination of circumstances which permitted it to occur as it did – immemorial individualism and parliamentary absolutism, for example – were replicated nowhere else. Where market institutions did develop elsewhere on English lines, as in North America and Australasia, it was in virtue of the fact that English cultural traditions and legal practice had been exported there more or less wholesale. Market institutions of the English variety failed to take root where, as in India, their legal and cultural matrix was not successfully transplanted.

The first reason why the market institutions of the post-communist countries will not be those of Anglo-American capitalism is that they do not have the luxury of several centuries of legal evolution in a context of massive and almost uninterrupted political stability in which the English were so fortunate. Further, their underlying cultural and legal traditions are nowhere those of the common law; where these traditions have survived the communist period more or less intact, as in the Czech lands, they are German. Where their indigenous legal traditions have been destroyed during the communist period, as in Romania, say, they will have no alternative to attempting to graft a foreign legal code on the stem of whatever institutions retain any legitimacy – in Romania, probably only the institution of monarchy. If they follow this latter course, they will not be entirely without precedent. The Scots adopted a wholly novel, Romano-Dutch legal code, in less than a generation, around the start of the eighteenth century, at the initiative of a handful of lawyers inspired by a single man, James Dalrymple, the first Viscount of Stair;[9] modern Turkey was founded when a foreign legal code was imposed on it by fiat by Kemal Atatürk; Meiji Japan adopted important elements of German legal practice; and so on. In these and similar cases, the legal framework of market institutions, and of a civil society, is not a spontaneous emergence from a long period of incremental and evolutionary change, but the result of swift and radical initiatives, undertaken in favourable circumstances. Most of the post-Soviet states have no option but to follow this latter course, with all its uncertainties; the English path, with its leisurely pace and fortunate historical context, is not an option for them.

Nor, if they consider the recent record of Anglo-American capitalism, is it an especially promising option for them. It has, in particular, nothing to tell them as to how to avoid, or cope with, the large-scale unemployment that goes with the transition process, when, in Britain and even in the United States, much smaller levels of structural economic change, followed by a weak resumption of growth, have not significantly dented long-term unemployment. Again, the policies of privatization and marketization, undertaken in the English-speaking countries during the era of Thatcherite and Reaganite hegemony, against background conditions that were incomparably less adverse, have not achieved their avowed goal of massively reducing state economic activity, as measured by the resources pre-empted by government in taxation and expenditure. On the contrary, both government expenditure and taxation remained virtually unaltered as fractions of national income in the United States and in Great Britain, after a decade of policy animated by neo-liberal ideology; and, at present, in the wake of the predictable political wreckage of neo-liberal policy, both are rising fast.

The failures, or the abandonment under the pressures of democratic political competition, of neo-liberal policies in Britain and the United States should be a warning for anyone who seeks to model transition policy in the post-communist countries on the flawed exemplars of Thatcher and Reagan of the political costs, and ultimately self-defeating consequences, of attempting to implement the utopian paradigm of market liberalism. Such a warning may not be needed in the post-communist world itself, where Anglo-American capitalism is widely perceived to be in rapid and precipitate decline, and where there are now few who expect to learn anything of importance from it; but it unfortunately remains necessary for those Western advisers who model their policy prescriptions on idealized versions of the Anglo-American model and of its history of aborted market reform in the 1980s, and who remain captivated by the delusive simplicities of market liberal ideology despite its miserable record in the Western countries where policy was for a while animated by it. It would be a pity if the post-communist countries, where the political stakes and human costs are incomparably higher than in any Western country, became laboratories for ideologies whose central beliefs have already been tested to destruction in Western societies where the conditions for their implementation were far more favourable.

We may be briefer in our consideration of the Swedish model. It is worth recalling that, as recently as the late 1980s, the Swedish model was strongly favoured, both by Gorbachev and his advisers, and by modish opinion in the West, as the chief

Western exemplar for the development of market institutions in the Soviet world. This adoption of the Swedish model was an absurdity for at least three reasons. First, it underestimated the instability of Soviet institutions, holding out a prospect of their reformability which, though almost universally endorsed by Western opinion at that time, was completely delusive. As I wrote in the *Financial Times* in September 1989:

> The danger is that the decay of the totalitarian system built up by Lenin and Stalin will not result in the reconstitution of a stable civil society, but in mounting chaos and economic collapse. . . . If this is so, then what we are witnessing in the Soviet Union is not the middle of a reform, but the beginning of a revolution, whose course no one can foretell.[10]

The appeal of the Swedish exemplar as a model for development in the Soviet world rested on the illusion that its difficulties were not terminal – on the illusion, propagated by the Soviet *nomenklatura*, and imbibed uncritically by all sections of Western opinion, including notably Western Sovietology, that its crisis could be overcome by the reformist programme of *perestroika* – and on the appeal, irresistible both to the Soviet elite and to Western opinion-formers, that the path of development for the Soviet Union was a 'third way' between capitalism and socialism. This appeal has been destroyed by the collapse, political as well as economic, of the Swedish model in 1991, and the progressive dismantling, in the early 1990s, of its most distinctive institutions and policies. There is now no Swedish model which the post-Soviet states could emulate – which is the second reason for its inappropriateness as a paradigm for post-communist development.

Even before its collapse, the Swedish model could be considered a feasible paradigm for the post-Soviet states, only if its nature and historical development were thoroughly misunderstood. Consider its inception. From 1870 to the 1920s, Sweden was ruled by a small, old-style liberal government, with a political base in limited suffrage, whose economic interventions amounted to little more than mild agricultural and industrial tariffs. It was under these institutions and policies that the decisive early phase of Swedish economic development occurred. Or consider the later evolution of the Swedish model. In the first forty years after the Swedish Social Democrats came to power in 1932, the role of government in the economy was on most measures smaller than that in many other Western states. In 1960, government spending was 31 per cent of GNP in Sweden, only three points higher than that in the United States, and tax levels were not markedly different in the two countries; for the whole of the period of Social Democratic rule, governmental economic regulation was far less restrictive than in most other countries, and vastly less so than in the United States: capital gains tax was non-existent or slight; government ownership of industry was negligible; and so on.[11] The fact is that, even at its most interventionist, Sweden had a more comprehensively capitalist economy than most other Western countries. The downfall of the Swedish experiment occurred only as a result of policies initiated in the 1970s, when radically redistributionist income tax and transfer schemes were imposed on highly capitalist market institutions which were already weakened by emerging stagflation. It is noteworthy that, until its collapse in 1991, the Swedish model performed well in respect of what was, perhaps, its principal achievement, an active labour policy that kept long-term unemployment very low, and so effectively prevented the growth of an estranged underclass of the multi-generationally unemployed.

This distinctive historical context and development of the Swedish model provides the third reason why it is, in general, a wholly inappropriate one for the post-communist states. The crucial early stages of economic development occurred under institutions of limited franchise and liberal government that exist nowhere in the post-Soviet world, and they took place against a background of legal institutions – a law of property and of contract, for example – that in the Soviet world have been systematically uprooted. Further, Sweden had the not inconsiderable advantage of over a century of capital accumulation uninterrupted by the destruction occasioned by two world wars. Yet again, the successes of the Swedish experiment, such as the active labour policy, were achieved against the backdrop of conditions – a highly culturally homogenous population with strong habits of law-abidingness, and an uncorrupt tradition of public service – none of which is to be found in the post-communist lands. Finally, and most obviously, the welfare institutions, for which Sweden was justly famous, proved too expensive to be sustainable in Sweden, one of the world's richest countries; they are entirely beyond the reach of the post-communist countries, the most fortunate of which cannot expect to reach Western living standards in less than a generation. The plain fact is that social democracy on the Swedish model is a non-starter for the post-communist societies, even as it is crumbling throughout most of Western Europe. Indeed, social democracy, as that was traditionally understood, is probably nowhere on the political and historical agenda, even in Western Europe, where – except perhaps in Spain – moderate socialist parties are in deep decline, and the historic institutions and policies of social democracy are under threat everywhere.

By far the most powerful exemplar of Western market institutions in the post-communist countries is the German model. Nor should this be surprising. The legal and cultural inheritance of many of the East Europeans is German, and the composition of foreign investment, both in Eastern Europe and in Russia, is overwhelmingly German. If Germany emerges from the trauma of reunification as the hegemonic power in Eastern Europe few there will be surprised. Despite its recent difficulties. Germany is still regarded as the real economic success story of the post-war world, and it is Germany, not the English-speaking countries, which sets the standard of normality in the economy and in society to which the post-communist countries aspire. The German economic miracle appears to many to be a precedent far more appropriate to post-communist circumstances than any other Western exemplar. It arose on the ruins of a totalitarian political system and its associated command economy and it did so relatively quickly, over a period of a few years, by dramatic acts of deregulation and legislative activism – initiated, incidentally, against the advice and wishes of the Allied occupying powers, by Erhard under the influence of indigenous German traditions of Ordoliberalism and Catholic social theology – not by any slow incremental process. Further, as one of its principal founders himself asserted, 'The economic system had to be consciously shaped'.[12] This explicit recognition of the necessity for the reconstruction of market institutions by a far-reaching programme of legislative activism accords far better with the needs and circumstances of the post-communist states than anything in the Anglo-American experience. For all these reasons, it is undeniably the case that of all the Western exemplars the German model has by far the most resonance in the post-communist world. None the less, as with the Swedish model, the singularities of the German post-war pattern of development preclude its transplantation to any of the post-communist countries. In the first place, the Nazi regime was short-lived by Soviet standards, and the degree of totalitarian control it achieved correspondingly weaker. In particular, the legal infrastructure of civil society and of market institutions in Germany, though it was greatly damaged, was not comprehensively devastated there as it was in most of the countries of the Soviet bloc. A body of commercial and corporate law, of contract and property law, remained substantially intact, as did institutions of banking and finance. In short, the legal and institutional matrix of market institutions did not need to be created *ex nihilo* in post-war Germany, as they do throughout the post-communist world: they required legislative renovation and redefinition rather than reinvention. In the second place, the complete destruction of the National Socialist regime in a total war was followed by the destruction or dispersal of the body of the Nazi *nomenklatura*. Post-war Germany was not burdened, as the post-communist states are burdened, by a ubiquitous and resourceful caste of nomenklaturists, skilled at turning market reform to its advantage, and at manipulating the fledgling democratic institutions. It had the good fortune that sometimes comes from national catastrophe, that it brought about a scattering of the collusive interest groups that otherwise thwart, or capture, the process of transition to new institutions. By contrast, the post-communist states, even Russia, have the disadvantage that comes from not enough of their old social structure having been destroyed. These two factors taken together – the survival in Germany of much of the old legal and civil infrastructure and the comprehensive dissolution of the previous Nazi regime – mark a disanalogy between the circumstances of post-war Germany and of the post-communist states that is decisive for the prospects, and appropriate strategies, of market reform in the wake of the Soviet collapse.

There is another circumstance of crucial importance that prevents any transposition of the German model into the post-communist states.[13] This is the fact that the post-war German economic miracle arose on the basis of an *ad hoc* political settlement, wholly indigenous in character, that is not replicable elsewhere, and may indeed now be breaking down in Germany itself. The German or Rhine model of market institutions, as it developed in the post-war period up to reunification, was not the result of the application of any consistent theory, but rather of a contingent political compromise between a diversity of theoretical frameworks, of which the most important were the

Ordoliberalismus of the Eucken or Frankfurt School and Catholic social theology. It represented a political settlement, also, between the principal interest groups in post-war Germany, including the newly constituted trade unions. (The reconstitution of the trade unions in post-war Germany is another important point of contrast with the post-communist countries, in many of which – particularly Poland – the old communist unions have managed to renew themselves without any radical changes in their leadership or organization.) In other words, it reflected, or embodied, the most influential traditions of economic and social thought in pre-Nazi Germany, in the forms in which they had survived the National Socialist period, and it expressed a profound national consensus, embracing all the major interest groups, in Western Germany. It was this national consensus which supported modes of co-operation or co-determination between worker and employer which were unimaginable in Anglo-American contexts, and which made of corporatist institutions in Germany an engine of economic growth rather than an economic deadweight, as in the United Kingdom in the 1970s. The shock of reunification has broken this undergirding consensus, at least for the foreseeable future, and will necessitate a reworking of the Rhine model over the coming years, in which a new political settlement will need to be forged.

This is by no means to underestimate the German post-war achievement, or to pass over its theoretical genesis in Walter Eucken's seminal article of 1948 'On the Theory of the Centrally Administered Economy: An Analysis of the German Experiment', in which Eucken at the same time showed the incompatibility of central economic planning with the practice of a *Rechtstaat* and for the same reason rejected any policy of *laissez-faire*. On the contrary, the German experiment in Ordoliberalism was far more successful than any of the recent experiments in economic liberalism in the Anglo-American world. As Hutchison observes, no less truly in the mid-1990s than in 1981:

so persistent, and seemingly ineluctable, has been the extension of the role of government in so many economically advanced, democratic countries, that it is difficult to cite any case from such countries where a significant rolling back of the inter-ventionist tide has been achieved, except after major wars. Even there, the role of government in the economy has usually only been reduced as compared with the all-pervasive central regulation of wartime, and not nearly pushed back to the previ-ous peacetime level. To these generalisations the Social Market Economy of the German Federal Republic has provided the outstanding exception among the leading Western democratic countries.[14]

The point is that the political settlement on which the German achievement rested was a contingent historical phenomenon; and that it has been broken, or weakened, and will need to be renewed in another form, as a result of German reunification.

This is hardly surprising: which other economy could have withstood an exogenous shock as deep as that arising from the absorption of the bankrupt GDR? The magnitude of the shock itself was not entirely unpredictable. In July 1989, I wrote in the *Times Literary Supplement*:

Whatever the outcome of current negotiations, it is safe to assert that neither the division of Germany in its present form, nor West Germany's current relationship with NATO, can be sustained for long. As it stands, the political and military pos-ture of Western Germany disregards both the realities of history and legitimate German aspirations for unification; and the pressures for a separate settlement between West Germany and the Soviet Union are probably irresistible. . . . The darker side of the dissolution of the post-war settlement is in the prospect of . . . West Germany prised loose from NATO only to inherit the rusting industries and the indigent pensioners of the GDR.[15]

Even this dark assessment did not anticipate that – very ominously, for the other post-communist states – much of the GDR's industrial plant cannot be privatized on any terms that are acceptable to the world market, but only liquidated, at vast cost in transitional unemployment. The huge economic trauma of reunification is undoubtedly the chief factor in Germany's current economic malaise, and will demand a renegotiation of the post-war German economic settlement on terms we cannot at present foresee. In addition, there are doubtless other factors, such as its very high labour and welfare costs, that will necessitate radical revisions in the inherited Rhine model in the near and medium-term future.

The point relevant to our present purpose is that no post-communist state, with the possible and partial exception of the Czech Republic,[16] has either the degree of consensus, or the potential wealth, to replicate the Rhine model in any foreseeable future. They do not have the convergence of interests that facilitated German corporatism, and they cannot afford the welfare institutions whereby the political stability of German corporatism was guaranteed. As we shall later see, this does not mean that the social market perspective which draws, among other sources, on German Ordoliberalism, is not the most fruitful point of departure for the post-communist states in transition, since, though it acknowledges a large debt to the German model, the social market perspective must not be identified with that, or any other model. It does mean that there is no prospect of exporting to Eastern Europe a German model that, in this respect like the other Western models, has its historical roots in circumstances that cannot be replicated elsewhere and which may no longer exist in Germany itself. It is, indeed, perhaps not too much of an exaggeration to say that the German model is now engaged in a process of metamorphosis which in certain respects runs parallel with the transition process in some of the post-communist states themselves.

The difficulties of combining the vast dislocations of market reform in the post-communist countries with democratic institutions have led some, particularly in Poland and Russia, to look favourably on the prospects of constructing market institutions under authoritarian political auspices. Such proposals have come largely, but not exclusively, from within the communist oligarchies. In Poland such communist thinkers as B. Lagowski have looked with favour on the Chilean example,[17] while in Russia figures such as the so-called 'black colonel', Victor Alksnis, an animating force of the 'Soyuz' group of military officers and others dedicated to the maintenance of the Soviet state, have done likewise.[18]

There is little doubt that the model of Pinochet's Chile will exercise a continuing fascination on political elites in some of the post-communist countries, above all in Russia, where the likelihood of recourse to political authoritarianism is highest. There is, however, little more reason to suppose that the Chilean model is exportable to Russia, say, than there is to think that Western models of the development of market institutions in tandem with democracy can be successfully transplanted. The notion that there is an exportable Chilean model probably arises from a misinterpretation of the Chilean experience itself. It is arguable that the historical role of the Pinochet dictatorship was not – as Western neo-liberals imagine – to install any model of market institutions in Chile. It was instead to return Chile to political traditions which the Allende regime threatened to overturn. (I do not mean here to try to justify, or otherwise to pass judgement on, the complex and tragic political events that led up to Pinochet's coming to power. My point is that the long-term significance of the Pinochet period is easily overestimated both by its critics and by its defenders.) Crucially important here is the fact that in Chile there was a highly developed civil society, complete with the legal infrastructure of market institutions, and a political tradition of democratic rule longer than that of many

European states. The historical project of the Pinochet dictatorship was not, then, the construction of market institutions, or of a civil society, in Chile, since both already existed; it was their protection from destabilization by the Allende regime. This interpretation of the Chilean experience is supported by its upshot, which has been the return in Chile after Pinochet to the political traditions that were normal before Allende – an outcome that was decisively confirmed in December 1993, with the election of the centre-left president Eduardo Frei.

This interpretation suggests the fundamental reasons why the Chilean experience cannot be replicated in the post-communist states, even in Russia. Russia lacks the legal infrastructure of market institutions and the political traditions of a civil society. It is inherently unlikely that these would emerge from a military dictatorship, given that the task of such a regime would not be the feasible one of returning Russia from traditions from which it had been briefly deflected, but rather the heroic one of reconstructing anew, rebuilding *de novo*, institutions that were destroyed generations ago and of which no living memory or tradition remains. It is far from clear that Russia possesses any longer armed forces equal to the task of imposing for a protracted period a stable military dictatorship, let alone one with such an ambitious project of institution-building. At present, Russia's armed forces are demoralized and fragmented, lack a coherent chain of command and are fully occupied in containing violence in Russia's 'near abroad'. If the project of constructing market institutions in Russia under the auspices of a military dictatorship were attempted, it would demand leadership of the genius of Peter the Great or Atatürk to have any real prospect of success. In comparison, Pinochet's project was a modest one. Should a military regime emerge in Russia – most plausibly by a mutation of policy in the present leadership rather than by a coup – its goals are likely to be the staving off of anarchy in the Russian Federation and the preservation of established interests, particularly those of the military-industrial complex, rather than market reform. Such an outcome is far from being the worst imaginable for Russia, in which anarchy – a repetition of the dreaded 'Time of Troubles' in the early seventeenth century, recalled in Mussorgsky's *Boris Godunov* and Glinka's *A Life for the Tsar*, when Russia descended into anarchy – is a real danger; but it is unlikely to achieve, by authoritarian means, objectives – the construction of market institutions and of a civil society – in which a democratic or quasi-democratic regime has already failed. If this is true of Russia, an authoritarian regime is likely to be no more promising in Poland, where a Pinochet-style authoritarian regime has in any case been taken off the historical agenda by the coming to power of a neo-communist coalition.

Because, for all of these reasons, even authoritarian Western models have poor prospects in those post-communist states whose problems of transition are greatest, except as devices for staving off anarchy, it is natural that the political elites of the post-communist countries should – especially in Russia – have looked East, for non-Occidental models of economic development. Of these, the example of Japan in the post-war period has by far the most relevance to the present circumstances of Russia and to its pre-communist history. This is so, partly because economic growth took off in post-war Japan against a background of demilitarization, which strikingly resembles the task of civilianization of the military-strategic sector now confronting the Russian government. (The most ominous implication of the political success of Vladimir Zhirinovsky's Liberal Democratic Party in December 1993 may, however, turn out to be the abandonment or slowing of the civilianization programme that had been pursued, fitfully enough, by Yeltsin until then.) Further, it was propelled by deep governmental involvement in all the most decisive areas of the economy – a fact that has echoes in the pattern of economic growth of Tsarist Russia[19] – and not by anything resembling *laissez-faire*. Finally, the astounding Japanese economic success of the post-war period was achieved, in part, by a policy of not opening Japan's economy to world markets – a fact of the closest relevance to the situation of Russia and the other post-Soviet states, upon which free trade is urged by Western advisers and institutions, but who have no realistic hope of competing in world markets. The Japanese example is, in fact, considerably closer to the historical experience and present circumstances of Russia than any of the Western models, or indeed than any of the other non-Western models, including that of China; and it merits the most careful study by policy-makers in Russia, in Central Asia and perhaps elsewhere in the post-Soviet world. There are important disanalogies between the two contexts, nevertheless, which entail that there are real limits to the extent to which the lessons of the Japanese experience can be applied in the post-Soviet world, and especially in Russia.

It should never be forgotten that the decisive period of industrialization and economic development in Japan was not the post-war period, but the Meiji period, from the second half of the nineteenth century onwards, during which Japan industrialized, earlier than most Western states, and built up a navy which destroyed the Russian fleet at Tsushima in 1904. In achieving this extraordinary feat, Japan had two advantages not possessed by any other Asian people: an intact social structure, which had never been subject to Occidental invasion or colonization; and a subtle and purposeful elite, which created a highly competent and skilled bureaucracy. Decisively, by contrast both with other Asian powers in the nineteenth century, such as India, and with Russia in our own time, Japan possessed not only a social structure and elite that was intact and vital, but also a massive degree of cultural and ethnic homogeneity, which allowed for national policy to be pursued unswervingly for long periods. By contrast with Japan, Russia today is ethnically and culturally heterogenous to an extreme degree, its social structure has been devastated by generations of Soviet rule, and it lacks anything resembling an honest or competent bureaucracy or even a coherent ruling elite. The Japanese path to development cannot be replicated in Russia because these necessary conditions for its success are lacking there. As with the German model, this is not to undervalue the Japanese achievement, which encompasses a level of full employment which has been matched, or maintained, by no Western country. Nor is it to neglect the most distinctive feature of this achievement – a degree, and depth, of successful governmental concertation of the economy that reveals the narrow cultural parochialism of much Western economic theory and policy analysis. It is partly in order to maintain this unique achievement that any Japanese government should – and will – reject out of hand the demands of the US-inspired Structural Impediments Initiative, which amount to little more than the project of Americanizing the Japanese economy. It should, most especially, resist the importation into Japan of Western, and especially US, policies on employment, which run against Japanese traditions of lifetime employment and Japanese concern for communal harmony. This is not to say that the Japanese model can be renewed in its present form, any more than the German model can be so renewed. It is to say that its likely, and desirable, future lies in an evolution in which its most distinctive and extraordinary achievements are preserved. There can be no doubt that the Japanese model merits close study in Russia. Nevertheless, it cannot sensibly be denied that many of the necessary conditions for the unparalleled success of the Japanese model are absent in Russia. For similar reasons, including especially the absence in Russia of a skilled and uncorrupt bureaucracy, the South Korean model of *dirigiste* market development cannot be emulated either.

The Chinese model seems to many to be most pertinent to Russian circumstances for two reasons. First, economic reform was adopted and pursued, with a considerable measure of success, before political reform, that is to say, it was promoted under authoritarian political auspices; and, second, with respect to economic policy, agrarian reform was pursued before the reform of industry. As it is commonly put, in China *perestroika* was pursued before *glasnost*, and the crucial first phase of economic restructuring occurred in agriculture, not in industry. True as these common observations may be, they do not show that what has been achieved in China was ever possible in Russia. Consider China's successful agrarian policy. This depended crucially on the fact that the Chinese communist regime had not succeeded in the Bolshevik project of destroying the peasant family and the peasant cultural tradition, as did the Soviet regime. It is doubtful if a policy of agrarian reform on Chinese lines could ever have been initiated in Russia, since the Russian agricultural proletariat lacks both the skills and the ambitions of a peasantry; for the most part, it neither wants, nor has the capacity, to own and farm its own land, its entrepreneurial activities being restricted to niches in the collective farm system, such as the private plots from which much of Russia's food supply derives. It is certain that if a Chinese-style agrarian reform had been launched in Russia its results would have been very different from those in China: such is the measure of Bolshevik success in exterminating peasant cultural traditions in Russia. A more modest agrarian reform might have had a measure of success, and might do so even now, but not plausibly on the scale of China's, and not sufficiently to alter radically the prospects of market reform in Russia.

Both the political and military environments in Russia are in any case too divergent from those in China to allow for a replication there of the Chinese success. The key difference is the massively smaller level of divisive ethnic diversity in China. It would be false to imagine that China lacks ethnic conflict, or separatist movements. As a portent for the future, there appears to be an Islamic separatist movement in the far-western 'autonomous region' of Xinjiang, which has borders with the new republics of Kyrgystan, Kazakhstan and Tajikistan, and with Afghanistan and Pakistan; and there are undoubtedly strong separatist movements in neighbouring Tibet and Mongolia. None of these movements currently mounts a threat to the integrity of the Chinese state such as is constituted by the ongoing savage war in Tajikistan, by the secessionist state of Chechnya, or by separatist demands in Tatarstan and the Russian Far East. Of course, it would not be entirely surprising, but would in fact rather accord with long-term patterns in Chinese history, if the Chinese state were to fragment in the coming years, perhaps after the death of Deng Xiaoping; but the strength of the army, which has been all-important in China since the Cultural Revolution weakened the Party apparatus there, counts heavily against that scenario. The very weakness of the Party since the Cultural Revolution means that economic reform has not encountered in China resistance of the strength it has come up against in Russia, particularly now that the Party has reasserted itself at the levels of local government in Russia, where the only real power now lies. So far, at any rate, China has succeeded in its project of fostering market institutions under a Hobbesian peace. In short, in comparison with Russia, China is a strong unitary state; for this reason it has been able to promote market reform while steadfastly refusing, or successfully repressing, demands for political reform, and without allowing the emergence of the institutions of a Western-style civil society. In addition, unlike Russia, China has not adopted any Western-based model of economic policy in which government relinquishes control of overall economic development; as in the other East Asian exemplars, strategic involvement of government in industry is pervasive, and normal. It is partly its resistance to Western advice, and to Western exemplars, that accounts for the Chinese economic achievement.

The Chinese success may be approached from another angle. The Chinese reform project is not that of copying any Western model but of building market institutions *without* any corresponding civil society. It is that of building market institutions under the shelter of a Hobbesian peace but not of a civil order.

If there is a model for it, it is not Western but anti-Western, that of Singapore, in which *dirigiste* market institutions are reinforced by political and cultural authoritarianism. Further, in Singapore as in Japan, South Korea and Taiwan, the policy-forming elites have wisely resisted the Western prescription of unfettered free trade – an aspect of Singaporean policy that has not been lost on the Chinese elite. The Singaporean achievement of maintaining virtually unparalleled levels of economic growth against a background of social peace and political stability is especially pertinent to the Chinese circumstance because, unlike Japan but like China, Singapore is not ethnically homogenous. Further, China and Singapore have in common – in this respect along with Japan – cultural traditions, Confucian in origin, which are favourable both to political stability and to market institutions. In promoting economic development on this authoritarian model, accordingly, China has the inestimable advantage of strong indigenous traditions (Confucian in origin) which support political authority and are congenial to market institutions. It is this fact, probably more than any other, that explains the astounding success of the Chinese economic reform. It also accounts for the difficulties of emulating it, especially in Russia.

Russia has no such cultural traditions, that of Orthodoxy being weak and compromised, and in any case having no fondness for the market. If, as is a real possibility, following the strong electoral showing of Russian neo-fascist groups in December 1993, the Russian regime were to fall back on Russia's endogenous cultural traditions, this would not be as a stimulus for market reform but as a means of replenishing its faltering legitimacy. Such a nativist move in Russia would not advance, but, because of central elements in the Russian religious and cultural tradition, would more likely retard the development of market institutions in Russia. For better or worse, the prospects of market institutions in Russia lie, now and in the future, with Westernizers, not nativists. (Such Westernizers can, to be sure, lay claim also to a legitimate Russian tradition. Most ethnic Russians have long considered themselves to be Europeans in their cultural inheritance, notwithstanding its many unique features. At the same time, there has always been in Russia another, anti-Western tradition, which has resurfaced, especially in the armed forces, in a 'Eurasian' ideology, which conceives Russia as midway between Western and Oriental cultural traditions. It would be frivolous and dangerous to suppose that this other Russian tradition, now embodied in an electorally successful neo-fascist party, cannot in the coming years have a profound influence on policy, especially in circumstances of Weimar-like economic collapse and national humiliation.) The Chinese scenario, in which indigenous cultural traditions are used to bolster political authority and market reform at one and the same time, cannot be duplicated in Russia because the cultural tradition of Orthodoxy, though it is favourable to authority, is hostile to commercial civilization. It follows that, along with the major Western models, the Chinese model is inapplicable in Russia.

The non-Western exemplars have more relevance to the post-Soviet states, and especially to Russia, than any of the Western exemplars other than Germany, principally because they are built on the recognition of the necessity of active governmental involvement at every stage in the development of market institutions. They recognize, in other words, the utter unrealism of exposing the post-communist economies to the rigours of market competition, when their communist economic inheritance means that they cannot survive unsheltered in global markets, and lack even the institutional infrastructure for domestic market competition on Western lines. Further, the non-Western models have the advantage of a track record that, unlike most of the Western economies apart from Germany, and particularly unlike that of the Anglo-American countries, combines rapid economic growth with social harmony and stable communal life. All these factors should commend the non-Western models to the policy-forming elites of the post-communist countries for the lessons they can teach, particularly of the advantages of resisting Western advice; but they do not mean that any of these models can be duplicated or replicated in the post-communist world.

From the social market perspective which I shall try to set out, it is entirely understandable that there should be no model, Western or East Asian, which can be replicated in the post-communist states. This is not merely because Russia, say, lacks the solidaristic traditions and the ethnic homogeneity that distinguish some of the East Asian exemplars; nor because even the Czech Republic, whose cultural and legal traditions have so much in common with Germany's, cannot afford to implement the generous measures of social welfare that have been distinctive of the German model, for example. It is the very idea of a model for all the post-communist states, or even for any one of them, that is suspect. This idea springs from a conception of market institutions that is overly abstract and general, which neglects their various structures and diverse histories, and which severs them from their supportive cultural matrices, where it does not implicitly, and illicitly, invoke one species of them – 'democratic capitalism', perhaps – to stand for all of them. It is just this suspect conception of market institutions, as all being approximations to a single ideal type, that the social market perspective, as I understand it, is concerned to reject. The idea of a model or exemplar for the post-communist states, or even for any one of them, is mistaken for another reason: it underestimates the unique and unprecedented problems associated with transition from central planning institutions as comprehensive, and as long-standing, as those in the Soviet bloc. The developmental paths of market institutions in other parts of the world, and in other historical milieux, cannot be replicated anywhere in the post-communist world, because the inheritance of central planning does not vanish with the regimes which sponsored it. It lingers on pervasively, not only as habits of thought and expectation in the population, and as coalitions of groups with diverse and often conflicting interests in the market reform process, but also as physical plant, as logistical and distribution systems, as energy supply arrangements and – last but by no means least – as a terrible inheritance of pollution and environmental degradation. This inherited deformation of the institutional and natural environments is a common feature of every post-communist state, whatever their many differences may be. It does not disappear along with the system which produced it. This fact rules out, even as a possibility, the development of market institutions in post-communist states tracking or mirroring that in other historical contexts, such as post-war Germany, or South Korea. It also makes dangerously inappropriate, as we shall see, policies for the post-communist states that are modelled on policies of market reform that have been implemented, however successfully, in very different contexts – such as that of Bolivia in the mid-1980s.

What are the key ideas that define the social market perspective? There are, so far as I can see, six ideas that animate this intellectual tradition, as it is found among the German Ordo-liberals who are its principal intellectual progenitors, and as it is echoed in other, kindred thinkers such as Maynard Keynes. First, the social market theorists reject the view that markets are, or should be, the unplanned outcomes of cultural or institutional evolution. For these thinkers, market institutions are not forms of spontaneous order, which we receive as gifts from history, but instead human artefacts, created – in all their varieties beyond the most rudimentary – by legal artifice and political intervention. Second, and following from the first point, market institutions are not to be theorized, as they are commonly in the United States and by those who think of themselves as Lockeans, as being constituted by a structure of fundamental rights. Market freedoms are not best theorized as shadows cast by basic human liberties, and market institutions are not justified by their embodiment of any structure of supposed fundamental rights. Rather, market institutions are justified by their contribution to individual and collective well-being, and their structure – unlike, presumably, any structure of fundamental rights – is perpetually open to revision and reform. Third, on this view, market institutions must be complemented by other institutions, and by modes of public policy, which confer on market participants forms of security that market institutions by themselves cannot, or do not adequately, provide. Market institutions are not free-standing, but come to us – if they are at all stable – embedded in such other institutions, which both define their limits and confer legitimacy upon them. Among these institutions and policies are not only welfare institutions conferring entitlements on people but also macroeconomic policies designed to secure a stable economic environment – of both employment and prices – within which market participants can effectively operate. In some national and historical contexts, the policy framework may legitimately and desirably encompass an industrial policy which seeks to confer a measure of concertation on the research and development and on wage-bargaining. Market institutions are not then free-standing but part of a larger nexus of institutions from which they derive whatever stability and legitimacy they possess.

Fourth, and as an implication of the last point, market institutions have as their matrices particular cultural traditions, without whose undergirding support the frameworks of law by which they are defined are powerless or empty. Such cultural traditions are historically very diverse: in Anglo-Saxon cultures they are predominantly individualistic, in East Asia solidaristic or familial, and so on. The idea that there is a special or universal connection between flourishing market institutions and an individualistic cultural tradition is an historical myth, an element in neo-conservative folklore, especially in the United States, rather than the result of any disciplined historical or sociological investigation. Moreover, among the Scottish thinkers, such as Adam Smith and Adam Ferguson, who not unreasonably generalized from their own historical experience to such a connection, this result of their inquiries evoked anxiety as to the eventual fate of market institutions, since – like later thinkers such as Joseph Schumpeter – they feared that individualism would consume the cultural capital on which market institutions relied for their renewal across the generations. Our experience suggests that such fears as to the ultimately self-defeating effects of market institutions that are animated by individualist cultural traditions are far from groundless.

Fifth, market institutions legitimately and necessarily vary according to the diverse national cultures of the peoples who are their practitioners. There is no universal or ideal-typical model for market institutions, but instead a variety of historical forms, each rooted in the soil of a particular common culture. In the modern age, this common culture is that of a people or nation, or a family of such peoples. Market institutions which do not express, or accord with, an underlying national culture will be neither legitimate nor stable; they will mutate, or be rejected, by the peoples that are subject to them.

Sixth, and as a consequence of the last point, market institutions will not have popular acceptance or political stability if they do not meet standards of legitimacy set by their underlying cultures. In East Asian cultures, they must be compatible with the maintenance of social consensus and communal harmony. Among European peoples, they must – contrary to neo-liberal ideologues such as Hayek[20] – satisfy vague, but pervasive and deep-seated norms of equity and fairness; and they must be reconciled with the political demand for forms of common life, and a public environment, that are rich in choice-worthy options, that is recurrently generated through democratic institutions.[21] This last point is generalizable, and of considerable importance.

In all those cultures where democratic institutions are themselves elements in the common conception of legitimacy, market institutions will be stable and flourishing only in so far as their forms and workings are acceptable, ethically, culturally and economically, to the underlying population. Contrary to neo-conservative messianism about 'democratic capitalism', there is nothing to suggest that the combination of market institutions with political democracy, particularly in their Anglo-American forms, is at all universal. In China, and perhaps in parts of the post-Soviet world, market institutions may exist, and flourish, in combination with non-democratic regimes, for generations. They will do so, however, only if they accord with the cultural traditions of their practitioners. In countries where democratic conceptions of legitimacy are deep-seated, and democratic institutions themselves stable, market institutions will flourish only in so far as they match conceptions of fairness, community and for that matter of efficiency which find expression in democratic political life. Projects of market reform which are insensitive to the cultural norms of fairness to which democratic institutions give political expression are fated to ignominious failure. Whether or not democratic norms are deep-seated, projects of market reform in which governments relinquish overall strategic direction of the economy, and in which the course of rapid economic change is for that reason uncontrolled, will fail, and the regimes that preside over them will fall. In the post-communist world, weak democratic regimes which sponsor projects of market reform that result in economic dislocation that violates popular standards of acceptability will be swept away, and replaced by regimes whose commitments are neither to market reform nor to democracy.

One programmatic result of the foregoing analysis of Western and non-Western exemplars, and of the statement of the social market perspective that has been given, is that there can be no highly specific policy prescriptions that apply to all the

post-communist states. Despite their common communist inheritance, their present circumstances and their historical traditions
vary too greatly for any such advice to be sensible. Nevertheless,
there are some results of the argument of a fairly general sort
that have considerable leverage on current Western policy and
opinion regarding the post-communist states, and which are
illuminating in exemplifying the uses of a social market perspective or approach on these issues. There is first of all the result that
'shock therapy' of the sort advocated by Jeffrey Sachs for Poland
and Russia on the basis of its application in Bolivia is very
unlikely to be successful in any post-communist context. Enterprises subjected to market forces by a drastic stabilization policy
will confront an economic environment deformed by decades,
and in Russia generations, of communist central planning, and
lacking much, if not all, of the infrastructure of market institutions which enabled enterprises to adjust in Bolivia. A 'big bang'
policy on the lines that worked in Bolivia cannot work in any
post-communist state, because such a policy in Bolivia was
substantially one of legitimizing a huge parallel private economy
that was already in existence, and which required only deregulation to be legitimized. A policy of deregulation is meaningless
when the economy is dominated by elephantine state enterprises
that have never been subject to market forces and in which the
parallel economy, though large, is secondary in that it flourishes
in the interstices of the command economy. The result of shock
therapy as applied to the post-communist economies will only be
slump. This is recognised even by other free-market economists,
such as Sir Alan Walters, who has written:

> A damning report has been issued by the European Commission
> in Brussels and the London-based Centre for Economic Policy
> Research. It details what went wrong with economic reforms in
> Eastern Europe. The villains of the piece are the 'shock thera-
> pists' such as Harvard's Jeffrey Sachs. They recommend the

use of massive monetary squeezes to shock these economies into life. Shock therapy worked in Germany after World War Two, when applied to a free market economy with a social infrastructure in place. But Russia and Eastern Europe in 1993 are not Germany in 1948. Their economies are rigid, unreformed and bureaucratic. Instead of bringing them back to life, shock therapy just imposes pain.[22]

It is not only that shock therapy causes a big slump in output and employment. While such therapy is supposedly taking effect, large state enterprises will be able to protect themselves against its effects to a degree by constraining banks and suppliers to keep credit lines open to them. This in turn chokes off credit to the nascent private sector. Rather than assisting in the growth of the private sector in post-communist countries, shock therapy is far more likely to strangle it at birth. An analogous argument applies to the absurd demand that the post-communist econo- mies be opened to the full rigours of the world market. Such a policy would not only speed the death of the old state enter- prises but also prevent the birth of new private businesses. In most cases only a gradualist policy is likely to allow conditions to come about in which private enterprises can come to birth and flourish. The oft-repeated argument of economic radicals schooled in Western free-market ideology, which asserts that a gradualist strategy of market reform will only allow established interests to act collusively to thwart the process, or turn it to their own advantage, overlooks the fact that in Russia attempts at shock therapy have so far resulted in a wild, 'spontaneous' or 'Hayekian' privatization that is in fact only the latest episode in nomenklaturist expropriation and rent-seeking, and that the economic system it has yielded is a sort of anarcho-capitalism of competing mafias.[23] That these economic institutions are not perceived to be legitimate, and are not in fact politically stable, has been dramatically confirmed by the election results of

December 1993, which have produced a shift away from shock therapy. Indeed, the elections of December 1993 are proof, if proof were needed, that the political result of neo-liberal economic policy in Russia is massive instability. This is not a recipe for foreign investment, or for the political legitimacy or stability of market reform. It is rather a recipe for the shipwreck of the project of market reform itself.

A second general result of our analysis and of the social market perspective is that market institutions will not emerge, or survive, in the post-communist countries unless economic reform is accompanied, or complemented, by measures to offset its high transitional costs in terms of dislocation and unemployment. We have seen already that welfare institutions on any Western model are unlikely to be affordable anywhere in the post-communist world – if indeed they remain sustainable in the West – for at least a generation. A safety net of some sort for the relief of unemployment arising during the transition period is nevertheless indispensably necessary, if the market reform is to be politically tolerable and not attended by too large a drop in demand. One scheme suggested for Russia by George Soros is for an internationally financed safety net, distributed directly to unemployed and needy people in the form of Western hard currency.[24] Whether this particular scheme is feasible in currently prevailing Russian monetary conditions does not matter. The key point is that provision for a safety net, assuring elementary forms of material security to the common people, is a necessary condition of the political viability of market reform in post-communist contexts. This is only a particularly clear instance of the general truth, stated in our exposition of the social market perspective, that market institutions are not free-standing or self-justifying; they depend for their legitimacy on other institutions and policies, and on their workings conforming with popular norms of acceptability. Market institutions will not survive, without massive political coercion, if the early stages of their development in post-communist societies bring ruin or severe deprivation to millions, even by comparison with the miserable living standards endured by them during the communist period. That a safety net for such societies need not be prohibitively costly will be understood by those who know that the communist systems had very little that was comparable with the Western welfare state (a fact that should have commended them to Western neo-liberals, if it had been understood by them). A safety net could be affordable in many of the post-communist states, provided it was not modelled on those which exist in the West. This is only one fairly obvious respect in which the growth of market institutions in the post-communist world will be facilitated by the abandonment there of Western models of development.

A third general result of our inquiry concerns the legitimacy of the governments that sponsor market reform in post-communist societies. One of the lessons of historical experience is that a painful and protracted period of adjustment can be endured during the transition process provided the government overseeing it possesses popular legitimacy. The successful eradication of hyperinflation in Poland is a case in point: the legitimacy of the post-1989 government, its perceived character as an embodiment of Polish nationhood, enabled that phase of the stabilization process to be carried off with a good measure of success. That there are clear limits to such legitimacy is shown by the fate of the Landsbergis government in Lithuania, where even intense nationalist sentiment, deep rooted and progressive in the first people to break away from the Soviet state, could not prevent its toppling by economic hardship arising from Lithuania's energy dependency on Russia. If such experience is any guide, post-communist governments – in this respect no different from their Western counterparts – need to deliver a reasonable degree of economic security to the general population if they are to survive. They need to do this if they are to be able to afford the safety net to cover the transitional costs of dislocation discussed earlier. Their success in this depends partly on the wisdom and prudence of the macroeconomic policies they pursue, which it is no part of my purpose to discuss in any detail here. The success of post-communist governments in securing a reasonably stable economic environment during the transition period depends on another, and yet more vital factor – their ability to secure national security, to protect their citizens from foreign attack, civil strife, and organized criminality. In the absence of success in these Hobbesian tasks the whole agenda of market reform of any post-communist state is forfeit.

This is, perhaps, the hardest problem for most of the post-communist states to resolve. Almost all of them confront irredenta and national minorities whose dangers to peace are only compounded by the artificial territorial boundaries and the displacement of peoples they inherit from the Stalinist period. That this difficulty is a deadly serious one is evidenced not only by the Balkan war, and by conflicts in the Caucasus that have virtually destroyed the state of Georgia and that encompass an intractable war between Armenia and Azerbaijan over the disputed region of Nagorno-Karabakh, but by the dissolution of the Czechoslovak state and the questions over the borders of Hungary raised by the presence of significant Hungarian minorities in adjacent countries – separatist and irredentist issues that arise not at the periphery but at the very heart of Europe.

The hardest problem of all concerns Russia, which has never been a nation-state in any normal sense, and whose political embodiment, the Russian Federation, already shows unmistakable signs of the fissiparous tendencies which spelt ruin for its parent, the Soviet Union. Here the lessons of history are again being neglected. The history which is most relevant is that of the forgotten period between the collapse of the Russian Empire in 1917–18 and the foundation of the USSR in 1922–3. During that period both the Ukraine and Siberia declared independence.

Ukrainian independence was recognized only by Germany, but it was surrendered to the Bolsheviks only after the capital, Kiev, had changed hands fifteen times. It is difficult to believe that present demands for full Ukrainian sovereignty and for Siberian autonomy do not augur a period of political disintegration comparable to that which occurred in Russia between 1918 and 1922. The war in Tajikistan, which is virtually ignored by the world media but which may have already claimed well in excess of one hundred thousand lives, does not support the hope that this process of fragmentation will occur peacefully. At the very least, the prospect of fragmentation of the Russian Federation may evoke a radical nationalist political backlash in Russia, whose political and strategic objectives may not be confined to the maintenance of the integrity of the Russian Federation but may encompass the reclaiming of 'lost' territories of the former Soviet Union, including the Baltic states. The risk is that, if the Hobbesian danger of reversion to a 'Time of Troubles' is avoided in Russia, it may be at the cost of partially recreating, in an altered form, an old-style Soviet Leviathan, shorn of Soviet ideology, but not of much of the vast Soviet war machine. This is a prospect in which the danger to peace in Russia is tempered, but only by enhancing the risk to world peace.

Not all the post-communist states are imperilled equally by the strategic uncertainties generated by the Soviet collapse: Slovenia and the Czech Republic are, so far, virtually untouched. It is in the case of Russia that the Hobbesian problem is most urgent, and most intractable, compounded beyond imagination by the decomposition of the Leviathan of the strategic-industrial complex and by the flood of weaponries – including perhaps nuclear weaponries, or elements thereof – which it is releasing into the world. It is compounded yet further by the real possibilities, amounting by now to likelihoods, of environmental catastrophes, arising from the ongoing decay of the unsafe civilian nuclear power programme, on a scale as great, or probably greater, than that which occurred at Chernobyl. I have detailed elsewhere the almost apocalyptic environmental destruction which is perhaps the most catastrophic, because the most irreversible, inheritance of the Soviet system.[25] Evidence subsequently available suggests that the cost of environmental clean-up in the former USSR would cost around US$800 million over a period of a decade *aside from the cost of dealing with existing nuclear pollution*.[26] (This is, of course, in addition to the ordinary capital needs of Russia, which have been estimated at between $80 billion and $120 billion per annum for several years to come.[27]) It is obvious that no such sums will be forthcoming from any source, and that the threat not only of large-scale war but also of environmental catastrophe will continue to compound the Hobbesian dilemma of the Russian Federation for the foreseeable future.

The magnitude and severity of the Hobbesian problem in Russia, and its multifaceted character, is such that it conditions every other policy that may be pursued there. The rule of law, which is a necessary condition both of developed market institutions and of a civil society, was the first practice of civilized life to be destroyed by the Bolshevik dictatorship; it will probably be the last to be reinvented. In much, perhaps most of Russia, it may well – if the armed forces prove equal to the task, and another 'Time of Troubles' is avoided – reappear in the form of martial law. The growth of lawlessness in Russia, the threat posed to social and business life by organized criminality,[28] and the apparent powerlessness thus far of the Yeltsin government in the face of this threat, suggest that an authoritarian turn in Russian political life, whether by the Yeltsin government or by a successor, and whether or not the army has a decisive role in any subsequent authoritarian regime, would be in accord both with the exigencies of current circumstances and with Russian historical precedent. Authoritarian government is likely to emerge in Russia both in response to the dangers of fragmentation of the state and ensuing civil strife and as a response to growing criminal violence in everyday and business life. In such circumstances, any government will have perceived legitimacy that restores law and order and facilitates ordinary social and economic life, regardless of whether it develops a rule of law or other institutions characteristic of a Western-style civil society. It is in these respects, more than in any others, that the Chinese project of promoting market institutions under a Hobbesian peace, without the development of anything resembling a civil society, may be most pertinent to the case of Russia.

The Soviet collapse is an event of world-historical significance which will condition economic and political developments everywhere in the world, for decades or for generations; it is not an episode in Western privatization policy. It is wrongly perceived if it is seen as a moment in a global convergence on Western institutions. It cannot be the latter, for two large and mutually supportive reasons. First, the economic development of the post-communist societies cannot replicate or track that of Western market institutions, since the point of departure for all such societies is a common inheritance of communist central planning, physical and social, that figures at no point in the economic development of the West and is in fact unprecedented in history. Further, the post-communist countries, unlike the Western exemplars with which they are conventionally compared, lack almost entirely the legal and institutional infrastructure of the market on which economic take-off was based, and which policies of economic liberalization in Western countries presupposed as necessary conditions of their chances of success. We cannot know what economic development in the post-communist countries will be like; we can be certain that it will be unlike that in any Western country. It is unfortunate that the Soviet collapse occurred at a time when economic policy in the West was animated by a species of free-market fundamentalism, since the lingering in public consciousness of remnants of that mesianic creed has made the actual course of events in the post-communist lands even harder to comprehend, or to influence.

The second major reason why the Soviet collapse does not represent a mere extension of existing Western institutions is that it has plunged both the principal institutions of Western transnational co-operation and the domestic political settlements of the leading Western states into a crisis. The Soviet collapse, far from enhancing the stability of Western institutions, has destabilized them by knocking away the strategic props on which they stood. The prospect of the orderly integration of the post-communist states into the economic and security arrangements of the Western world is a mirage, not only because of the unprecedentedly formidable difficulties each of them confronts in its domestic development, but also because the major Western transnational institutions and organizations are themselves in a flux, amounting sometimes to dissolution. Such flux offers opportunities as well as creating dangers for policy. In the European Union, for example, the shattering of the federalist project creates the opportunity for some of the post-communist states of Eastern Europe, beginning perhaps with the Czech Republic, to enter a European Union that is decentralist and open in character. It is far less clear that membership of NATO is feasible for any of the post-communist states, if only because of the territorial guarantees that such membership confers. The key point is that, in destroying the post-war settlement, the Soviet collapse has thrown all Western transnational institutions into a flux that is not easily stabilized. The post-communist countries cannot, then, hope for admission to a club that no longer exists. Indeed, as with the European Union, only further change in Western transnational institutions will allow them a fuller integration into Western economic life. The risk is that, as the illusions of the 'New World Order' give way to the realities of a chaos of nations, there will be no overarching framework of Western institutions into which integration of the post-communist states might proceed.[29]

The very currency of the discourse of post-communist econo-mies and societies in transition encourages expectations of an orderly convergence on a Western model which, if the argument of this chapter is sound, are supported by nothing in historical experience or in theoretical analysis. Of the exemplars that have been proposed for the post-communist states, that of Germany has most relevance to the European states, and – especially in virtue of the strategic role government must adopt in the econ-omy in a context of demilitarization – that of Japan to Russia; but no exemplar, including that of China, itself a post-communist state in all but name, is adequate to the historical singularities of the post-Soviet societies, especially of Russia. The social market perspective set out here aims not to protract the vain search for exemplars or paradigms which the post-communist countries could emulate or instantiate but to put to an end that fruitless search. It tries to do so by presenting a general conception of market institutions in which they are theorized not as self-enclosed systems but as human practices that always come deeply embedded in matrices of cultural tradition and in legal and political frameworks, to which they owe all their stability and legitimacy. On the social market perspective advanced here, market institutions are like natural languages in that it is their very nature to be plural and diverse. To model economic policy on the tacit supposition that there is a single, ideal-typical exemplar for all varieties of market institutions, to which all real-world cases do or should approximate, is like modelling language teaching on the premise that all natural languages have a tendency to converge on Esperanto.

In the real world of human history as distinct from the illu-sory history postulated in Enlightenment philosophies, no such convergence is to be expected. If there is a global trend that is presently afoot, it may well be one in which economic initiative is shifting from the Western nations, from whose historical experience standard economic theory takes its bearings, to the non-Occidental cultures of East Asia. In this larger historical context, the Soviet collapse will be seen not as another surge in an irresistible movement of Westernization but as the beginning of the world-historical reversal of that movement.[30] In that event, Western theoretical models and Western market institutions themselves will confront many difficult problems of adjustment. The goal of the social market perspective sketched here is the humble one, not of prescribing for any people or polity, but of rendering the changes that are afoot in the world more readily intelligible, by breaking the hold on the understanding of a crude and monistic conception of market institutions in which they are misconceived as self-contained and free-standing systems. The premise of this chapter is the belief that so long as policy remains in the grip of this conception it condemns itself to incomprehension and impotence regarding the real development and problems of the post-communist states.

6

AGONISTIC LIBERALISM

In all of its varieties, traditional liberalism is a universalist political theory. Its content is a set of principles which prescribe the best regime, the ideally best institutions, for all mankind. It may be acknowledged – as it is, by a proto-liberal such as Spinoza – that the best regime can be attained only rarely, and cannot be expected to endure for long; and that the forms its central institutions will assume in different historical and cultural milieux may vary significantly. It will then be accepted that its role in political thought is as a regulative ideal, to which political practice can hope only to approximate, subject to all the vagaries and exigencies of circumstance. None the less, the content of traditional liberalism is a system of principles which function as universal norms for the critical appraisal of human institutions. In this regard traditional liberalism – the liberalism of Locke and Kant, for example – represents a continuation of classical political rationalism, as it is found in Aristotle and Aquinas, where it too supports principles having the attribute of universality in that they apply ideally to all human beings.

This universalist claim of classical political philosophy in the central Western tradition is transmitted to the political thought of modernity, which in all its varieties, liberal and otherwise, is an application of the Enlightenment project – the project of giving human institutions a claim on reason that has universal authority. This is the project inaugurated by the first political thinker of the Enlightenment, Thomas Hobbes – not himself a liberal, but, like Spinoza, anticipating many of the central themes of liberal thought – when he sought to found political authority on the rational choice of its subjects rather than on tradition or local prescription. In the political theories of the Enlightenment, the universalist content of classical political rationalism reappears as a philosophy of history which has universal convergence on a rationalist civilization as its *telos*. The idea of progress which the Enlightenment project embodies may be seen as a diachronic statement of the classical conception of natural law. This is the modern conception of human social development as occurring in successive discrete stages, not everywhere the same, but having in common the property of converging on a single form of life, a universal civilization, rational and cosmopolitan. Modern liberalism, in all its conventional forms, from Locke to Kant and from John Stuart Mill to the later Rawls, is inextricably linked with the philosophy of history, and the idea of progress, that were embodied in this Enlightenment project.

My starting-point is the failures of the Enlightenment project in our time, and their implications for liberal thought. The failures to which I refer are in part historical and political rather than theoretical or philosophical: I mean the confounding of Enlightenment expectations of the evanescence of particularistic allegiances, national and religious, and of the progressive levelling down, or marginalization, of cultural difference in human affairs. It is the empirical falsification of this Enlightenment philosophy of history to which Stuart Hampshire alludes, when he refers to a positivist theory of modernisation, a theory that is traceable to the French Enlightenment. The positivists believed that all societies across the globe will gradually discard their traditional attachments to supernatural forces because of the need for rational, scientific and experimental methods of thought which a modern industrial economy involves. This is the old faith, widespread in the 19th century, that there must be a step-by-step convergence on liberal values, on 'our values'.

Of this old faith Hampshire concludes: 'We now know that there is no "must" about it and that all such theories of human history have a predictive value of zero'.[1] The world-historical failure of the Enlightenment project – in political terms, the collapse and ruin, in the late twentieth century, of the secular, rationalist and universalist political movements, liberal as well as Marxist, that that project spawned, and the dominance in political life of ethnic, nationalist and fundamentalist forces – suggests the falsity of the philosophical anthropology upon which the Enlightenment project rested. In this philosophical anthropology, cultural difference was conceived as an ephemeral, even an epiphenomenal incident in human life and history. The falsification of this view by historical experience is a phenomenon that conventional liberal thought, for which cultural difference is either a form of atavism or else of subjective preference whose place is in private life, has found too threatening to explore. On the alternative view that I shall develop, the propensity to cultural difference is a primordial attribute of the human species; human identities are plural and diverse in their very natures, as natural languages are plural and diverse, and they are always variations on particular forms of common life, never exemplars of universal humanity. This alternative philosophical anthropology, owing much to the Romantic movement and to other thinkers of the Counter-Enlightenment late eighteenth and early nineteenth centuries, conceives humankind as being a species that is only partly determinate in its nature, that is for that reason unavoidably self-defining and self-transforming, and which exercises its distinctive powers of self-invention in the creation of identities that are not only diverse but also typically exclusive in their natures. The task for liberal theory, as I see it, is not vainly to resist the historical falsification of the universalist anthropology that sustained the Enlightenment philosophy of history, but to attempt to reconcile the demands of a liberal form of life with the particularistic character of human identities and allegiances – to retheorize liberalism as itself a particular form of common life.

The failures of the Enlightenment project that are my point of departure are intellectual as well as world-historical, though these intellectual failures are inevitably repressed in conventional liberal thought: I mean the inability of liberal theorists to deliver on the foundationalist promises of the Enlightenment project, by giving the principles of a liberal society a universal claim on reason.[2] It is the contemporary intellectual failure of the Enlightenment project which has led liberal thought to take in the work of the later Rawls a Deweyan relativist and historicist turn. (That this Deweyan turn in Rawls's later work has not been accompanied by an abandonment of a Kantian agenda of determinacy and fixity for liberal principles is an inconsistency in the later Rawls I have explored elsewhere.[3]) Unfortunately the bankruptcy of the philosophy of history by which the larger relevance of Deweyan liberalism was assured has rendered the later Rawlsian project of no more than local academic interest. It is evident that liberal political philosophy in this traditional mode has reached a dead end in which its intellectual credentials are negligible and its political relevance nil. It is exhausted, even as other forms of the Enlightenment project, such as Marxism, are exhausted.

This conclusion will doubtless be resisted by Old Believers in the Enlightenment project, and by fundamentalist liberals of all varieties, for whom the political and intellectual failures of the Enlightenment to which I have referred are greatly exaggerated, or are at least not sufficiently unequivocal to warrant the radical step of abandoning the Enlightenment project itself. It is not my intention here to enter into dialogue with this view, which I construe as a kind of rationalist fideism, a humanist variation on Pascal's wager, which nothing in our actual historical experience supports. Instead I wish to consider the prospects for liberal theory on the supposition that the Enlightenment project – whether it be in the hubristic forms it assumed in the French *philosophes* and in Marxism, or in the more modest, and sometimes pessimistic, but nevertheless illicitly universalist, modes in which it was undertaken by the thinkers of the Scottish School – has indeed foundered. My argument will be that traditional varieties of liberalism are all exemplars of conceptions of rational choice. They are also all exemplars of a universalist anthropology for which cultural difference is not an essential but only an incidental and transitional attribute of human beings. The progenitor of the modern liberal intellectual tradition is Thomas Hobbes, since, though he did not share the later liberal concern with the limitation of political power and the promotion of individual liberty, he modelled political allegiance on a conception of individual rational choice by which all subsequent liberalism, be it rights-based, utilitarian or contractarian in its undergirding moral theory, is animated. Further, Hobbes inaugurated the modern tradition – prefigured in the Sophists – for which the local historical identities of human beings are artifactual and superficial, and only humans' pre-social nature is authentic. This rationalist and universalist tradition of liberal political philosophy runs aground, along with the rest of the Enlightenment project, on the reef of value-pluralism – on the truth that the values embodied in different forms of life and human identity, and even within the same form of life and identity, may be rationally incommensurable. The truth of value-pluralism suggests another mode of liberal theorizing, in which not rational choice but radical choice among incommensurables is central, and in which the particularistic character of human identity and reasoning is fundamental.

This other liberalism differs in decisive respects from any species of traditional liberalism. Since it does not claim a universal authority in reason, it understands commitment to a liberal form of life to be a matter of historical contingency and loyalty, not rationality. Since it recognizes that incommensurabilities may break out even in the heart of liberal ideals of liberty and equality, it rejects the legalist model that dominates American liberal thought, according to which the structure of basic human liberties or equalities can be prescribed by a jurisprudential or constitutional theory, in favour of a political model, in which these liberties and equalities cannot be made fixed or determinate by any theory or legalist device, but are themselves changeable episodes in political conflict and the results of provisional political settlements. Since it denies that liberal forms of life have a universal claim on reason, it denies also that allegiance to a liberal political order can ever be, solely or even primarily, allegiance to abstract or universalizable principles: instead it must always be allegiance to a particular common culture, where this is itself a concrete historical form of life, not an abstract ideal. In these, and perhaps other respects, agonistic liberalism diverges profoundly from those liberalisms, mainly Kantian in inspiration, that have prevailed in Anglo-American political philosophy, and from the earlier liberalisms that take their cues from Locke or Mill.

It differs from these standard liberalisms in its assertion of the limits of rational choice, which is to say, in its critique of rationalism in politics; but it differs no less from the conservative critique of political rationalism[4] whose object is a return to an uncorrupted text of common life that has not been 'scribbled on' by rationalist philosophers. It differs from this familiar conservative critique of political rationalism, in that – unlike Maistre, who hoped to find in the Russians a people that *philosophes* had not scribbled on, until his visit to the French-speaking *salons* of

St Petersburg shattered his hopes – it does not imagine that a pre-reflective form of common life is to be found anywhere which lacks experience of deep political conflict, and so has not confronted occasions for radical choice in which tradition, like reason, fails to give guidance.

It differs from both of these standard positions, liberal and conservative, in its stress on political conflict, both within liberal forms of life, and between these and other forms of life, as being an ineliminable and therefore permanent feature of the human condition; and in its understanding of liberal forms of life as having no special leverage on reason or history. This other liberalism, as I try to sketch it here, borrows from the thinkers of the Counter-Enlightenment in its critical rejection of the Enlightenment project; but, because it takes the Enlightenment project to be, in world-historical terms, an anachronism, a thing of the past, it is not a mirror-image of the Enlightenment, in the way that the thought of Burke or Oakeshott, say, is a mirror of the Enlightenment. It aims to have truly passed over the Enlightenment project, taking both from it and from its critics what may be valuable in each, but viewing it as we now view the Renaissance or the Reformation, from a standpoint of historical distance.

But can there be a post-Enlightenment liberalism? Can there be a form of liberal theory and practice which renounces the rationalist and monist moral theory, and relinquishes the universalist anthropology and philosophy of history, that are foundational in the Enlightenment project? My question may be of interest as a thought-experiment to those who remain unpersuaded by its point of departure in the ruin of the Enlightenment project in our time.

AGONISTIC LIBERALISM AND VALUE-PLURALISM

I use the term 'agonistic liberalism' to refer to the variety of liberal theory I have found in the work of Isaiah Berlin.[5] Here my

aim is not to interpret Berlin's writings, nor to maintain fidelity
to his views, but to expound and develop the unfamiliar and, as
it seems to me, highly promising form of liberal theory – the
'other liberalism' to which I have already alluded – that is intimated in his work. The term 'agonistic' comes from the Greek
word *agon*, which has the meaning both of a contest, competition
or rivalrous encounter, and of the conflict of characters in tragic
drama. Agonistic liberalism is that species of liberalism that is
grounded, not in rational choice, but in the limits of rational
choice – limits imposed by the radical choices we are often constrained to make among goods that are both inherently rivalrous,
and often constitutively uncombinable, and sometimes incommensurable, or rationally incomparable. Agonistic liberalism is
an application in political philosophy of the moral theory of
value-pluralism – the theory that there is an irreducible diversity of
ultimate values (goods, excellences, options, reasons for action
and so forth) and that when these values come into conflict or
competition with one another there is no overarching standard
or principle, no common currency or measure, whereby such
conflicts can be arbitrated or resolved. This anti-monistic, anti-
reductionist position in ethical theory may appear innocuous or
even trivial, with a cutting edge only against forms of classical
utilitarianism that few moral philosophers take seriously now-
adays; and value-pluralism may seem to have no important
implications for liberal political philosophy – but both of these
appearances are thoroughly deceptive. Value-pluralism imposes
limits on rational choice that are subversive of most standard
moral theories, not merely of utilitarianism, and it has deeply
subversive implications for all the traditional varieties of liberal
theory. In particular it has the implication that we often face
practical and moral dilemmas in which reason leaves us in the
lurch and in which, whatever we do, there is a wrong or an
irreparable loss of value; it implies that the fundamental rights
or basic liberties of liberal thought cannot be insulated from

conflicts among incommensurables, as liberal thinkers in both Lockean and Kantian traditions imagine; and it renders the Enlightenment conception of the historical progress of the species meaningless or incoherent. These are far from trivial results – indeed, for many, they are deeply counter-intuitive. Let us try to gain a better grip on the elusive idea of value-incommensurability and see how it comes to have these strong implications.

Joseph Raz has put the central idea of incommensurability very clearly:

> Value-pluralism is the doctrine . . . which takes the plurality of valuable activities and ways of life to be ultimate and inelimin-able. This radically changes our understanding of pluralism. On a reductive-monistic view when one trades the pleasures (and anxieties) of a family life for a career as a sailor one is getting, or hoping to get the same thing one is giving up, be it happiness, pleasure, desire-satisfaction, or something else. One gives up the lesser pleasure one would derive from family life for the greater pleasure of life at sea. If value-pluralism is correct this view is totally wrong. What one loses is of a differ-ent kind from what one gains. Even in success there is a loss, and quite commonly there is no meaning to the judgement that one gains more than one loses. When one was faced with valu-able options and successfully chose one of them one simply chose one way of life rather than another, both being good and not susceptible to comparison of degree.[6]

In his most systematic statement of the idea of incommensurabil-ity among values,[7] Raz has distinguished it from indeterminacy or incompleteness in options, and from their rough equality. Incommensurability among options means their rational incom-parability. We are most sure of its presence when we have elimin-ated or discounted indeterminacies and incompleteness in them.

Where incommensurability exists it shows itself as a break-down in transitivity in practical reasoning. As Raz puts it: 'The test of incommensurability is failure of transitivity. Two valuable options are incommensurable if 1) neither is better than the other and 2) there is (or could be) another option which is better than one but not better than the other.'[8]

Contrary to moral theorists such as Aristotle and Kant, such a mark of incommensurability does not signify any imperfection in our understanding; it marks a feature of the world. As Raz puts it, 'where there is incommensurability it is the ultimate truth. There is nothing further behind it, nor is it a sign of imperfection'.[9] Incommensurability marks imperfection neither in our understanding nor in the world; rather it signifies the incoherence of the very idea of perfection. Incommensurability is not, then, the Augustinian idea of the imperfectibility of human things, which is a familiar cliché of conservative thought; it is the radical denial of the very meaning of perfection. For religions and metaphysical systems in which the idea of the perfection of the deity or of the world, the project of theodicy and the idea that there is one way of life that is right or best for all human beings, are centrally important, this may be a result of no small importance.

Incommensurability may break out among goods that are combinable; when it does, it means that there is no best combination of them. Or it may break out among goods that are constitutively uncombinable, goods that in their very natures cannot be jointly realized; then it means that there is no right ranking of them. Either way it marks a limit to rational choice, and an occasion for radical choice – for the kind of choice that is not, and cannot be, reason-based, but consists in making a decision or a commitment that is groundless. The deepest form of incommensurability occurs among goods that are constitutively uncombinable. This may happen when – contrary to the Aristotelian doctrine of the unity of the virtues – one good or excellence drives out another; as when increased self-knowledge in an artist depletes powers of artistic creativity whose vitality depended on unresolved or repressed emotional conflicts; similarly, the virtue of compassion is rarely to be found in people with a rigorous sense of justice. In this case incommensurability is true as a matter of moral psychology or philosophical anthropology. Or it may occur when the goods, virtues or excellences are elements in whole ways of life that depend on uncombinable social structures as their matrices; then incommensurability is a truth of cultural anthropology or social psychology. The important point to note here is that, if value-pluralism is correct, then these are truths, correct moral beliefs about the world. The thesis of the incommensurability of values is then not a version of relativism, of subjectivism or of moral scepticism, though it will infallibly be confused with one or other of these doctrines: it is a species of moral realism, which we shall call *objective pluralism*. Its distinguishing features are that it limits the scope of rational choice among goods, affirming that they are often constitutively uncombinable and sometimes rationally incommensurable. It is a logical truth about any claim about value-incommensurability that it is a claim to moral knowledge. As Bernard Williams has observed:

> Insofar as we are drawn towards the objectivity of ethics by an impression which is borne in on us in moral experience, the experience of ultimate moral conflict is precisely one which brings most immovably with it the impression of objectivity: that there is nothing one decently, honourably, adequately *can* do in a certain situation seems a kind of truth as firmly independent of the will or inclination as any truth of morality seems.[10]

How does value-pluralism so understood bear on the claims of liberalism?

VALUE-PLURALISM AND TRADITIONAL LIBERALISM

A common argument of traditional liberal theorists – particularly those influenced by Kant – is that liberalism is untouched by value-pluralism. This argument rests on the claim that value-pluralism is a position in axiology, the theory of value or the good, whereas liberal principles are deontic principles, principles of right which do not depend on any particular theory of value or any specific conception of the good. It is urged that liberal principles do not designate substantive goods or values which may come into conflict with one another or with other goods and values; they designate regulative principles which specify the terms and constraints under which substantive goods may be promoted and pursued. To suppose that value-pluralism, the thesis of the incommensurability of ultimate values, if true, threatens liberalism in any way is, on this view, to commit a sort of category mistake; it may also be to conflate intellectual disciplines by assimilating political philosophy to moral theory. Indeed it may even be argued that, far from threatening or undermining traditional liberalism, value-pluralism is actually congenial to it. For the implication of value-pluralism – that in many cases the project of maximizing value is not even a logical possibility – removes any obstacle to the adoption of purely deontic principles of right or justice which might be posed by aggregative utilitarian principles. According to this argument, then, traditional liberalism – the liberalism of Kant or his latter-day disciples, say – is uncompromised by, and may even be strengthened by, the truth of value-pluralism.

This common line of reasoning turns on the possibility of a pure philosophy of right that both Berlin and Raz deny. It is a fundamental contribution of Raz's political philosophy to have shown that a rights-based political morality is an impossibility.[11] Raz demonstrates that both the scope or content and the ground and weight of fundamental rights are given by their contribution to the protection and promotion of vital human interests. It is by appeal to further claims about human interests that disputes about rights are settled – when they can be settled at all. Rights discourse, for this and other reasons, cannot – as the proponents of a pure philosophy of right suppose – be insulated from controversy about the content of human well-being or flourishing and the relative place in it of different human interests. Indeed different conceptions of human well-being will generate different views of human interests, or at least divergent rankings of human interests. To understand this is to understand that rights claims are never primordial or foundational but always conclusionary, provisional results of long chains of reasoning which unavoidably invoke contested judgements about human interests and well-being. It is to grasp – what in political philosophy before Kant was a commonplace – that rights are never the foundation of any political morality. In so far as traditional liberalism seeks to insulate itself from the force of value-pluralism by attempting to seal off rights discourse from dispute about the human good it does so only by recourse to illusion – the legalist and formalist illusion that in political philosophy the right can have priority over the good. For, if Raz's argument is sound, human rights have neither substantive content nor moral weight until their impact on human interests, their contribution to human well-being, has been specified.

Berlin gives another, and yet deeper reason why liberalism cannot be insulated from the force of value-pluralism.[12] The liberties specified by traditional liberal theory cannot – except by a sleight of hand – be rendered harmonious, compatible or mutually compossible. Liberties – including the negative liberties which Berlin believes to be central to liberalism – are not elements in a structure of compossible rights; they are often competing and conflictual in their implications for practice. One may indeed maintain, after the fashion of Hohfeld or Rawls, that claim rights or basic liberties cannot as a matter of logic conflict:

they must, as Rawls puts it,[13] be 'contoured' so that conflicts among them are contoured away and they constitute an harmonious set. This is only to redescribe in legalist terms what in ordinary language is more perspicuously described as a conflict of liberties. Such a redescription may be legitimate within the conventions of contemporary US jurisprudence – in which conflicts among liberties whose trade-offs are appropriately matters of political decision are given a spurious legalist resolution – but it is not in others. In Canada, for example, the Constitutional Charter explicitly allows for conflicts among liberties and rights, and seeks to specify the conditions under which rights or basic liberties may be overridden, rather than to contour away their conflicts. In any case, jurisprudential conventions are never decisive considerations in philosophical controversies of the sort we are now considering.

If liberties can and do conflict with one another, how are the conflicts to be resolved? Here Berlin's most radical move is made, when he maintains that liberties – in this case, negative liberties – are not only rivalrous but also sometimes incommensurable values. It was in response to H. L. A. Hart's criticism that Rawls had acknowledged that when liberties conflict their competition cannot be resolved by a neutral judgement as to which structure or combination of liberties 'maximizes' or 'best promotes' liberty; such expressions are indeterminate to the point of emptiness, until the importance or worth, the weight or value, of the various liberties is put in the scales. Berlin's argument is more fundamental: it is that we lack the scales whereby the liberties could be weighed. When liberties conflict we have no option but to try to settle their conflict by assessing their impact on human interests and so their contribution to human well-being. As soon as we do this, however, we find that we are confronted by different conceptions of human well-being which spawn divergent judgements of human interests and thereby of the weights or values of the rival liberties. Even an agreed conception of human well-being will yield different rankings of the same interests as it is applied by different people. How is the human interest in privacy to be weighed against that in freedom of information, when the two conflict? It is clear that, in this as in similar conflicts of liberties, we have on Berlin's view a radical choice among incommensurables. Such conflicts have no uniquely rational solutions, since the liberties at issue will be valued differently depending on divergent conceptions of the good. In Berlin's view, then, liberalism cannot be sealed off from the radical choices forced on us by the truth of value-pluralism. On the contrary, value-conflict among incommensurables breaks out at the very heart of liberalism as he conceives it, that is to say, within the idea of liberty itself. If this is so, traditional liberalism is undermined by the truth of value-pluralism, and liberalism itself is transformed.

AGONISTIC LIBERALISM VERSUS TRADITIONAL LIBERALISM

The truth of value-pluralism defeats traditional liberalism, contrary to those who maintain that it is untouched by it. It remains to consider the implications of the defeat of traditional liberalism for liberal theory, and to answer the question, how must liberalism be amended, if it is to be reconciled with value-pluralism? It is manifest, first of all, that conceptions of the priority of the right over the good in political philosophy, of justice as the first virtue of social institutions and of the neutrality of justice (and of the liberal state) with respect to specific conceptions of the good life, must all be abandoned. The existence of conflicts among basic liberties and fundamental rights, the consequent impossibility of anything akin to a pure philosophy of right, and the sensitivity of principles of justice and liberty to divergences of judgement about human interests and well-being, rule out all such legalist doctrines.

The upshot of the truth of value-pluralism for political philosophy is not merely that the structure of basic liberties, or the content of fundamental rights, is massively underdetermined by any general theory or principles; it is that, in virtue of the radical choices that are occasioned by conflicts among rights or liberties expressing incommensurable values, hard cases abound. Indeed, if value-pluralism is true, hard cases, undecidable by reasoning from any overarching theory, are the rule, not the exception, in political life. Now it must be observed that nothing follows inexorably, as a matter of strict implication or logical necessity, for the design of liberal institutions, from the truth of value-pluralism. The anti-universalist implication of value-pluralism should itself caution against any general inferences from it about the character of institutions. At the same time, it seems to me that the undermining of traditional liberalism by value-pluralism also undermines the implicit model of a liberal state intimated in recent liberal political philosophy, as exemplified in the work of Rawls, Dworkin, Ackerman and their followers. In this model, which draws heavily on an idealized version of US jurisprudence, basic questions about liberty and the restraint of liberty are decided by legal and not by political reasonings; by judicial review, not by legislation. Now if, as the truth of value-pluralism implies, hard cases undecidable by general principles are pervasive in questions having to do with liberty, then there seems a natural presumption in favour of dealing with such questions by political reasoning, which is inherently and avowedly inconclusive, and which admits of compromises and of provisional settlements that change over time and which vary from place to place, rather than by legal reasoning – especially that species of legal reasoning that invokes grand jurisprudential or moral theories of the sorts that value-pluralism subverts. If the truth of value-pluralism is assumed, such that there are no right answers in hard cases about the restraint of liberty, then it seems natural to treat questions of the restraint of liberty as political, and not as theoretical or jurisprudential questions. To do so would be in accord with a view of political reasoning as being essentially circumstantial, as being not a reasoning from first principles that could ideally be demonstrative but instead a form of practical reasoning in which no step is necessitated, of which intimations can be found in Aristotle. And it appeals to a conception of political life as a sphere of practical reasoning whose *telos* is a *modus vivendi*, to a conception of the political in which it is a domain devoted to the pursuit not of truth but of peace, that has the authority of Hobbes.

The conception of political life that goes best with agonistic liberalism derives, nevertheless, not from Aristotle or from Hobbes, but from another thinker, whose relations with traditional liberalism are at best oblique, to whom I shall turn in the last section of this chapter. Both Aristotle and Hobbes hold to forms of rationalism, classical and modern, which value-pluralism defeats. There is in each of them, at the same time, a conception of politics as an autonomous sphere of practical life, which is congenial to agonistic liberalism as I am developing it here. For, by contrast with traditional liberalisms, including that of the later Rawls, agonistic liberalism is truly a 'political liberalism' in which *the primacy of the political* – over the legal or the theoretical, say – is strongly affirmed.

The contrast with Rawlsian liberalism is instructive. In the latter, all important questions about liberty and distribution are decided pre-politically, by theoretical reasonings whose results are entrenched in constitutional law, and they are not subsequently politically alterable. Now it is true that Rawls, entirely rightly from the perspective of agonistic liberalism, insists that the principles and institutions that govern a liberal society are not applications of any comprehensive moral theory, or conception of the good, of the kind we find in John Stuart Mill, for example. Indeed the self-interpretation of Rawls's view as a species of 'political liberalism' is intended to mark a divergence between traditional liberalisms in which principles about liberty and justice are derived, perhaps even deduced, from a comprehensive moral philosophy, and Rawls's own liberalism, which conceives itself not as applying first principles but as teasing out the presuppositions and implications of an actually existing overlapping consensus in society on important issues about liberty and justice. It is on the basis of this self-interpretation that Rawls characterizes his mode of reasoning as practical and as keeping on the surface in philosophical terms.

There are many difficulties with this self-understanding of Rawlsian liberalism, some of them fatal. One difficulty, to which I have referred already parenthetically, concerns the tension in the work of the later Rawls between the self-interpretation of his theorizing as a quest for practical agreement which proceeds by uncovering the tacit structure and content of overlapping consensus and the strong determinacy of the principles which this method is supposed to deliver. It seems implausible in the extreme to suppose that, even in the parochially United States context to which apparently he confines himself, the overlapping consensus is broad or deep enough to be capable of yielding results as strongly determinate as those he advances. Who can plausibly maintain, for example, that Rawls's account of the basic liberties, his defence of the difference principle, or his treatment of the abortion issue as an issue that can be resolved by appeal to provisions about equality that are supposedly laid down in the Fourteenth Amendment, are uncontroversial applications or developments of an overlapping consensus that exists even in the narrow confines of the United States? It is not only that Rawlsian liberalism grossly exaggerates the strength of overlapping, or underlying, moral consensus, even in his best-case example of the United States, and thus of the determinacy of the principles that are derivable from it. It is also thoroughly unclear how the results of the method of seeking practical agreement on the basis of any such consensus could have the fixity he attributes to the principles of justice. Does not any consensus change over time? If so, why should any moment in its development be privileged as the source of fixed principles?

The explanation for these anomalies arises from the anti-political character of Rawls's avowedly political liberalism. Its method is the elucidation of the content or underlying coherence of an overlapping consensus, the formulation of that content in terms of highly determinate prescriptive principles and the entrenchment of these principles so that they are immune from the contingencies of political life. The key move in Rawlsian political liberalism, in other words, is the removal from political life of the principles specifying the basic liberties and justice in distribution. These are not upshots of political discourse, or aspects of any real settlement or agreement achieved in actual political practice, but theorems, products of the peculiar species of theoretical reasoning that Rawls's method entails. Neither the method of reasoning, nor the results of Rawlsian political liberalism possesses any of the marks of indeterminacy and contingency that distinguish political discourse and practice. On the contrary, the object of Rawlsian political liberalism is the removal of these distinguishing marks of the political from both its method and its results. In consequence political life is in Rawlsian political liberalism void of substance.

Despite its self-description as political liberalism, then, Rawls's is a liberalism that has been politically emasculated, in which nothing of importance is left to political decision, and in which political life itself has been substantially evacuated of content. The hollowing out of the political realm in Rawlsian liberalism is fatal to its self-description as a form of political liberalism and discloses its true character as a species of liberal legalism. The liberal legalism of Rawls and his followers is, perhaps, only an especially unambiguous example of the older liberal project, or illusion, of *abolishing politics*, or of so constraining it by legal and constitutional formulae that it no longer matters what are the outcomes of political deliberation. In Rawlsian liberal legalism, the anti-political nature of at least one of the dominant traditions of liberalism is fully realized.

According to the value-pluralist perspective which animates agonistic liberalism, the liberal legalist project of abolishing politics is utopian and unrealizable. This is so, not merely or primarily because of the imperfectibility of constitutional and legal arrangements, but because legal reasoning can never avoid the indeterminacies and incommensurabilities that pervade political reasoning. The idea of a constitutional or jurisprudential theory, in which the *ad-hoc* judgements of political discourse are supplanted by disciplined legal decisions on major questions in the restraint of liberty, is merely an illusion. In historical practice, the effect of attempting to abolish or to marginalize political life has been – especially in the United States, where legalism is strongest – the politicization of law, as judicial institutions have become arenas of political struggle. The end-result of this process is not, however, the simple transposition of political life into legal contexts, but rather the corrosion of political life itself. The treatment of all important issues of restraint of liberty as questions of constitutional rights has the consequence that they cease to be issues that are politically negotiable and that can be resolved provisionally in a political settlement that encompasses a compromise among conflicting interests and ideals. In conflicts about basic constitutional rights, there can be no compromise solutions, only judgements which yield unconditional victory for one side and complete defeat for the other. It is plain that this is not a recipe for civil peace but rather for the loss of civility. The history and prospects of the abortion dispute in the United States, where it remains wholly intractable and a standing threat to civil peace, by contrast with its treatment in other countries – such as New Zealand, the United Kingdom, France, Portugal and Italy – in which it is an issue in legislative policy and not in constitutional law, and which have achieved a variety of political settlements on it, is a compelling illustration of the dangers of liberal legalism. It suggests that the hegemony of legalist rights discourse in public life has the effect of rendering non-negotiable issues that are susceptible of compromise. The liberal legalist project of abolishing politics is utopian if it means that politics will be supplanted by law; it is all too realistic if it means the destruction of the political realm, the domain of public reasoning about public matters, and its replacement by a sort of low-intensity civil war, in which the capture of legal institutions is only an episode. The utopian liberal project of abolishing politics is not then an innocuous one, since its pursuit contributes to the erosion of the virtues of civility on which a stable modus vivendi among us depends.

The utopia of liberal legalism tends to undermine the achievable condition of civility in which moral and other conflicts which cannot be resolved are politically mediated and contained. It is this achievable and desirable condition to which Stuart Hampshire refers, when in a comment on Rawls's *Political Liberalism* he asks:

> If the moral and religious sentiments of human beings are in their essence exclusive and divisive, how is the war of all against all to be avoided and how can that degree of consensus necessary for public order ever come into existence? The most plausible and historically defensible answer is by political compromise, by rule-governed negotiation, by arbitration, sometimes adjudication, in institutions that have grown up to serve this purpose, usually by slow stages over a long period of time. This is the sphere of public reason, of political values and virtues, and of the duties of civility . . . fairness and justice within a liberal society . . . require that there should exist respected institutions for adversarial argument, and equal access to them, accepted manners of negotiation, and entrenched rules and habits of advocacy, a full ritualization of public conflicts.[14]

It is precisely the political character of the civil virtues that sustain liberal institutions of the sorts to which Hampshire refers that is denied, or compromised, in Rawlsian liberal legalism.

The liberal legalist project of abolishing, or sterilizing, politics, and of replacing politics by law, has another effect, which illuminates the contrast between traditional liberalism and agonistic liberalism, and which concerns the nature of political allegiance in a liberal state. Whereas for traditional liberalism, especially in its Anglo-American varieties, allegiance to a liberal state is allegiance to the rationally defensible principles it exemplifies, for agonistic liberalism this must be an illusion. Such allegiance will be in part an attachment to particular institutions, having the purpose of mediating conflicts and achieving a tolerable settlement of them, which are characteristic of liberal states in general. It will in part also, and always, be an attachment to a particular political community and its animating common culture, with the actual history and distinctive characteristics that it contingently has. Allegiance to a liberal state is, on this view, never primarily to principles which it may be thought to embody, and which are supposed to be compelling for all human beings; it is always to specific institutions, having a specific history, and to the common culture that animates them, which itself is a creature of historical contingency.

There is here another instructive contrast between agonistic liberalism and Rawlsian liberalism. It is true that they have something in common in that each of them precludes the political embodiment of any comprehensive moral doctrine. Both rule out John Stuart Mill's version of qualitative hedonism, or eudaemonistic utilitarianism, with its associated values of autonomy and individuality,[15] for example; but they do so for very different reasons. The political embodiment of comprehensive moral doctrines, or conceptions of the good, is excluded by Rawlsian liberalism because justice, understood as demanding equality of respect among persons, dictates legal and political neutrality with regard to specific conceptions of the good life. Agonistic liberalism, though it is bound to acknowledge the existence of substantive comprehensive conceptions of the good life, denies that there can be any comprehensive theory which might rationally arbitrate their conflicts, where – as will often be the case – the goods recognized in such rival comprehensive conceptions are incommensurable with one another. The first view, in demanding the neutrality of the law in respect of specific conceptions of the good, thereby demands the legal disestablishment of morality. In so doing it demands the legal disestablishment of any common culture, in so far as that incorporates – as inevitably it must – specific conceptions of the virtues, and of the good life. Rawlsian liberalism is bound then to treat political allegiance to liberal institutions as entirely a matter of recognition of the principles of justice they embody: indeed it will deny liberal institutions such recognition in so far as they illicitly embody the values distinctive of a particular common culture. Political allegiance to any particular common culture is not only no part of liberal justice on the Rawlsian view of it, but also forbidden by liberal justice. In this crucial respect Rawlsian liberalism remains faithful to its Kantian lineage in affirming that only that which can be universalizable by rational agents can be a just and legitimate object of political allegiance.

In the perspective of agonistic liberalism, by contrast, it is recognized that the exemplars of the liberal form of life are always particular common cultures, and that it is to them, rather than to any universalizable principles which they might embody, that allegiance is owed. Such common cultures may be, and in any modern context of pluralism will be, highly internally complex, embodying subtle adjustments among a variety of traditions and styles of life; but on the agonistic view allegiance will always be to a particular form of common life, not to abstract principles which may be elicited from it. This is so, on the agonistic view, if only because there is no impartial or universal standpoint from which the claims of all particular cultures can be rationally assessed. Any standpoint we adopt is that of a particular form of life and of the historic practices that constitute it; it is the expression of a human identity that is historically specific, not of one that is universally and generically human. This is, in effect, to deny the philosophical anthropology of the Enlightenment, by affirming that human identities are always local affairs, precipitates of particular forms of common life, never tokens of the universal type of generic humanity. It is also to give the central thesis of value-pluralism, which is that of the constitutive uncombinability and incommensurability of values, a political statement, by observing that the conflict of values arises in political life, most fundamentally, as the rivalry of ways of life that are mutually exclusive, even where they are also internally complex.[16]

In the modern world, such common cultures are typically those of nations, common ways of life recognized by themselves and others as constituting distinct peoples, whose claims give rise to divergent, and sometimes tragically conflicting, allegiances. (I leave aside, as – unfortunately – historically obsolete, the question of the nature and sources of allegiance to a liberal empire, such as that of the Habsburgs. I think it too is intelligible only in terms that are particularistic, though they are not those of particular national cultures.) On the view being developed here, allegiance to a liberal state is always allegiance to the common culture it embodies or expresses, and, in the late modern context in which we live, such a common culture is typically a national culture. The common culture on which allegiance to a liberal state depends need not, and indeed should not, be conceived as an 'integral' culture, of the sort theorized by reactionaries such as Charles Maurras, in which cultural minorities are denied full citizenship; and it was not so conceived in the thought of those liberal thinkers in an older tradition, including John Stuart Mill, who recognized that allegiance to liberal institutions always rests on participation in a shared national (or, perhaps, sometimes imperial) culture. In this respect, agonistic liberalism returns to an older and a wiser tradition in liberal thought, encompassing Constant and Tocqueville as well as Mill, though without endorsing the philosophy of history that these thinkers hold in common with other traditional liberals. By contrast with American liberalism, especially its Rawlsian variety, agonistic liberalism has an ineliminable communitarian dimension, in that it understands both human identity and political allegiance in terms of participation in common forms of life.[17] Such forms of life are not, as in much communitarian theorizing, ideal-typical abstractions, as remote from history and practice as the disembodied Kantian subject rightly criticized by communitarian critics of liberalism;[18] they are concrete historical practices – the only things, on the account here defended, that *can* command allegiance. In our world they are nations, or the common forms of life which national cultures encompass and shelter. The point may be put in another, and perhaps a simpler way: there can be no form of allegiance that is purely political; political allegiance – at least when it is comparatively stable – presupposes a common cultural identity, which is reflected in the polity to which allegiance is given; political order, including that of a liberal state, rests upon a pre-political order of common culture. If this is a general truth, then it follows inexorably that a liberal polity will depend for its successful renewal over time on the common cultural identity of its subjects. Among us, in the historical context of late modernity, the stability of any liberal polity will usually depend on its expressing a shared national culture.

Since belonging to a people or a nation is a matter of historical memory and thus of historical contingency, it follows that allegiance to a liberal state cannot avoid being also a matter of contingency. This has the large implication that allegiance to a liberal form of life must always be a matter of cultural solidarity, not of universalizing rationality.

LIMITS OF THE LIBERAL AGON

The argument against liberal universalism which has been developed so far is easily confused with relativism. It is wrong, however, to conflate the theory of objective pluralism which underpins claims about value-incommensurability with any sort of relativism or subjectivism in ethics. That this is a mistake is shown in the work of Isaiah Berlin, who has always affirmed the reality of goods and evils that are not culture-specific but generically human. As Berlin has put his position:

> The fact that the values of one culture may be incompatible with those of another, or that they are in conflict within one culture or group or in a single human being at different times – or, for that matter, at one and the same time – does not entail relativism of values, only the notion of a plurality of values not structured hierarchically; which, of course, entails the permanent possibility of inescapable conflict between values, as well as incompatibility between the outlooks of different civilisations or of stages of the same civilisation.[19]

He sums up his view: 'Relativism is not the only alternative to universalism ... nor does incommensurability entail relativism'.[20]

The claim that a liberal form of life cannot be grounded in universal reasons does not entail, nor does it presuppose, any variety of cultural relativism; but it does mean that liberal forms of life are underdetermined by the universal minimum content of morality – by what H. L. A. Hart called 'the minimum content of natural law'.[21] Three points of importance are worth making here as to the relations between the universal minimum content of morality and liberal forms of life. First, the conception of the universal minimum content of morality that figures in the work of an agonistic liberal such as Berlin differs sharply from that of classical natural law. It differs because on Berlin's view, and surely correctly, the elements or values that go to make up the universal minimum may conflict with one another, and even such conflicts may be conflicts among incommensurables. The universal minimum content of morality might contain such goods as freedom from the threat of violent death, such virtues as human sympathy, and such norms as are embodied in ideas of fairness. Berlin's point, which is surely correct, is that there may be a specifiable minimum universal content to morality, and some forms of life may be condemned by it; but the items which make up the minimum content may, and sometimes do, come into conflict with one another, there being no rational procedure for resolving such conflicts. (I do not wish here to address the question of what is the universal moral minimum, or how this can be known to us. Plausibly, it would contain certain norms of procedural fairness, and certain generically human virtues, though the forms these would assume in different cultures would be diverse. A useful, if not altogether satisfactory account of this is given in Stuart Hampshire's book, *Innocence and Experience*.[22]) Radical choice breaks out even within the universal minimum – between, say, the demands of justice and mercy – and at that point reason deserts us – a truth denied in the classical natural law tradition.

Second, and as a consequence of the first point, among the many regimes or forms of life that satisfy the universal minimum requirements of morality, conflicts among incommensurable elements within the universal moral minimum will be resolved in different ways, in accordance with their different cultural traditions; and, because the universal minimum in all of its variations underdetermines any liberal form of life, many of the regimes that meet the test of the universal minimum – probably the vast majority of such regimes to be found in human history – will not be liberal regimes. This is a truth denied in traditional liberalism, all of the varieties of which specify that the requirements of liberal justice come within the universal minimum.

Third, there is the possibility – by far the most threatening for fundamentalist or traditional liberals – that liberal regimes may sometimes satisfy the minimum universal requirements of morality less well than some non-liberal or post-liberal regimes do. This could be so, when a regime which protected liberal freedoms of expression and conscience, say, and whose political institutions met liberal criteria for public accountability, nevertheless failed to maintain a level of civil peace and freedom from ordinary criminality necessary for a decent human life for most, many or a significant minority, of its subjects. What is intellectual liberty worth, if it has to be exercised in city environments that have become states of nature? What is the value of choice, if choice must be exercised in a social environment, such as the Hobbesian environment of some US cities, in which there is little that is worth choosing? In such a circumstance, a non-liberal regime, whose political institutions lack public accountability and which does not assure liberal intellectual freedoms, but which assures the security and protects the everyday liberties of its subjects, might legitimately be judged to satisfy the universal minimum better than some weak liberal regimes. There is, to be sure, nothing of necessity in such a judgement, if – as is likely – the goods under assessment in the two regimes are, some of them, incommensurables; the point is not that such a judgement is inevitable in a case of this sort, but that it is intelligible and defensible.

This last possibility reveals the stark implausibilities of the standard Enlightenment philosophy of history on which all traditional liberalisms rest and, in so doing, it discloses the limits of the liberal *agon* itself. The thought of the late 1980s and early 1990s, intoxicated by the collapse of some of the principal totalitarian regimes of our century, has witnessed a revival of Enlightenment philosophy of history in its most *simpliste* forms.

In the writings of Francis Fukuyama, for example, the Soviet collapse has fuelled a Western triumphalism in which modernization and Westernization are conflated, the spread of market institutions and the globalization of Western civil society are confounded, and the 'final triumph' of 'democratic capitalism' is announced.[23] Here the fundamentalist liberal expectation of a universal convergence on liberal values, 'our values', which Hampshire has incisively criticized in the Enlightenment *philosophes*, is atavistically revived. The counter-examples to this liberal expectation that are most relevant to the present argument are not the failures of many of the post-Soviet societies to achieve anything akin to a Western civil society, nor the spread of Islamic fundamentalism in countries such as Algeria and Egypt, nor even the increasing likelihood that the secular state in India will be abandoned in favour of a Hindu fundamentalist regime, since in all these cases it is arguable that the regimes which are emerging not only will confound Enlightenment expectations of a convergence on liberal values but also will fail to satisfy minimal conditions of moral acceptability for their subjects. These are examples of states, regimes and movements that plausibly violate both liberal norms and the universal minimum content of morality.

The examples most relevant to the present argument are different: those of the East Asian countries, such as Singapore, where market institutions have been combined with political *dirigisme* and pervasive authoritarianism to yield both social stability and extraordinary economic development; mainland China, where the avowed project is that of promoting market institutions *without* developing a Western-style civil society; and Japan, where the Meiji reforms, initiated over a century ago, have produced a modernized society which remains wholly non-Occidental in its cultural traditions and forms of life, despite its many superficial borrowings from the West, and despite the political inheritances – now in a degree of flux – of the post-war period. These examples are centrally relevant to our current purposes inasmuch as they suggest the real possibility, in the late modern context, of regimes that clearly meet the test of the minimum universal content of morality, and do as well or better than liberal states on other criteria relevant to human flourishing, without adopting liberal institutions or social norms, and without converging on the universal civilization anticipated in the Enlightenment philosophy of history. These regimes, if they continue to perform well without converging on Western forms of life, may be regarded as the most radical empirical falsification of the Enlightenment project hitherto and so of traditional liberalism, since they are examples of the successful adoption of Western technologies by flourishing non-Occidental cultures that remain deeply resistant to Western values.

If history is any guide, then the predictive value of the old faith of the Enlightenment is as Hampshire suggests – zero. Worse, from the standpoint of traditional liberalisms which all embody variations on the Enlightenment project, we may be witnessing the emergence of regimes which outperform liberal societies on all those criteria, including the requirements of the universal minimum morality, that are not internal to the liberal form of life itself. Liberal forms of life, for these reasons and for the reasons explored in earlier sections of this chapter, cannot be underwritten by Enlightenment philosophy of history or anthropology. Political philosophy which aims to underwrite them in such a fashion is apologetic in character, like the philosophies which Wittgenstein stigmatized as 'bourgeois' in the sense that they sought to provide 'foundations' for the practices of particular communities.[24] Rather than persisting in the futile project of an apologetic liberal foundationalism, we should instead recognize liberal forms of life as being constituted by contingent human identities in contingent communities, both of which are just like any others in their contingency. We thereby recognize that liberal selves and liberal cultures are particular social forms that are granted no special privileges by history or human nature: in Richard Rorty's idiom, we acknowledge the contingency both of selfhood and of community.[25] This is not to endorse the relativistic view that liberal, or other forms of life, can be subject only to immanent criticism, since it remains a real possibility that some liberal forms of life may do less well than some other, non-liberal forms, from the standpoint of the universal content of human well-being. It is rather to recognize that the contribution of liberal forms of life to the well-being of liberal subjects, even where this is a reality, is not an argument for the universal adoption of such forms of life.

If we achieve this measure of self-understanding, of liberal forms of life as particularistic cultural traditions, then we shall be able to see the liberal *agon* – the rivalrous encounter of ideas and values in a context of peaceful coexistence – as a special case of the larger rivalry between whole forms of life. This agonistic pluralism is the deeper truth of which agonistic liberalism is only one exemplar. For the incommensurabilities among uncombinable goods on which agonistic liberalism stands is nowhere starker than among the incommensurable goods whose uncombinability derives from their being embedded, as their indispensable matrices, in uncombinable social structures, of which some are non-liberal. The conflict between *these* goods cannot be other than conflict between the whole ways of life in which they are indissolubly rooted. Such conflict cannot be contained within the liberal *agon* since it is a conflict in which the prospects of liberal forms of life are themselves at stake. It is also a conflict in which non-liberal forms of life may shelter goods that are weak or absent in liberal regimes.

Here an idea of Joseph Raz's may be helpful. Raz has shown in his conception of an *inherently public good*[26] that the activity of choosing has little value if there is not available to the chooser a range of worthwhile options, as embodied in a rich public culture or form of common life. This is a perfectly general truth, applicable to all societies and regimes, regardless of how they fare as to liberalism. Its application in the argument here is that there are valuable options, genuine goods, authentic forms of human flourishing, whose matrices are the social structures of non-liberal societies. Such values are crowded out or driven out, or survive only as pale shadows of themselves, in liberal societies, once their undergirding social structures have been knocked away. The larger pluralism which the thesis of incommensurability among objective values captures is the rivalry among whole cultural forms carrying with them uncombinable goods and excellences, in which liberal forms of life appear as only one constellation of incommensurable goods among many others, actual, historical and as yet hypothetical.

Deploying Raz's notion of an inherently public good, an example which may elucidate the logic of the present argument may be that of the prospects of Western societies whose political institutions and cultural traditions are those of liberal individualism by comparison with those of the East Asian societies in which modern market institutions have been grafted successfully on to the vital stem of a cultural tradition that is not individualist and which has imbibed none of the illusions – rationalist and universalist – expressed in the Enlightenment project.[27] The likely prospect, on all current trends, is not only of the East Asian societies overtaking Western liberal individualist societies in the economic terms of growth, investment, savings and living standards; it is also of their doing so while preserving and enhancing common cultural forms which assure to their subjects personal security in their everyday lives and a public environment that is rich in choiceworthy options. By contrast, the prospect for the Western individualist societies is one of economic development that is weak and feeble in a context of cultural impoverishment in which the remnants of a common culture are hollowed out by individualism and legalism. The prospect for the Western liberal societies, and particularly for those in which individualism and legalism have by now virtually delegitimized the very idea of a common culture, is that of a steep and rapid decline in which civil peace is fractured and the remnants of a common culture on which liberal forms of life themselves depend are finally dissipated. The self-undermining of liberal individualism, which Joseph Schumpeter anticipated in the mid-1940s, is likely to proceed apace, now that the Soviet collapse has removed the legitimacy borrowed by Western institutions from the enmity of a ruinous alternative, and the East Asian societies are released from the constraints of the post-war settlement to pursue paths of development that owe ever less to the West.[28] The liberal societies that are best placed to weather the storms of a period in which the end of conflict among Enlightenment ideologies means not the end of history but the end of the Enlightenment project as a political force in the real world are those liberal societies in which liberal traditions and a common national culture go together. If the argument of this chapter has any force, the liberal societies which will do worst will be those in which the political influence of a hubristic liberal ideology – an ideology which succours the illusions of legalism and rationalism, and spurns the historical realities of particular forms of common culture for the sake of the mirage of universalism – has been greatest.

CONCLUSION

Why is personal liberty worth pursuing? Only for what it is in itself, because it is what it is, not because the majority desires freedom. Men in general do not seek freedom, despite Rousseau's celebrated exclamation that they are born free; that, remarks Herzen (echoing Joseph de Maistre), is as if you were to say, 'Fish are born to fly, yet everywhere they swim.' Icthyophils may seek to prove that fish are 'by nature' made to fly; but they are not.[29]

If we have no reason to expect a peaceful *agon* among different cultures neither do we have reason to expect convergence on a universal liberal culture. Instead we do well to recall the other meaning of the Greek word *agon*, which is the conflict of characters in tragic drama. Such tragic conflicts are not conflicts between good and evil but (as Hegel saw) between right and right. The conflicts in which liberal societies and states find themselves mired in the coming decades are most unlikely, on the whole, to have the moral simplicity of the conflicts that the twentieth century has witnessed between Western liberalism and National Socialism and Soviet communism. They will be conflicts in which at least some non-liberal regimes and cultural forms possess genuine virtues and harbour authentic excellences that are weak, or lacking, in liberal regimes. This is, surely, the vision of human life expressed by Berlin, when he says of the true originator of what I have called agonistic liberalism, himself no liberal:

> Machiavelli's cardinal achievement is . . . his uncovering of an insoluble dilemma, the planting of a permanent question mark in the path of posterity. It stems from his *de facto* recognition that ends equally ultimate, equally sacred, may contradict each other, that entire systems of value may come into collision without possibility of rational arbitration, and not merely in exceptional circumstances, as a result of abnormality or accident or error – the clash of Antigone and Creon or in the story of Tristan – but (this was surely new) as part of the normal human situation.[30]

It would be to indulge an optimism that is alien to the agonistic perspective I have defended here to express the hope that the tragic conflicts that are surely to come might be moderated if, contrary to the hallucinatory perspectives of traditional liberalism, Western liberal societies were to conceive the liberal form of life as only one form of life among many, neither better nor worse than some others, but merely different. It is an implication of my argument that Western liberal forms of life are not, in truth, always worthy of allegiance: they may not be the forms of life that best meet the demands of the universal minimum content of morality, and their adoption may entail the loss of precious and irreplaceable cultural forms. A further implication is that, where the liberal form of life is worthy of allegiance, it is so not because it is the form of life blessed by reason, or the one in which human beings as such best flourish, but simply because it is an incident in a choice-worthy tradition or form of life, to which some human beings find themselves constitutively, but at the same time contingently, attached.

7

THE UNDOING OF
CONSERVATISM

CONSERVATISM IN RETROSPECT

The undoing of conservatism has come about as an unintended consequence of Hayekian policy. The hegemony, within conservative thought and practice, of neo-liberal ideology has had the effect of destroying conservatism as a viable political project in our time and in any foreseeable future. Traditional conservatism is no longer a realistic political option when inherited institutions and practices have been swept away by the market forces which neo-liberal policies release or reinforce. When our institutional inheritance – that precious and irreplaceable patrimony of mediating structures and autonomous professions – is thrown away in the pursuit of a managerialist Cultural Revolution seeking to refashion the entire national life on the impoverished model of contract and market exchange, it is clear that the task of conserving and renewing a culture is no longer understood by contemporary conservatives. In the context of such a Maoism of the Right, it is the permanent revolution of unfettered market processes, not the conservation of traditional institutions and professions, having each of them a distinctive *ethos*, that has become the ruling project of contemporary conservatism. At the same time, neo-liberalism itself can now be seen as a self-undermining political project. Its political success depended upon cultural traditions, and constellations of interests, that neo-liberal policy was bound to dissipate. In adopting the neo-liberal programme of a permanent institutional revolution as their own, contemporary conservatives not only have abandoned any claim to be guardians of continuity in national life; they have at the same time linked their fortunes to a political project which all the evidence suggests is self-defeating.

In the late 1970s, and throughout the earlier years of the 1980s, neo-liberalism was a compelling response to otherwise intractable dilemmas. The manifest failings of corporatist policy in Britain and the collapse of central planning throughout the Soviet bloc vindicated market institutions as the chief organizing structures in any modern economy. The old 'systems debate', between 'planning' and 'markets', was resolved decisively on the terrain of history. By the late 1980s, however, that old debate receded, and a new debate began to emerge – a debate about the varieties and limits of market institutions, and about their cultural and political preconditions. In this new debate, neo-liberal thought has little to contribute. Further, conservative policy that is animated by neo-liberal ideology finds itself baffled and powerless when confronted by the political challenges to market institutions that distinguish the 1990s – well exemplified in the success of neo-communist parties as the principal political beneficiaries of market reform in the post-Soviet world. In Western democracies, such as Britain, Canada and New Zealand, conservative governments animated by free market ideology look, impotent and aghast, into an electoral abyss which their own policies have opened up for them. Yet the option of returning to

an older conservatism – 'One Nation' Toryism in Britain, say –
has been closed for them by the social effects of market forces
whose often destructive radicalism conservative policies have
only enhanced. As a result, conservatism, in Britain and elsewhere, has arrived at an intellectual and political impasse, from
which it can neither advance nor retreat. Except in societies, such
as Italy, whose special histories have given it a further lease of
life, conservatism is now a spent force in most Western countries. In an irony that will delight historians in years to come, the
political effect of the ephemeral intellectual hegemony of the
New Right, in Britain and similar countries, has probably been
to accomplish the political destruction of conservatism: it may
have rendered conservative parties unelectable, perhaps for a
generation.

The capture of conservative parties and governments throughout the Western world by free market ideology was an accomplished and familiar fact by the late 1980s. Its full implications
have yet to be properly understood. The conquest of modern
Western conservatism by a species of market fundamentalism –
Manchesterism *redivivus* – has transformed it profoundly and
probably irreversibly. A political outlook that in Burke, Disraeli
and Salisbury was sceptical of the project of the Enlightenment
and suspicious of the promise of progress has mortgaged its
future on a wager on indefinite economic growth and unfettered
market forces. Such a bet – Hayek's wager, as it might be called –
scarcely exhibits the political prudence which was once revered
as a conservative virtue. It leaves the governments and societies
that have staked their patrimony on such a throw defenceless
and without resources when, in the normal fortunes of markets
everywhere, or because economic growth has come up against
insuperable social or ecological limits, market institutions fail
to deliver the goods expected of them. In such circumstances,
liberal civilization itself may be imperilled, in so far as its legitimacy has been linked with the utopia of perpetual growth

powered by unregulated market processes, and the inevitable failure of this utopia spawns illiberal political movements. Indeed, unconstrained market institutions are bound to undermine social and political stability, particularly as they impose on the population unprecedented levels of economic insecurity with all the resultant dislocations of life in families and communities. Market-driven economic change, especially when it is large-scale, rapid and unremitting, fosters insecurity also by marginalizing traditional forms and confounding established expectations. In the countries of continental Europe, the emergence of high levels of structural unemployment has been accompanied by the re-emergence of atavistic parties of the Right. In Britain, the desolation of communities by unchannelled market forces and the resultant pervasive sense of economic insecurity have not, and in all likelihood will not, evoke similar illiberal political movements; but they have been crucial factors in an epidemic of crime that probably has no parallel in national life since the early nineteenth century. It is only by the exercise of heroic powers of self-deception, or else by simple dishonesty, that British Conservatives can fail to discern the links between levels of criminality that have no precedent for generations and policies of marketization, pursued since 1979, which have ridden rough-shod over settled communities and established expectations. It is only a similar exercise in self-delusion or economy with the truth that can blind Conservatives to the links between the economic changes which their policies have reinforced and accelerated and the growth of the many varieties of poverty which are indifferently lumped together under the fashionable but deeply misconceived category of the underclass.

It is a general truth that, when they are disembedded from any context of common life, and emancipated from political constraints, market forces – especially when they are global – work to unsettle communities and delegitimize traditional institutions. This is a truism, no doubt; but it expresses an insight – that, for most people, security against risk is more important than the enhancement of choice – that conservative parties and governments have forgotten. For many people, perhaps most, the largely illusory enhancement of choice through freeing up markets does not compensate for the substantial increase in insecurity it also generates. More specifically, neo-liberal policies have worked to extend to the middle classes the insecurities and risks that have always plagued working-class life. By framing their policies with reference to an Enlightenment ideology of world-betterment through unconstrained global markets, Western conservatives may have given the rentier a new lease on life; but they have also brought about the euthanasia of the old middle classes. The political price to be paid for this dubious achievement is likely to be high, and, in the British case, may conceivably be the destruction of the Conservative Party – in its present form at any rate – as a party of government.

In throwing in its lot with the cult of the free market, Western conservatism has colluded with the spirit of the age, which is well summarized in Hayek's candidly nihilistic dictum 'Progress is movement for movement's sake'.[1] Conservatives who imagine that their parties can be recovered for traditional values are deluding themselves. New political groupings may arise, in which genuinely conservative ideas coexist with, and are fertilized by, ideas from other traditions; but the notion that established conservative parties can be reclaimed, and turned into vehicles for an older conservative philosophy, is in most countries a mere illusion. The result of conservative policy since 1979 has been to junk traditional practices of all sorts in the pursuit of the mirage of the wholly free market, with the evident fact that the workings of unconstrained market institutions are incompatible with the stability of any real-world society being treated as a taboo in conservative political discourse. Equally, the possibility – indeed, the reality – that policies predicated on the prospect of open-ended economic growth neglect the fragility of the natural world of which our species is but a part has been thoroughly exorcized from consciousness. Indeed, in attaching themselves to the utopia of perpetual growth in goods and services, conservatives have surrendered abjectly to the spirit of the age. To attempt to return conservative parties, or for that matter Western societies, to traditional forms of life at this stage in our history is to tilt at windmills, or else to enter into a dangerous flirtation with forms of cultural fundamentalism whose upshot will be – like the ephemeral 'Back to Basics' campaign of the Major government – at best farcical. The better way lies in the recognition that in our circumstances renewing genuine conservative values, and passing on the traditions of a liberal civilization, demand novel and radical policies and a willingness to think in unorthodox ways. Contemporary conservative thought is of no more assistance in this task than traditional socialist thought.

A central test of the readiness to think fresh thoughts is the way we think about market institutions. On the view defended here they are not ends in themselves but means or tools whose end is human well-being. Those who apply a model of the free market that was useful in the struggle against the stagnant corporatism of the 1970s to the radically different problems of the 1990s are misapplying liberal ideas in a fashion that is dangerous to liberal civilization itself. If the threat to a liberal form of life came in the 1970s from an invasive and overly ambitious state, in the 1990s it comes from the desolation and collapse of communities and the excesses of individualism, which have in fact been compounded by policies which conceive of marketization as an all-purpose cure-all for economic and social ills. If, in the 1970s, the principal danger to liberal civilization came from the hubris of government, in the 1980s and 1990s it has come from hubristic liberal ideology, in which a fetish is made of individual choice and the needs of solidarity and common life go unrecognized or spurned. The starting-point for serious political discourse in Britain in the 1990s must be in the recognition that the paleo-liberal celebration of consumer choice and market freedom as the only undisputed values has become a recipe for anomie, social breakdown and ultimately economic failure.

This is not to say that there are not areas of policy in which market institutions can still be usefully extended: there is a good case, as I shall suggest later in this chapter (p. 176), for the introduction of a version of the educational voucher that is different in crucial respects from those proposed by neo-liberals, with the aim of anchoring schooling more deeply in local communities. And, always provided such measures are fully and properly funded, there may be a useful role for analogous voucher schemes in some areas of welfare policy. Equally, not all curbs on market freedoms that are presently in place, or currently envisaged, are sensible, or defensible in any terms that are recognizably liberal: there is much in recurring EU proposals – for the restriction of vitamins as forms of prescription medicine and for the restraint of commercial expression, for example – that smacks of the moralism and paternalism that would immediately, and rightly, be rejected by liberal opinion in other areas of policy.[2] From the truth that market freedom is not a dogma it does not follow that current or proposed restraints on market freedoms are always acceptable. The deeper truth is that market institutions are useful devices, not articles of faith. Their scope, varieties and limits cannot be known *a priori*, but are to be assessed tentatively and provisionally. Such assessment will turn on the contribution they make to human well-being and their impact on valuable cultural traditions and forms of common life. Importantly, since cultural forms are various, the proper scope and limits of market freedoms will also be variable. Abstract notions of choice or rights are of very little use in sensible reflection on markets and their limits. Consumer choice, for example, is an important good, still sometimes wrongly curtailed, whose justification is in its contribution to individual empowerment. It cannot nevertheless be the basis of an entire political philosophy, or of the whole agenda of public policy.

When applied, or misapplied, in the context of a neo-liberal ideology that is insensitive to the human needs for community and cultural identity, the idea of consumer choice becomes positively pernicious. To make a fetish of free trade, for example, when it manifestly does not serve human needs, risks discrediting market institutions, and endangers the stability of liberal societies. Yet this risk will become a reality, wherever market institutions are presented not as indispensable instruments for the achievement of individual and communal objectives, to be shaped and curbed by reference to those ends, but as an all-or-nothing package, which has only an incidental (or coincidental) connection with the communities and cultures it serves. The real danger of paleo-liberal thought and policy in all of its forms is that it does not understand that market institutions are stable and enduring only in so far as they are embedded in the common cultures of those whose needs they exist to serve.

This is a danger that is being incurred not only by free market conservatism but also by traditional varieties of the Left project, all of which stake their policies on a resumption of economic growth – on a species of revived Croslandism. In so far as the Left project remains wedded to growthmanship, and fails to respond to the challenge of a situation in which a resumption of economic growth on conventional lines is unachievable or undesirable, it will suffer the same fate of political obsolescence that has befallen the market liberal doctrines of the New Right. Nor have attempts to reformulate a New Left project confronted the obstacles to socialist ideals presented by conventional prescriptions for global free trade.[3] At present, all conventional political thought seems fixated on assumptions, such as the possibility and desirability of resuming economic growth at the rates and of the sorts experienced in the 1980s or the 1960s, and on models, such as those of Anglo-American individualist capitalism or European

Social or Christian democracy, that are now in crisis and have clearly had their day. There is a real danger that the ossification of liberal thought resulting from the hegemony of discredited neo-liberal ideas in all mainstream parties opens a window of political opportunity for avowed enemies of liberal civilization. The gap between received political ideas and present political realities has rarely been wider, or more perilous. We shall best conserve our liberal patrimony if, as Maynard Keynes urged us to do, we seek new wisdom for a new age. The beginning of such wisdom is in the recognition that Western conservatism has come undone in its adoption of the policies and philosophy of the unfettered free market.

THE STRANGE DEATH OF FREE MARKET CONSERVATISM

The question 'What must be true for conservatism to be possible?' is likely to be received as a donnish diversion from serious political thought. Its implication – that, whatever the preconditions of conservatism may be, they may no longer exist among us today – may seem especially frivolous. For virtually all Western countries have political parties that avow themselves to be conservative; there are, or have been lately, groups which meet to consider the principles of conservative philosophy; and it has been cogently argued by one of our most modern and least nostalgist writers that a conservative disposition remains an essential element in any life that is recognizable by us, in whom the passion for novelty and the penchant for choice-making are notably strong, as worth living.[4] Given these familiar considerations, an inquiry into the presuppositions of conservatism may well appear to be ill-considered. And certain well-known features of conservative thought would seem to make an exploration of its general preconditions an especially unpromising venture. After all, what could be more misconceived than an effort at a transcendental deduction of a political outlook that disdains abstract principle, favours the local over the universal, and denies that practice needs support from philosophical 'foundations'? The search for the necessary preconditions of conservatism may even be dismissed as arising from a misunderstanding of conservatism itself.

Yet it will be my contention that the question with which I have begun is far from frivolous. I shall argue instead that the conditions under which conservatism as a coherent form of political thought and practice are possible exist no longer; that conservatism has for us a Cheshire Cat quality, in that what it proposes to conserve is a spectral thing, voided of substance, partly by the policies of recent conservative governments and partly by aspects of modern societies which such policies have reinforced; and that conservative parties and movements have in all Western countries been captured by neo-liberal ideas, more properly thought of as those of fundamentalist or classical liberalism, that in their utopian projects of world-improvement and their expectation of convergence on a universal civilization are alien to the forms of thought and practice most characteristic of a conservative outlook as that used to be understood. At the same time, I shall submit that any political outlook that is merely reactionary in its response to the dilemmas of the late modern period in which we live is bound to be a form of quixotry, or else of atavism. Ironically, and ominously, it is the capture of conservative parties by a primitive species of paleo-liberalism – which is what neo-liberalism and neo-conservatism really are – that enhances the prospects of truly atavistic illiberal movements. In a mirror irony, the hegemony within conservative thought and practice of market liberalism, when combined with the disruptive effects of unfettered market forces on settled communities and inherited social forms, has the result that unreflective adherence to tradition has been destroyed and replaced, if at all, by varieties of religious or cultural fundamentalism. In short, the

subversive effects of unhampered market institutions on traditional forms of life make free-market conservatism an inherently unstable and, over time, a self-undermining political project.
For these reasons, I conclude that a genuinely conservative form
of political thought and practice, the lineaments of which we can
discern as at least one element in our cultural history, is no longer
a real possibility for us. How has this strange circumstance come
about?

THE SELF-DESTRUCTION OF TRADITIONAL CONSERVATISM

The conquest in the 1980s of conservative parties throughout
the world by doctrines of market liberalism did not come out
of the blue. At least since the end of the Second World War
conservative parties in Western countries had relied upon policies which stimulated economic growth as the principal means
of securing the political legitimacy of market institutions. In
conditions of rapid economic growth, the destructive impact of
market forces on communities and settled practices is softened,
or compensated by, the new opportunities that such growth
affords. Further, the dislocations occasioned by market competition can in such conditions be palliated by welfare institutions
and more fundamental issues of distribution and livelihood
taken off the political agenda. This was, in effect, the Butskellite
settlement in post-war British political life: social conflict was
avoided by the pursuit of a full employment policy and by the
establishment of a welfare state in which the middle classes
participated fully and which was funded by the proceeds of
economic growth. Post-war British governments until 1979 conceived their task as that of extending their hold on office by
aligning the electoral and the political cycles in a context of sustained economic growth. Whether or not particular governments
were successful in this feat, the adoption of this conception of

their task by the two major parties in Britain produced a period of political and social stability in Britain that began to unravel only in the late 1970s. Moreover, the post-war settlement in Britain was paralleled by similar settlements in all the major Western countries, and began to show signs of strain in many of them in the late 1970s and early 1980s.

The chief innovation of early Thatcherism in Britain was to tear up the post-war social compact – at least as that concerned macroeconomic policies aiming at full employment and at a smooth meshing of the economic and political cycles – by the adoption of the Medium Term Financial Strategy (MTFS). The welfare state was left comparatively intact, but the political thrust of early Thatcherism was in the direction of the dismantlement of the corporatist policies of the 1960s and early 1970s, by the dissolution of the triangular relationship between government, business and the trade unions on which corporatist policy was based. It is important to note that these corporatist relationships started to come unstuck in Britain well before the coming to power of Margaret Thatcher in 1979. The Healey-IMF squeeze of the last Labour government was a clear portent of the fiscal austerity pursued in the early Thatcher years. It is no less important to be clear that when the collusive corporatism of the 1960s and 1970s foundered it was because it had issued in stagflation and social conflict, rather than yielding steady economic growth and social peace. Corporatism had failed to deliver the goods; but the idea that market institutions can secure political legitimacy in a democratic regime only against a background of steady growth in output remained firmly in place. The central project of early Thatcherism, whose intellectual inspiration came from rational expectations theory in economics, from the utopian notion of an economic constitution proposed in the Public Choice school and from the *mélange* of classical liberal and libertarian ideas that came together briefly under the heading of the New Right, was to secure the conditions of economic growth by the setting up of a stable framework of rules rather than by government acting directly as a pacemaker of economic expansion.

Though, predictably, the MTFS came to grief in the mid-1980s, the rewriting of the British social compact that it embodied had political resonance into the early 1990s. It is arguable that the result of the 1992 general election can be better explained by the decoupling in voters' perceptions of the performance of government from that of the economy than by mistrust of Labour's economic competence. This decoupling, in turn, was probably the most enduring trace of over a decade of Thatcherite rhetoric and statecraft focusing on the autonomy of market forces – a tribute to the success of Thatcherism, for a while at least, as a hegemonic political project whose objective was the transformation of British political culture. Whether this alteration in voters' perceptions is in fact irreversible or even long-lasting is another matter, but fortunately not one which anything fundamental in the present argument turns on. For, even if the correlation between voting behaviour and perceived economic well-being has been irreversibly weakened in British political life, the electoral prospects of British conservatism are not thereby necessarily enhanced. An upswing in the economy will not then work inevitably in favour of a sitting Conservative government, and elections will turn on other issues. Most likely, the traces of this Thatcherite legacy, in conjunction with the stubborn reality of persistently slow growth, will alter the terms of political trade by shifting the content of public discourse in Britain. The parties will be assessed by the voters on how they address issues having to do with the quality of life rather than on narrow issues of economic management. Specifically, they will be judged on how they propose to protect the quality of life in Britain more than upon their policies for the rekindling of economic growth. In other words, low growth – an annual growth rate of around 2 per cent or so, say – seems likely to be a presupposition of political debate in Britain, as perhaps in other European countries, for the foreseeable future. This is a prospect that bodes ill for the political fortunes of conservatism in so far as it continues to be wedded to the growth-oriented doctrines of market liberalism.

The deepest difficulty of contemporary conservatism is that of securing the political legitimacy of the unfettered market institutions to which it is committed in an age of low economic growth. In such an age, the gale of creative destruction blows less benignly, with the processes of entrepreneurship and technological innovation which distinguish unencumbered market institutions eliminating jobs without generating new ones of the same sort or at the same rate. The dystopian prospect – not so far, perhaps, from the present reality – is of a highly dynamic but low-growth economy in which a permanent revolution in technologies and productive arrangements yields large-scale structural unemployment and pervasive job insecurity. As Edward Luttwak has noted, in his provocative piece on 'Why Fascism is the Wave of the Future':

> Structural change, with all its personal upheavals and social disruptions, is now quite rapid even when there is zero growth, becoming that much faster when economies do grow. The engine turns, grinding lives and grinding down established human relationships, even when the car is stopped; and reaches Ferrari-like rpms at the most modest steam-roller speeds.

Luttwak comments:

> ... neither the moderate Right nor the moderate Left even recognises, let alone offers any solution for, the central problem of our days: the completely unprecedented personal economic insecurity of working people, from industrial workers and white-collar clerks to medium-high managers.[5]

The fact that the subversive dynamism of market institutions, particularly when these are globalized, destroys personal and communal economic security even in conditions of zero economic growth is of central importance not only in the Western liberal democracies of which Luttwak is speaking primarily, but also for the post-communist states. For, in the latter, the collapse of bankrupt institutions of central planning, and the subsequent ill-conceived adoption of neo-liberal policies of shock therapy, has replicated in grotesquely exaggerated form the Western problem of market-driven structural economic adjustments occurring in conditions of zero or even negative growth. Entirely predictably, though evoking the baffled incomprehension of Western opinion, the political beneficiaries of mass economic insecurity pervasive in such conditions have, virtually everywhere, been neo-communist parties and neo-fascist parties, sometimes in combination. In many, indeed most of the post-communist states, the political risk of unregulated market institutions that are exposed to the full gale of global market forces – that the liberal institutions that are supposed (according to Western theory) to accompany them will be repudiated or compromised – has already generated a powerful backlash against Western-imposed policies of shock therapy. It is paradoxical, but typical of the intellectual confusion of the times, that politicians and parties in the post-communist countries that seek to temper the impact of market reform on an already shell-shocked society, and thereby to preserve a measure of social and political stability, are denounced by Western conservatives for their deviations from neo-liberal orthodoxy. These developments in the post-communist countries have so far been little noted or comprehended in the West. They contain lessons that Western political elites and opinion-formers show few signs of learning. The fundamental truth that rapid and continuous market-driven economic change is inimical to settled community, and in the longer run to the stability of liberal and democratic institutions, has apparently yet to be grasped by most Western policy-makers.

The fact that the mobility of labour required of everyone in a society dominated by unconstrained market institutions is profoundly disruptive of settled communities and imposes severe strains on life in families is neglected, or repressed, by those contemporary conservatives – the vast majority – for whom the United States is the tacit or explicit model. It is true enough that, in the US case, all other values have been sacrificed for the sake of microeconomic flexibility, productivity and low labour costs. This US model, which is unlikely to be replicated as successfully anywhere else, has to its credit that the relentless pursuit of efficiency has kindled renewed economic growth, spurred technological advance and generated millions of new jobs. At the same time, the US model of individualist market institutions has been distinguished by levels of family breakdown and fractured community, of criminality and of incarceration, that are unknown in other Western countries. In addition, the successes in job creation in the United States have necessitated a large-scale casualization of work, a lowering of real incomes in the middle classes and a revolution of falling expectations in the younger generation that will not be tolerated in any European country. The US model, in which economic growth is restarted, against all the odds in a mature industrial economy, by restructuring and technological innovation in an atomized labour market, is not exportable to any society with a less individualist moral and political culture. Yet it is the paradigm for policy in all conservative parties in which market liberalism is dominant. Contrary to the US neo-conservative view which market liberals in other countries have endorsed, the United States is not in any sense a model for a universal civilization, but rather a singularity, a limiting case, whose lessons for others are chiefly negative. The significance of the American example for older and more rooted cultures is, in fact, of a warning to be heeded rather than of a model to be emulated. For the adoption in these older cultures of a US model for economic policy is bound to entail far greater cultural losses, with most of the economic gains being small, speculative or entirely illusory. If there can be such a thing as a coherent form of conservative thought and policy in the European countries – and it is an implication of my argument that that is at best an open question – then it can only be one that has decoupled, economically, politically and culturally, from the American exemplar which animates the New Right.

Market liberalism, as we have come to know it in Britain and elsewhere in the 1980s, fosters a privileging of choice and a cult of mobility that consort badly with the settled communities cherished by traditional conservatives. Indeed, among us, market liberalism is in its workings ineluctably subversive of tradition and community. This may not have been the case in Edmund Burke's day, in which the maintenance of the traditions of whig England could coexist with a policy of economic individualism, but in our age a belief in any such harmony is a snare and a delusion. Among us, unlike the men and women of Burke's day, markets are global, and also, in the case of capital markets, nearly instantaneous; free trade, if it too is global, operates among communities that are vastly more uneven in development than any that traded with one another in Burke's time; and our lives are pervaded by mass media that transform tastes, and revolutionize daily habits, in ways that could be only dimly glimpsed by the Scottish political economists whom Burke so revered.

For the Scottish thinkers to whom Burke owed allegiance, there was nevertheless no preordained harmony between the workings of a commercial society and the renewal of valued traditions. Adam Smith feared that the minute division of labour required in the emerging commercial society would stultify popular sensibility and intellectual development, and worried that the anonymity of great towns would lead to a breakdown in informal social monitoring; he conjectured that the dissociation of market success from the moral virtues in commercial societies could generate a new and perverse form of emulation, and that the hedonism of commercial societies would make the martial virtues unsustainable in them. As Smith himself put it, in one of his lectures on jurisprudence:

> There are some inconveniences . . . arising from a commercial spirit. The first we shall mention is that it confines the views of men. Where the division of labour is brought to perfection, every man has only a simple operation to perform. To this his whole attention is confined, and few ideas pass in his mind but what have an immediate connexion with it. . . . Another inconvenience attending commerce is that education is greatly neglected . . . we find that in the commercial parts of England, the tradesmen are for the most part in this despicable condition: their work through half the week is sufficient to maintain them, and thro' want of education they have no amusement for the other but riot and debauchery. So it may very justly be said that the people who cloath the whole world are in rags themselves . . . Another bad effect of commerce is that it sinks the courage of mankind and tends to extinguish the martial spirit. In all commercial countries the division of labour is infinite, and every ones thoughts are employed on one particular thing . . . In the same manner war comes to be a trade also . . . The defence of the country is therefore committed to a certain set of men who have nothing else to do; and among the bulk of the people military courage diminishes.[6]

These concerns, shared by other Scottish thinkers such as Adam Ferguson, have scarcely been shown to be groundless or exaggerated by the subsequent history of market societies. Most of Smith's latter-day epigones seem nevertheless not to have taken to heart his wise summary and conclusion: 'These are the disadvantages of a commercial spirit. The minds of men are contracted and rendered incapable of elevation, education is despised or at least neglected, and heroic spirit is almost utterly extinguished. To remedy these defects would be an object worthy of serious attention.'[7] These moral and cultural shortcomings of a commercial society, so vividly captured by one of its seminal theorists, figure less prominently, if at all, in the banal discourse of free market ideology.

The social and cultural effects of market liberalism are, virtually without exception, inimical to the values that traditional conservatives hold dear. Communities are scattered to the winds by the gale of creative destruction. Endless 'downsizing' and 'flattening' of enterprises fosters ubiquitous insecurity and makes loyalty to the company a cruel joke. The celebration of consumer choice, as the only undisputed value in market societies, devalues commitment and stability in personal relationships and encourages the view of marriage and the family as vehicles of self-realization. The dynamism of market processes dissolves social hierarchies and overturns established expectations. Status is ephemeral, trust frail and contract sovereign. The dissolution of communities promoted by market-driven labour mobility weakens, where it does not entirely destroy, the informal social monitoring of behaviour which is the most effective preventive measure against crime. It is odd that British conservatives, who have followed their US teachers in blaming the rise in crime in Britain on the disincentive effects of welfare measures, have not noticed that most forms of crime (apart from some sorts of property crime) are vastly commoner in the United States, where welfare institutions are far less developed, and market-driven labour mobility and its resultant anomie far more intense.

It is a general truth that has gone little noted by contemporary conservatives that the incessant change promoted and demanded by market processes nullifies the significance of precedent and destroys the authority of the past.[8] Indeed it is not too much of an exaggeration to say that market liberal policy delivers the *coup de grace* to practices of authority and of subscription to tradition already severely weakened during the modern period. Perhaps the most salient feature of our age is not a decline in individual liberty but the vanishing of authority, and a concomitant metamorphosis of moral judgements into a species of personal preferences, between which reason is powerless to arbitrate.[9] The tendency of market liberal policy is significantly to reinforce subjectivist and even antinomian tendencies which are already very powerful in modernist societies and thereby to render surviving enclaves and remnants of traditional life powerless before them.

The Old Right project of cultural fundamentalism is best understood as an ill-thought-out response to the modern dissolution of old forms of moral life that contemporary conservative policy has itself promoted or accelerated. This is not to say that all such older forms of community and moral life lacked value. On the contrary, the reactionary perception of cultural loss as a real historical phenomenon is sometimes well founded, and it is singularly lacking among contemporary conservatives; but that does not mean that the old forms of life can, or even should, be reconstituted. Not only is the current conservative clamour about family breakdown dishonest in repressing the role that market-driven economic changes – sometimes occurring over several generations, but greatly accelerated since the mid-1970s, as with female participation in the workforce – have played in transforming family life, but also it is self-deceiving in imagining that older forms of family life can conceivably be revived in which modern Western demands for choice and self-fulfilment – which are in other areas elevated by conservatives to the status of fetishes – are denied. The current neofundamentalist clamour for a return to the traditional family is, in other words, misconceived and frivolous in the highest degree. It expresses no serious concern for the needs of people in families, nor any understanding of the diverse forms in which the institution of the family is now to be found. Such vulgar clamour is symptomatic of contemporary conservative thought in the unreality of its perception of real people and their needs. The adoption by Conservative governments of a neo-fundamentalist stance on family policy is best understood as an act of desperation, reinforced by the remoteness from public sentiment bred by the hermetic culture of the new Tory *nomen-klatura*. Its political effect will be to speed Conservatives along the road to electoral oblivion.

THE POLITICAL ECONOMY OF EREWHON: THE MARKET LIBERAL UTOPIA

The desolation of settled communities and the ruin of established expectations will not be mourned and may well be welcomed by fundamentalist market liberals. For them, nothing much of any value is threatened by the unfettered operation of market institutions. Communities and ways of life which cannot renew themselves through the exercise of consumer choice deserve to perish. The protection from market forces of valuable cultural forms is a form of unacceptable paternalism. And so the familiar and tedious litany goes on.

Underlying this fundamentalist conception of market institutions is a model of society that in its rationalistic utopianism and its hubristic doctrine of global convergence on a universal civilization resembles nothing more closely than the most primitive forms of classical Marxism. Classical liberalism, or what I have termed market fundamentalism, is, like Marxism, a variation on the Enlightenment project, which is the project of transcending the contingencies of history and cultural difference and founding a universal civilization that is qualitatively different from any that has ever before existed. The conflict between fundamentalist liberalism and the European tradition of conservative thought is plain and incontrovertible, if only in the fact that conservatives as different as Burke and de Maistre defined their outlook in terms of enmity towards the central project of the Enlightenment. It was left to the conservatives of the late twentieth century to yoke conservatism, perhaps for the first time in its history, to an Enlightenment utopia. If, as I believe, we are now in circumstances in which conservative philosophy can no longer give us much guidance, this is partly because we live in a post-Enlightenment age, an age in which the best thought views the Enlightenment from a perspective of historical distance rather than setting itself in opposition to it. This is to say that we view the European Enlightenment, like the Renaissance and the Reformation, as an irreversible cultural transformation that has left permanent marks on all subsequent thought and practice. Nor, equally, can we found policy on Enlightenment expectations – of convergence on a universal civilization, and of progress in the growth of knowledge occurring in tandem with increasing human emancipation – which the historical experience of our century, and of humankind generally, renders incredible. Although it has transformed our cultures irreversibly, the Enlightenment cannot be for us – what it was for the French *philosophes*, and perhaps still is for a few Old Believers in the United States – an *ersatz* religion. Our situation, as late moderns, whether we wish it or not, is to belong to a post-Enlightenment culture, in which the rationalist religions of humanity are almost as archaic, as alien and as remote as the traditional transcendental faiths. It is therefore deeply ironic that conservatism should have surrendered its scepticism in regard to the Enlightenment at just the historical moment at which the Enlightenment project should be everywhere in evident disarray or actual collapse.

The kinship of market fundamentalism with classical Marxism is evident in at least three respects. Both are forms of *economism* in that their model of humankind is that of *homo economicus* and they theorize cultural and political life in the reductionist terms of economic determinism. A *reductio ad absurdum* of the reductionist analysis of social life on the basis of an abstract and in fact *a priori* model of market exchange may be found in the works of the Chicago economist Gary Becker, but less extreme versions of the same approach are to be found in the application of economic analysis to political and bureaucratic behaviour.[10] Second, this form of economic imperialism involves a marginalization of cultural difference in human life that grossly underestimates its political importance and even distorts our view of market institutions. It occludes our perception of political realities by treating nationalism and ethnic allegiance as ephemeral, and even epiphenomenal or derivative, episodes in modern life. It blunts our understanding of market institutions themselves by neglecting their cultural variability – a decisive mistake at any time, but especially momentous at present, when radically different East Asian market institutions are overtaking Occidental ones, particularly those of the Anglo-American varieties, on virtually any measure of performance. In general, it encourages the erroneous view of market institutions as free-standing entities, and the mistaken expectation that they will converge on a single model. Third, the economic imperialism of the fundamentalist conception of market institutions suggests a view of society, explicit in Hayek and before him in Herbert Spencer, in which it is nothing but a nexus of market exchanges, such that allegiance can be secured to a liberal political order that is universal and embodies no particular cultural tradition. In this paleo-liberal or libertarian view, the erosion of distinctive cultures by market processes is, if anything, to be welcomed as a sign of progress toward a universal rational civilization. Here paleo-liberalism shows its affinities not with European conservatism but with the Old Left project of doing away with, or marginalizing politically, the human inheritance of cultural difference.

That this perspective is a hallucinatory and utopian one is clear if we consider its neglect of the sources not only of political allegiance but also of social order in common cultural forms. Market liberalism, like other Enlightenment ideologies, treats cultural difference as a politically marginal phenomenon whose appropriate sphere is in private life. It does not comprehend, or repudiates as irrationality, the role of a common culture in sustaining political order and in legitimizing market institutions. It maintains that only a regime of common rules, perhaps embodying a shared conception of rights, is required for the stability of market institutions and of a liberal civil society. This species of *liberal legalism* overlooks, or denies, that market institutions will not be politically stable – at any rate when they are combined with democratic institutions – if they do not accord with widespread conceptions of fairness, if they violate other important cultural norms, or if they have too destructive an effect on established expectations. In short, they deny the evident facts that the wholly free market is incompatible with social and political stability, while the stability of market institutions themselves depends far more on their political and cultural acceptability than upon the legal framework which supposedly defines and protects them.

Market liberal responses to this criticism fall into two categories – the ideological and the pragmatic. Market liberal ideologists will argue that the stability of market society is only a matter of enforcing its laws. This thoroughly foolish reply need not detain us. It neglects the political fragility of the rule of law, and the frequent impossibility of enforcing it – points market liberals seem able to grasp in the context of laws which flout supply and demand, such as price controls, but which they appear incapable of generalizing. The pragmatic market liberal response is to argue that market institutions need no legitimation so long as they deliver the goods in terms of general prosperity. This argument is illuminating in that it reveals the dependency of market liberal thought on the permanent possibility of rapid and continuous economic growth. It shows also that market liberalism has few sources of legitimacy on which to call when market economies go through a bad patch. It is the dim or unspoken recognition of this problem of legitimation for market institutions in times of poor economic performance that has led many market fundamentalists to compromise the rationalist purity of their doctrine and to combine it with varieties of moral or cultural fundamentalism.

Market liberalism is a utopian ideology in that the free market institutions to which it is devoted cannot in the real world of human history be combined with social or political stability. (This result is corroborated rather than undermined by the US example, in which a highly individualist ideal of market institutions has been rendered compatible with social stability only by the adoption of protectionist and regulatory policies more restrictive and far-reaching than those of almost any other Western country.) It is utopian in its view of market institutions themselves – as perpetual motion machines requiring only a legal framework and government non-interference to deliver uninterrupted growth – and in its refusal to accept that sometimes an active macroeconomic policy is necessary to keep a market economy on an even keel. It is utopian in its neglect, or denial, of the truth that market institutions are stable when, and only when, they come embedded in cultural forms which constrain and inform their workings.

Market liberalism is at its most utopian, however, in its conception of a global market society, in which goods, and perhaps people, move freely between economies having radically different stages of development and harbouring very different cultures. Global free trade, as it is envisaged by economic liberals and embodied in the GATT agreements of late 1993, will subject both developing and mature economies to levels of strain and job dislocation severer than they have ever before known. The displacement of peasants in hitherto agrarian economies and of industrial workers in Europe by an untrammelled global market will unavoidably have consequences for the social and political stability of both kinds of economies that have not been addressed in the Panglossian scenarios of the supporters of world-wide free trade.[11] In Europe, the politically destabilizing effects of structural unemployment in excess of 10 per cent are already visible in electoral support for renascent radical parties of the Right; it does not need powers of clairvoyance to divine the political impact of further large job losses arising from an influx of goods produced at around one-tenth of European labour costs. Nor does it require more than a smattering of knowledge of twentieth-century history to guess what are likely to be the results of attempting to force on European peoples a structural economic adjustment larger, deeper and quicker, than any they have yet suffered other than as a consequence of war. Supporters of global free trade do not confront its systemic effects on the stability of families and communities. Global free trade imposes an inexorable downward pressure on workers' incomes in the First World for a variety of reasons, including demographic reasons. Further, it dislocates settled communal life by imposing unending job mobility on workers and their families. As Herman Daly has written:

> Given the existing overpopulation and high demographic growth of the Third World it is clear that equalization [of incomes] will be downward, as it has indeed been during the last decade in the U.S. ... Even with uniformly high wages made possible by universal population control and redistribution, and with uniform internalization of external costs, free trade and free capital mobility still increase the separation of ownership and control and the forced mobility of labour which are so inimical to community.[12]

These destabilizing effects of global free trade are not incidental but integral to it.

The political frivolity of the utopia of a frontierless global market of the sort that is embodied in the GATT agreements is perhaps matched only by that of proposals for the European Union that envisage a continental labour market operating under a single transnational currency. Such proposals for an unfettered single European market neglect not only the vast differences in economic development within the EU but also the embeddedness of the diverse market institutions that the EU harbours in divergent national cultures. At the same time, the project of a single European currency is bound to result in great stagnant pools of unemployment, regional and even national in scope, if it is not combined with an effective transnational labour market. Such a market has no precedent in modern history and there can be little doubt that the attempt to impose it will encounter a powerful political backlash. In general, attempts to steamroller the European peoples into an artificial and culturally disembedded single market can only work to strengthen political support for nationalism. Such a reinforcement of nationalism in Europe, arising from insensitivity to national cultures, can only have the effect of making more difficult those forms of European cooperation – on a common defence and foreign policy, for example – that Europe's present circumstances make desirable and indeed necessary.

Both visions, for GATT and for a federalist European Union, are neo-liberal rationalist utopias that will founder on the reefs of history and human nature, with costs in human suffering that may come to rival those of twentieth-century experiments in central economic planning. These and other similarly utopian projects of market liberalism neglect enduring needs of human beings, an understanding of which was once preserved in conservative thought. Human beings need, more than they need the freedom of consumer choice, a cultural and economic environment that offers them an acceptable level of security and in which they feel at home. Market institutions that deny this need will be politically repudiated. The project of constructing a market liberal utopia in which these needs for security and common life are not met has as its only sure outcome the spawning of atavistic movements that wreak havoc on the historic inheritance of liberal institutions. The challenge for thought and policy is that of abandoning once and for all the project of any such utopia and of applying the genuine insights of conservative thought to the novel circumstances in which we find ourselves. The results of this intellectual enterprise are bound to be radical and – for conventional Western conservatives – uncomfortable.

WHAT CONSERVATISM WAS

A central theme of this inquiry is that, partly because of the novelty of the times and partly because it has abandoned its most distinctive insights and concerns, conservatism may no longer for us be a viable political outlook. Conservative thought may well not be alone in suffering obsolescence and redundancy at this juncture in history, since it is plausible that both socialist thought, and the standard forms of liberalism, face a similar superannuation. In each of these traditions of thought there are insights that can and should be salvaged from the wreckage, but my aim here is to identify those grains of truth in conservative thought that retain a lasting value even as conservatism itself shuffles off the scene.

As it is expressed in such twentieth-century writers as Oakeshott and Santayana,[13] say, a conservative outlook on society and government encompassed three themes that are salient to our current circumstance and which are denied, or little understood, in the presently dominant schools of free market conservatism. There is first the belief that human beings as we find them are not individual specimens of generic humanity but practitioners of particular cultures. It is from these cultures that they derive their identities, which are never that of universal humanity, but

rather those conferred by the particular, and unchosen, inheritances of history and language. What is most essential about us,
accordingly, is what is most accidental, and what makes all of us
what we are is a local and not a universal matter.[14] Indeed, in this
conservative view the very meaning of anyone's life is a matter
of local knowledge, and the greatest disaster that can befall any
community is that the shared understandings – the myths, rit-
uals and narratives – that confer meaning on the lives of its
participants be dissipated in too rapid or too sweeping cultural
change.

> The Masai, when they were moved from their old country to the
> present Masai reserve in Kenya, took with them the names of
> their hills and plains and rivers and gave them to the hills
> and plains and rivers of the new country. And it is by some
> such subterfuge of conservatism that every man or people
> compelled to suffer a notable change avoids the shame of
> extinction.[15]

It was by such a subterfuge that the shamanists of Lake Baikal,
forbidden to worship their old gods by the Soviet communist
regime, renamed them after the Paris Communards, thereby
preserving from extinction both their religion and their very
identity.[16]

The conservation of local knowledge, because such knowledge is constitutive of our very identity, is a central value in
any outlook that is truly conservative. Local knowledge is threatened, or destroyed, by economic or cultural changes that are
large and incessant. It is by now recognized that agricultural
collectivization in Soviet Russia and the Ukraine resulted not
only in millions of deaths but also in a loss of the practical
knowledge of farmers, and a destruction of peasant cultural traditions, that are irreversible. Less commonly perceived is the loss
of local knowledge that comes about through constant business

reorganization, ephemeral job tenure, and unremitting mobility of labour, which are forced on contemporary societies by unrestricted market competition. There is a real paradox here, that has gone wholly unremarked in the banal discourse of contemporary conservatism, in that the epistemic argument for market institutions, which rightly stresses their superiority over planning institutions in utilizing dispersed local knowledge, must be supplemented by the observation that unfettered markets tend to destroy or dissipate local knowledge. They do so by rendering local knowledge increasingly obsolete or irrelevant to the operation of market processes that are themselves ever more disembedded. If, as I am inclined to think, conservatism is best stated not as a moral but as an epistemic doctrine – as the doctrine that the knowledge that is most important in the lives of human beings is local, practical, traditional and, as Edward Goldsmith has reminded us,[17] ineffable – then contemporary conservatism founders on the contradiction that it has committed itself to the hegemony of market institutions whose workings render traditional human knowledge worthless and the social world unintelligible in its terms.

A fundamental objection to the paleo-liberal regime of incessant economic change under unfettered market institutions, then, is that in devaluing traditional knowledge it renders social and economic life ever less understandable to its human participants. In so doing, unfettered market institutions tend to deplete the cultural identities of their practitioners – upon which these institutions themselves depend. Market institutions will enhance human well-being, and will be stably renewed across the generations, when they do not go against the grain of the particular cultures that harbour them, but on the contrary assist those cultures to reproduce themselves. By imposing on people a regime of incessant change and permanent revolution, unencumbered market institutions deplete the stock of historical memory on which cultural identity depends. The common cliché that globalized markets tend to yield cultural uniformity is therefore not without an element of truth. What such cultural homogenization signifies is perhaps less obvious: a breach in historical memory which disrupts, or empties of significance, the narratives in terms of which people make sense of their lives. If, as any conservative who is also a sceptic is bound to think, the meaning of life for all of us is a local matter, this junking of local knowledge by unencumbered market processes is no small matter. For these and similar reasons, the loss of historical memory brought about by globalized market forces will be recognized – on any view that is authentically conservative, or for that matter reflectively liberal – as a form of cultural impoverishment, not a stage on the way to a universal civilization. Let us call this first conservative belief *anti-universalism*, which is the insight that cultural difference belongs to the human essence, and its concomitant, the perception that the identities of human beings depend on the renewal of the particular cultural forms by which they are constituted.

A second conservative theme is what I shall call *non-progress*, or anti-meliorism. By this I mean the conservative rejection of the idea of indefinite world-improvement as either a realistic or a desirable end of political life. It is common among conservative thinkers to stress the Augustinian insight that, like all things human, political institutions are imperfect and imperfectible, so that the project of a *political providence* which promises to deliver humankind from mystery and tragedy – which was the project of Marxism-Leninism – is at once impious (from the standpoint of any religious believer) and impossible. The perception of human imperfectibility is, however, only one, and not in the end perhaps the most important, reason why conservatives will reject the idea of progress, at least as an animating idea in political and economic life. Conservatives will reject it because it presupposes a uniform standard of evaluation and improvement of human life, whereas it is an implication of their first belief that, limiting cases aside, such standards will vary across different cultures. If the bottom line in political and moral reasoning is a conception of human well-being, and if human well-being is bound up with participation in common cultural forms whose content varies to a significant degree, then there will except in limiting cases be no common measure for improvement in different cultures. It is not then the possibility of global betterment that the conservative rejects so much as its meaningfulness. Finally, for a conservative there is surely something anomalous in making progress, rather than the sustainability or stability of society, the end of political life. Any decent society will do what it can to alleviate the unavoidable misfortunes of human life, to enable and empower its members in coping with them and to ensure that those that cannot be avoided can nevertheless be borne with dignity and consolation. The politics of open-ended improvement, however, was, and is – or should be – alien to a conservative sensibility. Such a melioristic approach to human life cannot help encouraging unreal hopes of the human future and distracting us from dealing with the minute particulars of our lives as they are now.

> We all feel at this time the ambiguity of mechanical progress. It seems to multiply opportunity, but it destroys the possibility of simple, rural or independent life. It lavishes information, but it abolishes mastery except in trivial or mechanical efficiency. We learn many languages, but we degrade our own. Our philosophy is highly critical and thinks itself enlightened, but it is a Babel of mutually unintelligible artificial tongues.[18]

And the idea of indefinite progress is easily associated with the notion that social dilemmas are soluble by the generation of ever more resources through economic growth. This association is not a necessary or inevitable one, as we can see from the example of John Stuart Mill, who insisted that a stationary state need not be one in which human improvement has come to a halt;[19] but it is a common one which contemporary conservative thought does nothing to question. The fact is that in conservative thought, as we know it today,[20] a vulgar and unreflective meliorism about the human prospect is combined with a crudely economistic conception of what social improvement consists in. It is not from this thin gruel that we can hope for sustenance.

The third element in a conservative outlook I shall call *the primacy of cultural forms*, or anti-reductionism. By this I mean the idea, implied by much that has gone before, that neither market institutions nor political institutions can or should be autonomous in regard to the cultures they serve. Rather, they are themselves to be assessed, and controlled, by reference to the ends and norms of the cultures in which they are embedded. Market institutions which have been disembedded from their underlying cultures may increase the output of goods and services but they will not enhance human well-being through their activities.[21] Again, the idea that there is, or could be, a single model for market institutions is to be rejected, since they will properly vary according to their cultural matrices and social and political contexts. In this conservative view, the disembedding of market institutions from their parent cultures, and the conferring on them of functional autonomy, is one of the disasters of modern societies, since it amounts to a severance of markets from the ends they appropriately serve. The denial of the primacy of cultural forms is, of course, an implication of any neo-liberal view that makes a fetish of consumer choice, and of any more developed liberal philosophy which accords an intrinsic value to choice-making independently of the goodness of that which is chosen. And it is a necessary presupposition of the knee-jerk response of economic liberals which regards all political intervention in economic life as an evil that stands in need of justification.

The deeper import of the idea of the primacy of cultural forms is that it is not through the activity of choice-making that

values are created in our lives. The conception of the autonomous human subject, though it is a central one in contemporary
liberal thought, and one which I have myself deployed in earlier
work,[22] easily degenerates into a dangerous fiction. In its common uses, the idea of autonomy neglects the central role in
human life of chance and fate – of the unchosen accidents that
confer our identities on us and the further accidents that befall
us in life that choice has no part in and, where they are misfortunes, can do little or nothing to remedy. And it sanctifies that
fiction of liberal philosophy, the fiction of the unsituated human
subject, which is author of its ends and creator of the values in
its life. It is, indeed, this liberal fiction whose emaciated ghost
stalks the dim ruins of paleo-liberal ideology, gibbering of
global markets and economic efficiency.

In the subtlest liberal uses of the idea of autonomy, it is recognized that the exercise of autonomous choice depends for its
value on a cultural environment that is rich in choice-worthy
options and inherently public goods.[23] In this subtler liberal
perspective, value is not an artefact of individual choice, it is
discovered rather than created by us, and what has value in our
lives is often far from transparent to us.[24] It is arguable, and
plausible, that even this subtler liberal conception of autonomy
unreasonably privileges a particular Western ideal, whose costs
and illusions it has not fully perceived.[25] From the standpoint
being developed in this chapter, the ideal of autonomy has the
clear danger of reinforcing the excesses of individualism promoted in neo-liberal thought and policy by further undervalu-
ing the human need for common forms of life. All that is of
value in the subtler liberal conception of autonomy can be captured, without the excesses of individualism, in the ideas of
independence and enablement, where the human subjects that
are so enabled are not the noumenal fictions of liberal theory but
flesh and blood practitioners of particular, historically constituted forms of life. It is with the enablement of human beings

as they are in the real world of history and practice, embedded in their specific and diverse cultures, traditions and communities, rather than with the rights of the empty ciphers of liberal theory, that political thought and public policy ought rightly to be concerned. Such concerns are only obfuscated by the shallow discourse of choice and rights that has dominated British life since the 1980s.

AFTER CONSERVATISM

The conservative idea of the primacy of cultural forms is meant to displace not only standard liberal conceptions of the autonomous human subject but also ideas of the autonomy of market institutions that liberal thought has been applied – or misapplied – to support. It is not meant to support nostalgist and reactionary conceptions of organic or integral community which have no application in our historical circumstances and which, if they were implemented politically, could end only in tragedy or – more likely in Britain – black comedy. The idea of a seamless community – the *noumenal community*, as we may call it, of communitarianism[26] – is as much of a fiction as the autonomous subject of liberal theory. We all of us belong to many communities, we mostly inherit diverse ethnicities, and our world-views are fractured and provisional whether or not we know it or admit it. We harbour a deep diversity of views and values as to sexuality and the worth of human life, our relations with the natural environment and the special place, if any, of the human species in the scheme of things. The reactionary project of rolling back this diversity of values and world-views in the pursuit of a lost cultural unity[27] overlooks the character of our cultural inheritance as a palimpsest, having ever deeper layers of complexity.

Those who imagine that diversity and uncertainty of worldview are confined to the chattering classes are themselves captivated by the constructions of their own discourse. The healthy, unreflective folk culture of their imagination corresponds to nothing in common life; and the assertion of robust common sense against the depredations of 'theorists' and opinion-formers is itself made ridiculous by the bookish ignorance it displays. Among us, High Toryism can be only a pose, a playful or frivolous distraction from serious political reflection in a world in which authority and tradition are barely memories. Indeed, contemporary reactionary conservatives are reminiscent of no one so much as Joseph de Maistre, who set off for Russia in the hope of finding a people not 'scribbled on' by *philosophes*, only to discover a culture of Francophiles. For us a common culture cannot – and, for anyone touched by a liberal sensibility, should not – be a seamless web. It must consist of what the diverse traditions that our society harbours can recognize as a shared inheritance, which will reasonably change over time. The liberal legalist view and the reactionary or organicist view are equally removed from the realities and needs of our current circumstances. The effect of market liberalism has been to run down our common stock of cultural traditions by propagating the absurd liberal legalist view that we do not need a common culture but only common rules, while the patent failings of this paleo-liberal view have inspired the vain attempt to recapture a lost cultural unity. Cultural fundamentalism has emerged in a vain attempt to shore up the tottering edifice of market fundamentalism. Neither conservative position seriously answers to our present needs.

There is a contemporary conservative view – somewhat distinct from any reactionary or organicist posture, and argued in its most appealing and persuasive form by David Willets[28] – that holds that the disruptive effects of unfettered market institutions on the lives of communities have been much exaggerated. It is probably not an unfair caricature of this position to say that it is confident that in conditions of steady economic growth communities are pretty robust and can in most things safely be left to their own devices. It is hard to see what in contemporary conditions justifies such confidence. It may be true that communities were able to renew themselves in circumstances of rapid economic change in England in the latter part of the nineteenth century, say, but such circumstances cannot be replicated now. At that time, much of the English working class was subject to the influence of Nonconformist Christianity, with all the restraints on behaviour that that implied, including a form of family life in which duty and commitment had priority over self-realization and romantic love. Personal behaviour was subject to a level of social monitoring, to norms of respectability and to sanctions of ostracism and stigma that are unknown among us. Both neighbourhoods and churches were small, slow-moving face-to-face societies in which such sanctions were real and telling. None of these conditions obtains in Britain today or will exist in any realistically foreseeable future. They have been destroyed by a century and more of social changes which market liberal policies have only accelerated and deepened. Most of Britain is a post-religious, and in particular a post-Christian society, for good or ill, and the culture of marriage and the family is permeated by ideals of choice and self-fulfilment of the sorts celebrated by latter-day defenders of the free market. And, as I have noted, the fragmentation of family life which contemporary conservatives bemoan is, in very large part, a product of the culture of choice, and the economy of unfettered mobility, which they themselves promote.

It may be that the best prospects for traditional conservative values are to be found today not in any Occidental country but in the East Asian cultures. The absence, or weakness, in these cultures of the romantic and individualist conception of married life that characterizes Western bourgeois societies, and which are at their strongest in those societies, such as US society, in which family breakdown is most pervasive and extreme, may well go a long way toward accounting for their extraordinary economic achievements. It is ironical that the East Asian societies, which have been more successful than most Occidental countries in combining dynamic market institutions with stable communities, should have been so little studied by Western conservatives. No one imagines that the successes of the East Asian countries can be replicated in the very different cultural and historical milieux in which we find ourselves in Europe today. It is nevertheless a reflection on the poverty of Western conservatism that it should have failed to reflect on the experience of countries that have been more successful than any Western country in finding and maintaining the elusive balance between the claims of individual choice and the human need for a life in common.

For us, in Britain today, individualism and pluralism are an historical fate. We may reasonably hope to temper this fate, and thereby to make the best of the opportunities it offers us; we cannot hope to escape it. Yet it is just such an escape from our historical fate that is promised by those conservatives who seek answers to our social problems in the revival of religious and moral beliefs and disciplines – 'Victorian values' – that vanished generations ago. It is idle and silly to imagine that the resources of self-discipline, or the forms of social monitoring, exist among us which sustained the deferral of gratification among the mid-Victorians. The close neighbourhoods of Victorian times have been dissolved by the demands of labour mobility. Family life has changed utterly with contraception and the increased and sometimes predominant role of married women in the provision of the family income. Nor are these changes necessarily, or in fact, by any means, all for the bad. The point is that they remove many of the resources whereby mid-nineteenth-century communities renewed themselves in the face of rapid economic change. It is hard to understand the confidence of those who believe that communities without these resources will succeed in adapting to the impact of economic changes powered by far greater, and far more swiftly moving, global market forces.

Such confidence arises, in all probability, from a failure to perceive that the requirements of unfettered market institutions and those of stable communities may and do come into deep conflict. It expresses also, no doubt, resistance to the policy implication of such a perception, which is that communities need shelter from the gale of market competition, else they will be scattered to the winds. In the last resort, this contemporary conservative view regards communities as adjuncts to markets, optional extras in a society of market exchanges, rather than the sources of the needs markets exist to serve. It can therefore never accept that markets may need to be constrained, or channelled, so as to meet the needs of communities. For constraints on markets will presumably entail losses of efficiency, and so of output. And any loss of output, particularly if it is produced by political intervention aiming to protect something as elusive as the stability of a community, must be an error in policy. This contemporary conservative view is in the end, accordingly, a variation on a familiar theme of market liberalism, which is that market institutions are justified as engines of economic growth. The argument of this chapter, however, is that – as Aristotle anciently observed – economic activity is senseless unless it satisfies human needs. It is this old and homely truth that the new conservatism, even in its most intelligent forms, seems to have determinedly forgotten.

NEW MEASURES FOR CONSERVING COMMON LIFE

All strands of conventional political and economic thought are at one in staking our future on a continuation of economic growth as we have hitherto known it. They all thereby commit themselves to a political version of Pascal's wager – itself a celebratedly bad bet. It would seem more prudent to think and plan on the assumption that the common fate of the mature economies, at any rate – the economies of Western Europe and Japan, for example – is low economic growth, and to begin to consider how social and political life may best be organized when – doubtless willy-nilly rather than by any kind of premeditated policy – we find ourselves landed in something akin to a stationary state economy. The problems of legitimizing market institutions in a context in which no one can expect that his or her income or living standards will rise automatically have as yet hardly begun to be discussed.

The dilemmas opened up by the prospect of a near-stationary economy are not only political ones. The promise of an open horizon of growth and of an indefinite improvement in the human lot have served as a surrogate for religious conviction in an age in which the great political fact is the passing of Christianity. An inexorable consequence of the passing of Christianity – understood here not as a variety of personal faith but as the unifying world-view of a culture – is the waning of the secular religions of progress and humanity in which Christian moral hopes found political expression. The cultural void that yawns when the secular meliorism of the religion of growth founders is as yet too far away to be on any intellectual or political agenda. If it is thought of at all, it is as an element in a fundamentalist project for the rechristianization of Western societies which can be taken seriously by no one with a sense of historical perspective. The question of what is to be the content of the common culture in a country such as Britain, when it is no longer animated by inherited transcendental faith or by any variety of the Enlightenment project, is a deep and difficult one that I cannot consider here. It is clear only that, for us at any rate, a common culture cannot mean a common world-view, religious or secular. It is an implication of all that I have said, however, that we have no option but to struggle to make our inheritance of liberal traditions work. At present, the principal obstacle we face in the struggle to renew our inheritance of liberal practice is the burden on thought and policy of market liberal dogma.

Liberal dogmas work to occlude our perception of the dangers to liberal society arising from current policies. They dim our vision, most particularly, of the dangers to social and political stability arising from the ever greater autonomy of market institutions. Little serious thought has yet been given, for example, to the problems arising from the combination of a near stationary state economy with rapidly ongoing technological innovation which market institutions are producing in most, if not all, of the world's mature economies. This is a combination whose difficulties John Stuart Mill, writing on the stationary state in the mid-nineteenth century, could hardly be expected to anticipate. The central difficulty is that the enlargement of leisure that Mill, by contrast with the gloomier classical economists, expected to come from stability in population and output against a background of improvement in the industrial arts is occurring in the form of ever higher levels of involuntary unemployment. There can be little doubt that for the medium to longer term the agenda for thought is that of redefining full employment as a policy objective in terms that do not mean full-time jobs in an expanding economy. It may be that proposals for a basic or citizen's income, where that is to be distinguished from the neo-liberal idea of a negative income tax, and for a better distribution of capital among the citizenry, need reconsideration – despite all their difficulties – as elements in a policy aiming to reconcile the human need for economic security with the destabilizing dynamism of market institutions.[29] Even the outlines of a policy for such a new pattern of full employment, however, are as yet barely visible to us.

We can nevertheless be reasonably sure that the difficult transition to this new order of things will be made impossible if the relentless elimination of jobs by advancing technology is compounded by the job-destroying effects in the mature economies of global free trade. The proposition that Western labour forces can or must adapt to a global labour market in which their competitors earn one tenth of their wages is not one that commends itself either to good sense or political prudence. Nor is global free trade forced on us by anything in the Ricardian theory of comparative advantage, since a regional free trade area such as the EU is already larger than any that has ever before existed in human history and is diverse enough to satisfy all the Ricardian requirements. Indeed it is far from clear that Ricardian theory demands, or even supports, global free trade. Ricardo himself had doubts about the idea of comparative advantage, especially when it involves the technology-driven displacement of labour, that seem to have eluded his latter-day disciples. In Chapter 31 of his *Principles of Political Economy and Taxation* entitled 'On Machinery', Ricardo states that 'I am convinced that the substitution of machinery for human labour is often very injurious to the interests of the class of labourers.' Ricardo goes on:

> ... the discovery and use of machinery may be attended with a diminution of gross produce; and whenever that is the case, it will be injurious to the labouring class, as some of their number will be thrown out of employment, and population will become redundant compared with the funds which are to employ it.

Ricardo concludes:

> ... the opinion entertained by the labouring class, that the employment of machinery is frequently detrimental to their interests, is not founded on prejudice and error, but is conformable to the correct principles of political economy.[30]

It is fair to surmise that the force of Ricardo's doubts could have been increased only in a circumstance, such as ours, in which an untrammelled global market in labour-saving technologies is envisaged and on the way to implementation through the GATT agreements. It is, indeed, a circumstance of just such a sort – in which employers make productivity and profitability gains at the cost of unemployment and reduced incomes for workers – that Ricardo envisaged. For his followers, by contrast, the benefits of free trade are *a priori* truths, which mere observation cannot hope to bring into question.

On presently observable evidence, the likely result of the GATT agreements, if they are ever implemented, is not only ruin for Third World agriculture, with a billion or more peasants being displaced from the land in the space of a generation or less, but also – as Sir James Goldsmith has warned[31] – class war in the advanced countries as wages fall and the return on off-shore capital rises. It defies both common sense and historical experience to suppose that the economic and social dislocations produced by exposure to a global market larger, more dynamic and more uneven in development than any that has ever before existed can be absorbed by reductions in wages and shifts of personnel on a scale and at a rate that are wholly unprecedented, without a political backlash emerging in response to the devastating impact of this process of structural adjustment on working-class living standards. Such a backlash is made all the more likely given that this adjustment is demanded of working people at precisely the time when much of the social protection embodied in the post-war welfare state is being dismantled. In this historical context, global free trade is a recipe for social conflict and political instability on a large scale. A prerequisite for any policy that can hope to offer a decent measure of economic security to the population is accordingly an urgent reconsideration of the market liberal dogma of global free trade.

Market liberal policy is harmful to settled community in many other areas. Policy in regard to cities has in Britain been grotesquely poor, with their deformation as communities by the private motor car, and their hollowing out by such developments as warehouse shopping being particularly unacceptable examples.

Here the culprit is not primarily the influence of special interests, important though that undoubtedly has been, but rather neo-liberal blindness to the city itself as an institution and a form of life that is worthy of preservation and renewal. Cities – at least as these have been understood hitherto in the European tradition to which Britain belongs – are not congeries of strangers. They are not nomadic encampments, traffic islands or ephemeral aggregates of enterprises and households. They are long-standing human settlements, spanning the generations, whose welfare can neither be understood nor assured as an upshot of a myriad uncoordinated private decisions. Protecting cities as human settlements demands institutions for accountability and planning, devolved as far as is feasible and appropriate, which are anathema to neo-liberal dogma. This is only one example, but a vitally important one, of the way in which conservative policy cast in a neo-liberal mould has been inimical to the conservation of precious cultural achievements and forms of common life.

It is not my intention to try here to address the whole range of policy issues in which market liberal thinking has led us astray.[32] The key alterations in thought that must precede any such detailed re-examination of policy are scrapping the conception of market institutions as perpetual motion machines for economic growth and abandoning indefinite growth in output as a sensible objective of human effort. This is not to say that growth must be replaced as an objective by no growth. That would be hardly less nonsensical, since economic growth is itself a statistical abstraction that takes no account of the contribution to human well-being of the activities it purportedly measures. What it means rather is that economic activity is not an end in itself but must serve the needs and values of the cultures in which it is pursued. It must be sustainable in its longer-term impact on both the natural and the human environments, at least in the weak sense that it does not result in their irreversible degradation. And it must be sustainable in the stronger sense that it fosters, instead of undermining, stability in the communities it affects. Of course, stability is not fixity, and we cannot put the genie of technological virtuosity back into the bottle. But this is only to say that economic change is continuous and unavoidable and must therefore be channelled, not that it can be let to run its course with the devil taking the hindmost.

Such channelling of unavoidable economic change is unlikely to be successful so long as public policy and indeed the public culture are animated by the idea of the insatiability of ever-expanding human wants. I have argued elsewhere that a conception of satiable human needs has a central role in reasoned discourse about public policy.[33] The idea of a satiable human need will be workable in public discourse, however, only if the ruling ideal of the unending proliferation of human wants is relinquished and replaced by a conception of *sufficiency* in which it is the quality of social life, rather than the quantity of goods and services, that is the central objective of public policy. One of the themes of this chapter is that political parties in Britain and similar countries have been slow to recognize that, in conditions of low economic growth, political discourse is bound to focus increasingly on quality-of-life issues. A connected point is that, once we no longer expect or hope for a resumption of economic growth that can allow a return to full employment as that has conventionally been understood, we are free to consider how new forms of livelihood can be developed to supplement, or replace, older forms of job-holding. What is particularly important to note here is that the pursuit of sufficiency, in the context of providing people with opportunities for fulfilling livelihood and elsewhere, presupposes that market institutions be subject to political constraints. We have no hope of achieving fulfilling livelihood for all in the context of technology-driven displacement of labour by global free trade. The content of sufficiency, for any particular society at any particular time, must be a political judgement, arrived at by reasoned public discourse. Equally, the pursuit of sufficiency requires public policies in which the autonomy of market institutions is subordinated to political objectives of social stability and harmonious community.

Nothing advanced here is meant to cast doubt on the centrality and indispensability of market institutions in economic life. The point is that they must be harnessed and guided by political constraints if they are to serve human needs. Provided this condition is met, market institutions may well be extended in some areas of policy, where such extension helps to anchor institutions in local communities. There remains a good case for educational vouchers, not on the neo-liberal ground of promoting market competition, but on the ground that sensibly designed voucher schemes might render schools more sensitive than they are now to families and communities. Drawing on the ideas of Ivan Illich rather than upon neo-liberal thought, I have elsewhere advanced a version of an educational credit scheme in which it is not tied to any particular form of schooling and can be used by a diversity of institutions, traditions and communities.[34] A streamlined or minimalist National Curriculum could provide a common core of skills and knowledge as a standard for all families to meet, while they were otherwise free to meet the varying needs of their different communities. The details of such an educational credit scheme are less important than its objective, which is to harness market institutions to anchor schools, and other educational institutions, more securely in the communities they exist to serve. In some areas of welfare policy, also, voucher schemes can be defended as devices for devolving welfare institutions to the level closest to individuals, families and their communities. There are doubtless other, similar ways in which market institutions can be usefully extended. Such extension must always have the aim of embedding markets in the communities they serve and it must never concede to markets the autonomy and freedom from political constraint by which they have been privileged in neo-liberal theory.

CONCLUSION AND PROSPECT

The conquest of conservative parties by neo-liberal ideology, and the embodiment of that ideology in public policy, have altered irreversibly the social and political landscape of countries such as Britain. In delegitimizing traditional institutions, and confounding the expectations on which the lives of Conservative voters of all classes – but especially the middle classes – were based, neo-liberal policy has all but destroyed the social base of conservatism in Britain. A secular conservatism devoted to the protection of voters' economic interests – the only remotely plausible conservatism in a post-religious country such as Britain – has been taken off the political agenda for the foreseeable future by Tory policies which have ravaged and almost destroyed the traditional economic constituencies of British Conservatism. This undoing of conservatism by market liberalism is now an established fact of political life in Britain and in similarly placed countries. The likelihood that it augurs prolonged periods of electoral defeat for conservative governments and parties is, from the perspective of the present inquiry, less important than the exhaustion it betokens in conservative thought itself. That contingencies we cannot presently foresee will return Conservatives to government, at some time in the future, is a possibility that cannot definitively be excluded. Unlike the crazed neo-liberal ideologues of the 1980s, who pronounced that 'Labour will never rule again', we must never forget the phenomenon of chance in political life – the permanent political relevance of Cleopatra's nose – or neglect the related phenomenon of apparently deep-seated trends suddenly, and unpredictably, reversing themselves.

If, as I hazard the guess, the Conservatives face a long period of political marginality in Britain, conceivably lasting a generation, it could nevertheless be foreshortened considerably by errors and misfortunes occurring during a time of rule by the parties of the Left. It remains thoroughly unclear, however, what, if anything, a Conservative government arising from failures in government on the Left would be devoted to conserving. The paradoxical likelihood is that – in Britain at any rate – the task of conserving, perhaps in altered forms, the best elements in our institutional inheritance will pass to parties which presently think of themselves as being on the Left. If supposed conservatives succumb to the pseudo-radicalism of free market ideology, then genuine conservatives have no option but to become true radicals. And, if ordinary people cannot find in the party of the Right concern for their security from crime, economic risk and the breakdown of community, they will turn elsewhere for it. In so doing they will only be giving electoral expression to what has long been a fact – that conservatism in Britain has lost any clear perception of what it is that ordinary people are most concerned to protect in their lives. It is the demise of any recognizable Tory philosophy, far more than the fatigue and loss of the will to rule produced by too long a spell in power, that best explains the electoral rout currently facing British Conservatism.

What Left and Right may mean in the coming years, and whether these terms will retain much usefulness, is not yet clear. What is unmistakably clear is that the intellectual hegemony in political life of the Right, as we used to understand it, is over. Moreover, it has become evident that conservative thought, lacking the intellectual resources needed to cope with the dilemmas thrown up by the conservative policies of the 1980s, in effect created the conditions for its own demise. Neither the conservative denial that the conflict between unfettered market institutions and stable communities is real, nor the reactionary project of recovering a vanished past, are sustainable responses to our predicament. Both, in their different ways, evade the real challenge of the post-socialist age, which is that of harnessing market institutions to the needs of stable communities and so giving liberal civilization another lease on life.

The evident debility of conservative thought is only one sign of the obsolescence of the principal Western ideologies, which is mirrored in the ongoing meltdown, virtually world-wide, of the political and economic models which they sponsor. My focus here has been on the specious claims of paleo-liberal ideology, in which individual choice is elevated to the supreme value and at the same time emptied of all moral significance. Our present situation is the awkward one in which we can renew and extend liberal civilization only in so far as we recognize its embedded-ness in common forms of life unrecognized in liberal theory. It is unlikely that we shall succeed in giving liberal society another lease on life if our intellectual outlook does not become – at least by the standards of liberal theorizing – post-liberal. Within liberal thought, as within conservative thought, there are doubtless insights and truths that will survive the wreckage of liberal ideology; but the ruin of liberalism as an ideology is an undeniable fact of our present predicament. In so far as we accept this fact and thereby adopt a post-liberal perspective, we are bound to reject all those varieties of conservatism in which fundamentalist liberalism has found a political home.

An appropriate response to our present circumstance is a strategy of salvage and retrieval, of the kind attempted here with respect to the insights that have survived the wreckage of conservative philosophy. We shall cope best with the new dilemmas we confront if we accept the undoing of conservatism and learn the lessons its undoing has to teach us. We may then be able to summon up the readiness to think afresh about a world in which conservative thought no longer gives us guidance or illumination.

8

AFTER THE NEW LIBERALISM

As it manifested itself in the writings of its principal exponents, during its moment of ephemeral hegemony in contemporary political philosophy, the new liberalism was recognizable by virtue of its exhibiting a family of commitments and presuppositions, not all of them shared by every one of its theorists, but having resemblances enough in common to represent a distinctive and in some respects novel contribution to the liberal intellectual tradition. The new liberalism was an outlook, or a framework of categories, more than it was a doctrine, or a substantive philosophical position. Central among these categories were the notion of the person, conceived as the bearer of rights and the originator of plans of life and conceptions of the good; the idea of justice as the supreme regulative ideal for the assessment of political and social institutions; the conception of political philosophy as having a jurisprudential or legalist character, in that its agenda was the specification of the constitutional structure of political life, with its attendant basic liberties; and so on. Often, though not always, the philosophical inspiration of the new liberalism was Kantian. The Kantianism of the new liberals – of Rawls and his disciples, and of Dworkin, in his pre-hermeneutic phase at any rate – was, however, of a metaphysically neutered variety. It lacked altogether the apparatus of phenomenal world and noumenal selfhood by which the Kantian conception of universalizability, and thereby the political principles it supposedly generates, are accorded a universal authority. Instead, in all of the new liberals implicitly and in the later Rawls programmatically, the philosophical perspective that animated the new liberalism was a relativized Kantianism. It was a Kantianism relativized to yield a conception of the person disembedded from any cultural tradition that was found uncongenial to conventional liberal opinion. In emptying its construction of the person of any constitutive cultural identity, communal membership or ethnic allegiance, the new liberalism effectively relativized the Kantian subject, so that it became a rights-bearing cipher. The role of this cipher, as it can now be interpreted in the wake of the new liberalism, was that of a device whereby the warring cultural identities of latter-day United States could be passed over or suppressed. By voiding its central conception of the person of any constitutive history or community, the new liberalism was an historically highly specific, topical and local, response to the cultural wars of identity by which its parent culture is chronically convulsed. And, in seeking a history-purged and culture-blind resolution of conflicts and disorders arising from a moment in the history of its parent culture, the new liberalism showed itself to be distinctively, and indeed peculiarly American.

The cultural singularity of the new liberalism, as a peculiarly (if not parochially) US phenomenon, was nowhere more evident than in its uncritical endorsement of the Enlightenment project, by which US culture, more than any other in the contemporary world, continues to be animated. However methodologically relativized its Kantianism might be, the new liberalism unreflectively subscribed to a version of the Enlightenment philosophy of history in which universal convergence on a cosmopolitan and rationalist civilization – in other words, on the US model, as perceived through the fractured prism of US self-deception – was taken for granted as the *telos* of the species. Almost as significant in disclosing the Americocentric character of the new liberalism was its anaemic and impoverished conception of pluralism and cultural diversity. The incommensurability of values affirmed in doctrines of objective ethical pluralism was understood as arising in the formulation of personal plans of life rather than in conflicts among whole ways of life. And cultural diversity was conceived in the denatured form of a cornucopia of chosen lifestyles, each with its elective identity, rather than in the form in which it is found in the longer and larger experience of humankind – as the exfoliation of exclusionary forms of life, spanning the generations, membership of which is typically unchosen, and which tend to individuate themselves by their conflicts and by their historical memories of enmity. In its wholly unselfconscious endorsement of an Enlightenment philosophy of history, and of a highly attenuated and unhistorical notion of the pluralism of values, the new liberalism – in this respect like neo-conservatism, communitarianism and Straussianism, intellectual movements barely intelligible in any other context than that of their native America – betrayed naively its origins in indigenously American beliefs and values. More particularly it revealed its origins in the prevailing orthodoxies of the US academic class.

This, at any rate, is how the new liberalism begins to look, now that its political marginality becomes ever more apparent and its hegemony in political philosophy, at least outside the United States, is plainly over. Three central questions arise about the new liberalism, now that it is in manifest disarray and retreat. One concerns the Enlightenment project. Is there, or was there, such a project, and what were or are its defining commitments?

More particularly, what, if anything, can be saved from it, if – as I have claimed[1] – it is, in its political embodiments, in a condition of world-historical collapse? A second question concerns value-pluralism and cultural difference. How are these to be conceived, and how do they bear on Enlightenment doctrines in philosophical anthropology and the philosophy of history? The third question addresses the political implications of strong pluralism and of the failings of the Enlightenment project. Does a strong version of value-pluralism lend support to liberalism (however conceived) or to the democratic project? Each of these three questions approaches from a different direction the issue of how political thought is to proceed in the aftermath of the new liberalism and of its animating Enlightenment project. This central issue may be posed in the form of a single question: is a post-Enlightenment liberalism a possibility? And, to anticipate the negative answer that I shall give to this question, another follows: if a post-Enlightenment liberalism is *not* among the range of philosophical and political options available to us, and if – as I shall also contend – traditionalist and reactionary alternatives to the Enlightenment project are neither feasible nor desirable responses to its failure, what form of political theorizing emerges from this débâcle? These are the three questions which I shall address in this chapter.

What was the Enlightenment project? One answer to this question would contest the very idea that, from the diversity of intellectual and political movements and thinkers that are commonly grouped together as belonging to the Enlightenment, a single project can be established to which all, or nearly all, subscribed. Agnostics or sceptics as to the Enlightenment project, as I shall term these critics, point to the variety of historical contexts and intellectual and political traditions which the Enlightenment usually encompasses, and invoke the great divergences of doctrine and outlook that the Enlightenment thinkers of these different periods and circumstances exhibit.

The contexts and contents of the Scottish and the French Enlightenments – to take only the most obvious examples – differ substantially, with some French *philosophes*, such as Condorcet, affirming a commitment to human perfectibility, or at the least to the indefinite improvability of human institutions, that few, if any, of the thinkers of the Scottish Enlightenment accepted. Again, the conception of rationality favoured by Enlightenment thinkers varies significantly, with some adopting highly aprioristic conceptions (Spinoza, Leibniz) and others (Hobbes, Hume) advancing more empirical conceptions, with the dominance in human conduct of passion and sentiment being fully acknowledged in the latter. The forms or structures of the universal cosmopolitan society on which all peoples were expected to converge also diverge greatly among thinkers whose Enlightenment credentials no one would readily contest. If Auguste Comte anticipated and welcomed an organic, authoritarian social order in which most forms of human liberty had served their purpose and were accordingly redundant, John Stuart Mill asserted the permanent necessity, in all those societies that had emerged from 'barbarism', of the widest sphere of liberty for antagonistic modes of thought and diverse experiments in living. If Marx envisaged a form of communist society in which the necessity for justice had been transcended along with the institution of private property in the means of production, such thinkers as Herbert Spencer imagined the society of the future as one in which the maxims of justice were embodied in rigorously defined and enforced property laws. Moreover, Enlightenment thinkers differed greatly in their degrees of optimism and pessimism, with thinkers as different as Voltaire and Hume inclining to a pessimistic and cyclical interpretation of history, and others such as Paine and Godwin holding steadfastly to the conviction that the human future would be vastly different, and on the whole much better, than the human past. It would seem difficult, accordingly, to ascribe with confidence any doctrine of human perfectibility to Enlightenment thinkers *tout court*, with the greatest among them, such as Kant, unequivocally affirming human imperfectibility. Not even a doctrine of progress is common ground among the Enlightenment thinkers, as the example of Hume demonstrates. If, then, as such agnostics or sceptics about the Enlightenment project contend, there is so much diversity of doctrine and outlook among the thinkers of the Enlightenment, in what sense can there be a single identifiable Enlightenment project to which all, or virtually all of them subscribed? Is it not evident that there were many Enlightenments, and for that reason many Enlightenment projects?

Persuasive as this objection may sound, I do not think it need detain us for long. It is reminiscent of the arguments of those revisionist Marxists who claim that no trace of economic determinism can be found in Marx, or of those Christians who are wont to assert that the central tenets of Christian theism were never believed in literalist fashion as dogmas but always only as symbolic truths. In all three cases the intellectual strategy is to resist the overturning of a system of belief by experience or reasoning, by refining its content so that it is systematically elusive and thereby protected from overthrow or undermining. Contrary to such an agnostic, sceptical or revisionist view that there never was an identifiable Enlightenment project, it is not difficult to discern this project in the central Enlightenment thinkers, and to detect its presence in the new liberals, and its pervasive influence, almost as a universal unstated presupposition of discourse and policy, in the public culture of the contemporary United States. The core project of the Enlightenment was the displacement of local, customary or traditional moralities, and of all forms of transcendental faith, by a critical or rational morality, which was projected as the basis of a universal civilization. Whether it was conceived in utilitarian or contractarian, rights-based or duty-based terms, this morality would be secular and humanist, and it would set universal standards for the assessment of human institutions. The core project of the Enlightenment was the construction of such a critical morality, rationally binding on all human beings, and, as a corollary, the creation of a universal civilization. This is the project that animated Marxism and liberalism in all their varieties, which underpins both the new liberalism and neo-conservatism, and to which every significant body of opinion in the United States continues to subscribe. Despite its set-backs in our time, it remains one element among others in the public culture of all Western liberal democracies, and in the United States it functions as the civil religion, or hegemonic ideology, which is constitutive of American identity itself. It is this core project that is shared by all Enlightenment thinkers, however pessimistic or dystopic they may sometimes be as to its historical prospects.

In our time, it is the project which unifies such disparate liberal theorists as Nozick and Dworkin, Ackerman and Hayek, Popper and (at least the early, and arguably the later) Rawls. It is this project which inspires the libertarian minimum state as much as the egalitarian redistributionist state. The new liberalism, with its central category of the historyless and unsituated person, is merely the most recent reformulation of this Enlightenment project in the context of American thought. Though this Enlightenment project is a far weaker element in the public cultures of European countries, including Britain, whose cultural identity, unlike that of the United States, is not defined in terms of an ideology, a recent European attempt at reformulation of the same project is to be found in the work of Habermas.

As it appears in the new liberalism, and elsewhere, the Enlightenment project embodies a distinctive philosophical anthropology, for which cultural difference is an inessential, and – in its political manifestations, at any rate – a transitory incident in human affairs. It is not that the propensity of human beings to exhibit distinctive cultural identities is denied, or that a future condition of humankind is envisaged in which cultural difference has wholly disappeared; but, rather, that distinctive cultural identities are seen as chosen lifestyles, whose proper place is in private life, or the sphere of voluntary association. The demand that cultural identities have political embodiment – in sovereign nationhood, for example – is perceived as a form of atavism, inconsistent with modernity – in which, however, it is by far the most potent political force. This understanding of cultural identity, and of cultural diversity, by the new liberals expresses the philosophical anthropology of the Enlightenment, and has all of its flaws. This is my second concern – that in the new liberalism cultural difference is seen through the distorting lens of the idea of *choice*, as an epiphenomenon of personal life-plans, preferences and conceptions of the good. In the real world of human history, however, cultural identities are not constituted, voluntaristically, by acts of choice: they arise by inheritance, and by recognition. They are fates rather than choices. It is this fated character of cultural identity which gives it its agonistic, and sometimes tragic character. A German, an Austrian or a French Jew who believed that they had by choice assimilated to the cultural identity of these nations found that their self-conception and their perception by others were at odds. It was the recognition that assimilation was not a choice open to European Jews that, even before the Holocaust, was a principal motive for the project of establishing the state of Israel.[2]

According to the philosophical anthropology of the Enlightenment, the diverse and often rivalrous cultural identities manifest throughout human history are not expressive of any primordial human disposition to cultural difference. They are ephemeral, or at least developmental, phases in the history of the species. If they survived, as Marx thought national cultures would survive, it would be as politically marginal styles of personal or associational life, akin to ethnic cuisines, as we find them in the great North American cities, in their significance. Distinctive cultural identities, along with their constitutive histories, were like streams, whose destiny was to flow irresistibly into the great ocean of universal humanity. It might even be said that, just as the category of *civilization* is a central element in the Enlightenment project, so the idea of *a universal history of the species* is integral to it. Equally, the idea of *barbarism* is integral to the Enlightenment world-view, whether it encompasses a doctrine of historical progress or a cyclical interpretation of history, since it encapsulates the Enlightenment repudiation of the irreducible plurality of cultures in favour of the assertion that all civilizations are, or will be, exemplars of a single model. It is therefore worth stressing that the core Enlightenment project of a rational and universal civilization in which cultural difference has been politically marginalized informs Enlightenment philosophies of history at every point, whether or not they comprehend a doctrine of progress in which convergence on such a cosmopolitan civilization is a confident expectation. The foundation of the Enlightenment's marginalization of cultural difference is not in an expectation of convergence on a universal civilization – which Enlightenment exponents of a cyclical interpretation of history, such as Hume, do not share – but in its distinctive philosophical anthropology of generic humanity.

Rejecting or revising this anthropology, and the various philosophies of history which it supports, as in my view the evidences of history compel us to do, does not mean embracing any of the reactionary or traditionalist alternatives which have arisen in response to the Enlightenment project. Such alternatives, as we find them in Burke or de Maistre, say, are mirror-images of the Enlightenment and share many of its anachronistic features. Like the Enlightenment project, these reactionary and traditionalist views are europocentric in their supposed universalism, sharing with the Enlightenment – though in providentialist Christian form – a philosophy of history of which *we* are the *telos*. Moreover, such conservative responses to the Enlightenment project have in common with it a value-monism and a resistance to cultural difference which supports integralist or organicist conceptions of social and political order that, in the historical context of our age, are at best forms of reactionary quixotry and, at their not uncommon worst, are programmes for rolling back actually existing cultural diversity – that is to say, projects of cultural fundamentalism. It is true that such a project of cultural fundamentalism is very muted in the thought of the deepest twentieth-century conservative critic of the Enlightenment, Michael Oakeshott;[3] but his acceptance of the diversity of traditions and of conflicting cultural forms in contemporary society is equally muted, with the possibility that tradition may leave us in the lurch even as reason fails to give us guidance being scarcely considered. An explicitly anti-liberal programme of rolling back cultural diversity in favour of a sort of Eliot-like traditionalism or Maurrasian nationalism is found in the work of Scruton; but there its quixotic aestheticism is plain for all to see.[4] Rejecting the Enlightenment project, as it appears in the new liberalism and elsewhere, as I have done, on the grounds that it suppresses the truth of value-pluralism or else preserves it in the trivial and banalized form in which it figures in the American discourse of alternative lifestyles, does not and cannot imply support for the Right project of cultural fundamentalism, in which strong value-pluralism is equally repressed or denied.

The question remains: what *are* the political implications, if any, of the strong value-pluralism, and of the affirmation of the historicity of human subjects, that motivate the rejection of the new liberalism? It is, of course, a feature of the critique of the new liberalism that I have advanced that the programme of showing a single type of regime to be ideally the best for all humankind, and of enunciating a system of political principles applicable to all cultures and polities, is to be rejected. It follows inexorably that no single regime, or set of institutions, is privileged by value-pluralism of the strong variety I here intend. More particularly, value-pluralism will *not* support liberal forms of life

in any general or universal way. In so far as the thought of Berlin
or Raz, say, consists in an attempt to ground liberal practice in
strongly pluralist value theory – and I am by no means clear
whether, or how far, Berlin and Raz are to be interpreted as
engaging themselves in such a foundationalist liberal project – it
is to be *contrasted* with the position which I develop here and
elsewhere, in which liberal practice enjoys no theoretical privileges. The position defended here, on the contrary, though it is
wholly consistent with practical support for liberal institutions
in particular historical circumstances, is pluralist rather than
liberal in its theoretical orientation. That is to say that it affirms
the ultimate validity of a diversity of polities, moralities, forms
of government and economy and of familial and social life – of a
diversity of cultural forms, in short. And this is not the fathom-
lessly shallow cultural diversity that is invoked in the profession-
ally deformed discourse of numberless academic seminars on
race and gender, with its tacit agenda of global cultural homogenization on the US model; but rather the real diversity of
historic practices, often agonistically constituted, of which subordination, exclusion and closure of options are – in liberal
forms of life no less than in others – essential elements. It is a
central feature of this pluralist view that no universally authoritative prescriptions follow from it about forms of government or
economic or family life.

One particular implication of this pluralist view may be worth
stressing, even though it should be obvious – that the institutions
of 'democratic capitalism' have no claim whatever to universal
authority. Neither capitalist market institutions, nor the institutions of political democracy, are universally desirable, either in
all possible worlds, or in the real world of history in which we
actually live. The idea, propagated in absurdist form by Francis
Fukuyama but accepted in one form or other by virtually all of
Western opinion, that the post-communist period is one in
which Western institutions are extended throughout the world,

is likely to be, if anything, the very opposite of the truth. The Soviet collapse has, on the contrary, triggered a meltdown of political settlements in Western countries, that may amount in some cases to the legitimation crisis of Western capitalism for which generations of Western Marxists waited in vain. There is, in fact, no model of stable Western institutions for the post-communist societies to emulate or seek to replicate. Neither market institutions, nor political institutions are likely to evolve, in most of the post-communist countries, on any Western model. This is, perhaps, the significance of the most momentous political experiment currently underway in the world, that in China. Whatever its ultimate fate, its project is that of developing market institutions that are not modelled on any Western exemplar but are distinctively Chinese in their cultural matrix, and to develop such market institutions without the Western apparatus of democratic institutions, or a Western-style civil society in which 'human rights' are accorded privileged status. On the pluralist view here presented, in which neither liberal rights nor the democratic project has any special status, the possibility is, at the very least, left open that there should emerge in China a regime – a constellation of market and state institutions – that is legitimate precisely because it owes little or nothing to Occidental ideologies and promotes the well-being of its subjects as that is perceived by them from the perspective of their indigenous cultural traditions. The possibility of a diversity of irreducibly different regimes, liberal and non-liberal, is the most fundamental implication of the pluralist perspective, as that is applied in the global context.

The significance of such a pluralism of regimes for political thought and policy lies, of course, in the repudiation of the many varieties of neo-Wilsonianism that dominate Western foreign policy, especially in the United States. At this global level, the implication of pluralism is that of a modus vivendi among different regimes animated by divergent cultural traditions. A point of contrast with this pluralist view is found in the recent thought of Samuel Huntingdon, whose argument that future conflicts between states will be 'civilizational', if it means anything, means that cultural difference alone, in and of itself, will in future be a cause of war. This argument – which would probably be found remotely plausible only in a culture used to conceiving international conflict in ideological terms and which has been disoriented by the global dissolution of those ideologies – the pluralist view altogether rejects. Equally, it repudiates the view, common in both classical and newer liberalisms, that the incommensurable claims of peoples and polities will, or should be, dissolved into the universal commensurability of a global market.[5] The conception of international relations it sponsors is that of a peaceful *modus vivendi* among very different regimes, not the Kantian and Wilsonian prescription of the pursuit of perpetual peace through the globalization of Western institutions, political or economic.

At the level of particular polities, the view defended here as arising from the ruin of the new liberalism is that of a *modus vivendi* pluralism, not pluralist liberalism. This is a *political* pluralism, in that it seeks to avoid the legalist deformation of political thought that has occurred in the United States, and regards the pursuit of a *modus vivendi* within any polity as primarily a political rather than a constitutional or legal task. This is not to say that the pursuit of a *modus vivendi* among communities which share a single polity may not have legal and constitutional implications. It may well do so, as the historical examples of legal pluralism in the Roman empire, and in the Ottoman *millet* system, suggest. Moreover, in cultural milieux in which many or most subjects are constituted by plural inheritances and have no single or overriding identity, a legal order that is recognizably liberal in its structure may well be the best approximation to a *modus vivendi*. The crucial truth affirmed in the pluralist perspective is nevertheless that any legal order will promote or facilitate harmonious coexistence among different communities, only if it embodies and expresses a balance of claims and interests among the various communities that is relatively stable – only, in other words, if it rests on a successful political settlement. In political life, of course, no settlement is final, and only the provisional is permanent; so the legal framework in which any particular political settlement finds embodiment will be subject to recurrent revision, and eventual breakdown. But this is only to say that stability in political affairs is found in motion, if it is found at all, and not in the fixity of structures of basic liberties, and similar legalist constructions. It is to say that stability in political life is an artifice, necessarily fragile and easily destroyed, of the political arts – of statecraft.

This pluralist vision will, no doubt, be rejected as unduly disillusioned or overly modest, by those who seek entry to the sterile utopia of liberal neutrality, or who prize liberal ideals of individuality which make the pursuit of peace look a grubby and ignoble activity. That liberal individuality is, in practice, invariably a prescription for abject conformity to prevailing bien-pensant opinion is, on the view being presented here, not the chief objection to it. Nor is the incoherence of the new liberal ideal of neutrality the worst feature of it. The most disabling feature of these and other constitutive elements of the new liberalism is what they all betoken – namely, a rejection of the political enterprise itself, and of its animating value of peace. Now, to be sure, the pluralist commitment to the primacy of the political realm will be criticized by liberals of all varieties, especially in virtue of its detachment from any democratic project (at least in so far as such a project claims any universal authority). For liberals, the untransparency of the political arts, their inextricable connections with bargaining and dissimulation, are an objection to the political realm itself, and to the practice of statecraft. These ineradicable characteristics of political practice motivate the core project of liberal legalism, which is the voiding of political life of substantive content. For the pluralist, by contrast, the opacity of politics is vastly to be preferred – from a standpoint concerned with human well-being – to the clarity of war; and the liberal project of neutering political life is in any case a mere utopia. For the pluralist, the practice of politics is a noble engagement, precisely on account of the almost desperate humility of its purposes – which are to moderate the enmity of agonistic identities, and to generate conventions of peace among warring communities. The pluralist embrace of politics is, for these reasons, merely a recognition of the reality of political life, itself conceived as an abatement of war.

The pluralist position that arises with the failure of the new liberalism has little in common with communitarian critiques of liberalism apart from a shared perception of the limitations of liberal individualism. There is in the communitarian literature – inspired as it is by a conception of ideal or noumenal community as illusory as Kantian subjecthood – little of which I am aware that addresses with the supreme problem of communities in our time, which is that of finding terms of peaceful coexistence among themselves. In the world of human history, as distinct from that of communitarian theory, communities make rival claims on territories they inhabit together, they are animated by conflicting narratives and cultural traditions, they renew their identities across the generations by strategies of exclusion and subordination, and so on. The real agenda for political thought – ignored by the new liberals and by their communitarian critics – is given by the conflicting claims of communities, just as the agenda for ethics is the conflict among duties and among goods and evils. It is this agenda of relations among communities having irresolvably conflicting, and sometimes incommensurable claims, that the new liberalism, together with the standard criticisms of it, steadfastly ignores.

The pluralist perspective I have defended does not seek, after the fashion of the Enlightenment project, to abolish the fated or unchosen character of cultural identity by the construction of a universal cosmopolitan civilization in which all identities are elective. That Enlightenment project, with all of its costs in cultural impoverishment, has clearly failed. The pluralist, post-Enlightenment project defended here is a humbler one, that of diminishing the tragic character of cultural identities that will always be agonistic in their constitution by devising the institutions and practices of a *modus vivendi*. This perspective is Hobbesian in conceiving the avoidance of war as the rationale of politics, but Machiavellian – and so without the Enlightenment illusions latent even in Hobbes's thought – in recognizing that success in this project can always be only partial, temporary, and in part a gift of fortune. The agenda of political thought, after the new liberalism, is to return it to *politics*, so conceived.

In returning political thought to this agenda, the critique of the new liberalism I have sought to develop here seeks only to restore the sense of the primacy of the political, as we find it in the founders of modern political theorizing. For it is, after all, in Hobbes and in Machiavelli, in whose works liberal and republican traditions of modern thought have their modern origins, that the nature of the political realm as at once a continuation of and a partial transcendence of war is first achieved. It is in using this dual conception of the political realm to illuminate our current conflicts, our thinking no longer occluded by the hallucinatory perspectives of the Enlightenment, that the best way forward lies in the wake of the new liberalism.

9

FROM POST-LIBERALISM TO PLURALISM

The liberal project was the project of specifying universal limits to the authority of government and, by implication, to the scope of political life. The task of liberal theory was to specify the principles, and sometimes the institutions, in which this universal limitation on political power was expressed and embodied. To be sure, as a species of the Enlightenment project, the liberal project was often associated with, and dependent on, an historical philosophy of progress, which affirmed that different political regimes were appropriate and legitimate in different historical circumstances. None the less, the goal of liberal theory remained that of specifying principles for the limitation of political power which were universally authoritative in that they applied to the best regime for the entirety of humankind – if only in an unspecified future phase in the historical development of the species. It was acknowledged in liberal theory that the best regime might be unattainable in some historical milieux, and in such circumstances the task liberal thought set itself was that of providing a non-ideal theory of second-best arrangements, which approximated but did not try to meet the requirements specified for the ideally best regime. Again, liberal thinkers recognized that the institutional structure of the best regime might, and indeed would, legitimately vary in different historical contexts. Even where the best regime was attainable, its forms would properly vary, depending on their circumstances and antecedents. With these caveats, however, the goal of liberal theory was, and – in so far as the liberal project still lingers on – remains, the articulation of principles for the limitation of governmental and political power that have universal authority.

This liberal project animates all recognizable liberal theorists, including the later Rawls, but it is most self-conscious and systematic in the greatest of them, John Stuart Mill. In Mill's work there is exemplified the paradigmatic liberal programme of stating 'one very simple principle' (as he terms it in *On Liberty*) as governing the relations of state and society with the individual; this principle is defended by reference to a conception of man as a progressive being; and Mill makes entirely explicit his conviction that the principle he states is authoritatively applicable in all circumstances in which the species has emerged from barbarism.[1] Again, no doubt the principle will have novel applications, as circumstances, such as changes in technology, for example, throw up new contexts in which it must be applied. How Mill's principle of liberty, or harm principle, applies to the use of electronic bugging devices or long-distance cameras, or to new forms of video or computer-generated pornography, are obviously not questions that Mill could have answered, since such devices were unknown and unthought-of in Mill's time. If Mill's principle is to have the action-guiding force Mill demanded of it, however, it must have definite application in these new contexts. And, again, the applications of the principle will be universally authoritative, provided only that the society in which it is implemented is one that has emerged from barbarism. This liberal project, found prototypically in the work of John Stuart Mill, recurs in nearly all subsequent liberal thinkers. It informs Rawls's conception of the basic liberties, Feinberg's elucidation, restatement and emendations of the Millian principle,[2] Dworkin's account of equality and rights, and many others.

The liberal project is open to the criticism, which I have developed in earlier work,[3] that the principles it issues in are subject to disabling indeterminacies, arising not merely from the open-texture of their central concepts, but more seriously from incommensurabilities among, and within, the values they invoke. These disabilities in the principles to which the liberal project has given rise are so serious, I have argued, as to warrant its abandonment – the relinquishment of the universalist aspiration of liberal theory and the adoption instead of an historicist perspective on liberal institutions and practices. On this post-liberal view, the indeterminacies and incommensurabilities which afflict the principles articulated in liberal political philosophy are resolved, locally and provisionally, in a variety of recurrent political and juridical settlements achieved in the diversity of liberal regimes that are to be found in the real world of history. They are resolved in practice, typically in political practice, in settlements that vary from place to place and time to time. There is no overarching or synoptic normative theory from which these settlements can be derived – no delusive Archimedean point of privileged leverage whereby they can be generated. They arise, and are dissolved, in the contingencies and vicissitudes of practice. In this post-liberal perspective, the conflict of goods, their uncombinability and sometimes their incommensurability, is taken to be the central datum of political morality, and to support a form of theorizing in which the ephemeral but real settlements achieved in political practice are preferred to the delusive harmonies of liberal philosophy.

In the work of Isaiah Berlin and of Joseph Raz, the competitive moral pluralism marked by these deep conflicts among goods is invoked to support a novel and non-standard form of liberalism – what I have termed an *agonistic liberalism*.[4] What is most distinctive of this species of liberal theory is not its affirmation of the reality of rationally incommensurable values – which is a feature of standard or conventional liberalism of the Rawlsian variety – but its recognition that these incommensurabilities enter into liberal principles themselves and undermine the possibility of a comprehensive system of such principles. On this agonistic view, as on mine, conflicts within liberal political morality – conflicts among important liberties, say – cannot as a rule be decided by appeal to any theory or principle; they are decidable only in practice. Since it is characteristic of political practice, as distinct from that of law, that it issue in settlements that are open to renegotiation, embody compromises of interests and ideals, and carry no presumption of unique rational authority, agonistic liberalism is a genuinely *political* liberalism in a way that Rawlsian liberalism, in which political life is evacuated of virtually all substance, manifestly is not. This much is clear about the species of liberal theory we find, in markedly differing forms, in the work of Berlin and Raz. What is less clear is whether Berlin or Raz would follow me in the historicist move of theorizing liberal institutions and practices as particular forms of life having no universal authority whatever.

For my present purposes, I shall not at this stage in my argument pursue this last question, except to note my view that from the truth of a plurality of incommensurable values the priority of one of them – liberty, autonomy or choice-making, say – cannot follow.[5] Value-pluralism cannot entail, or ground, liberalism in any general, still less universal way. The historical fact of a diversity of conceptions of the good, or of world-views, in a particular society may be a good reason for the adoption of liberal institutions in that society; but, if value-pluralism is true, the range of forms of genuine human flourishing is considerably larger than can be accommodated within liberal forms of life.

As a matter of logic alone, it is safe to say that value-pluralism cannot mandate liberalism, where that is taken to be a theory or set of principles claiming universal authority. I shall, towards the end of this chapter, consider how a fully pluralist position differs from the agonistic liberal standpoint I have attributed to Berlin and Raz. My present purpose is not, however, to argue that value-pluralism cannot entail liberalism, but instead to take this result as a starting-point of a further inquiry – an inquiry into what forms of political order follow from acceptance of a strong form of value-pluralism.

In earlier work, defending a position I have termed post-liberal, I have argued that the institutions characteristic of liberal civil society are most congenial to the truth of value-pluralism, at any rate in the historical circumstances in which we find ourselves.[6] This was, in effect, a quasi-Hegelian defence of what I called 'the living kernel of liberalism', the historic inheritance of liberal civil society. Having interpreted liberalism as a system of ideas characterized by four values or theses – individualism, egalitarianism, universalism and meliorism – I argued that, whereas these values or theses could not be shown to be ration-ally compelling, they re-emerge as features of the constitutive practices and institutions of liberal civil society. I specified the four defining features of liberalism as follows:

> First, there is the idea of *moral or normative individualism* – the idea that, since nothing has ultimate value except states of mind or feeling, or aspects of the lives of human individuals, therefore the claims of individuals will always defeat those of collectivities, institutions or forms of life. . . . A second element in the liberal syndrome is *universalism* – the idea that there are weighty duties and/or rights that are owed to all human beings, regardless of their cultural inheritances or historical circum-stances, just in virtue of their standing as human beings. . . . This second idea leads, naturally enough, to the third element

in the liberal syndrome, namely *meliorism*. By this is meant the view that, even if human institutions are imperfectible, they are nonetheless open to indefinite improvement by the judicious use of critical reason. ... The fourth and final element of the liberal syndrome issues intelligibly from the first three – liberal *egalitarianism*. By this is meant the denial of any natural moral or political hierarchy among human beings, such as was theorized by Aristotle in respect of slavery and by Filmer of absolute monarchy. For any liberal, in other words, the human species is a single-status moral community, and monarchy, hierarchy and subordination are practices that stand in need of an ethical defence.[7]

I argued that

The four constitutive elements of liberalism as a doctrine ... re-emerge as characteristics of civil society. The legal structure of a civil society is bound to be *individualist* since none of us is (in the jargon of recent communitarian theory) a radically situated self whose identity is constituted by membership of a single community ... Here individualism is affirmed, not as any set of universal normative claims about the species, but instead as a necessary feature of any modern civil society ... Similarly with *egalitarianism*. Though a civil society presup- poses neither political nor economic equality, it does require equality before the law. For it is a necessary feature of a civil society that, just as no-one in it is above the law, so no-one is denied the protection of the law ... What of *meliorism*? ... Within the history of any particular civil society ... it makes sense to talk of improvement or decline and to frame projects of reform. ... Discourse as to amelioration or decline will in general be governed by standards that are immanent in the specific histories and traditions of the diverse civil societies ... The *universalist* element of liberalism survives, not by civil societies converging on any single model, but in virtue of the universality, or near universality, of civil society itself as a condition of prosperity and peace for any modern civilisation.[8]

By *civil society* I had specified regimes having three features: I contrasted it with the *weltanschauung*-states of ancient and modern times, maintaining that

In a civil society . . . diverse, incompatible and perhaps incommensurable conceptions of the good and the world can coexist in a peaceful *modus vivendi*. . . . A second feature of civil society is that, in it, both government and its subjects are constrained by *a rule of law*. . . . In any civil society, most social and political activities will take place in autonomous institutions that are protected by the rule of law but independent of government . . . A third feature of civil society is the institution of private or several property. The importance of several property for civil society is that it acts as an enabling device whereby rival and possibly incommensurable conceptions of the good may be implemented and realized without recourse to any collective decision-procedure. . . . The central institution of civil society – the institution of private property – has its rationale as an *enabling device* whereby persons with radically discrepant goals and values can pursue them without recourse to a collective decision-procedure that would, of necessity, be highly conflictual.[9]

In this argument that the defining features of liberalism as a doctrine re-emerge as constitutive features of modern civil societies, I was concerned to stress the diversity of forms in which modern civil societies may be found. Civil societies need not be liberal democracies – neither Whig England nor, in our own times, Hong Kong or Singapore are such, though they clearly fit the model of civil societies I have sketched – and they need not possess democratic institutions of any other sort. Civil societies need not be, and in their East Asian examples are not, associated with the moral culture of individualism which informs them in their European, and more particularly their US varieties. Nor need the economic system of a modern civil society be that of market capitalism; in parts of the post-communist world, especially Russia, market institutions are emerging that differ in fundamental respects from those of Western capitalism. Nevertheless, I concluded that: 'On the view presented here, civil societies, in all their legitimate varieties, are the living kernel of what was "liberalism".'[10] This was the core of the post-liberal view argued for in my earlier work – that, whereas the foundationalist, universalist or doctrinal claims of liberalism cannot be defended, the central elements of liberal political morality re-emerge as constitutive institutions or practices in modern civil societies. In other words, whereas any form of fundamentalist liberalism was rejected according to which liberal forms of life possess universal rational and moral authority, the post-liberal view affirmed the near-universality, in the late modern world, of varieties of civil society in whose institutions the elements of liberal political morality were preserved.

This post-liberal view seems to me now to be mistaken. It is mistaken in arguing that strong value-pluralism is, in contemporary historical circumstances, a good reason for the universal, or near-universal adoption of a Western-style civil society, in any of its varieties. In political milieux which harbour a diversity of cultural traditions and identities, such as we find in most parts of the world today, the institutional forms best suited to a modus vivendi may well not be the individualist institutions of liberal civil society but rather those of political and legal pluralism, in which the fundamental units are not individuals but communities. In polities that are plural or divided, the legal recognition of different communities, and of their distinct jurisdictions, may well be mandated on the Hobbesian ground that it promotes peace.

It may be justified on another, independent ground – that it enables practitioners of distinctive cultural traditions to have these mirrored in the legal orders to which they are subject, without necessitating the secessionist struggles that are unavoidable if a single polity or human settlement which encompasses many peoples also has only a single legal order to which all are subject. Such legal pluralism is justifiable, in other words, not only on the Hobbesian rationale of promoting the peace, but also on the Herderian ground that it allows even peoples who are commingled in the same territories or human settlements to recognize their cultural identities in the legal orders to which they are subject. Such legal pluralism is, in fact, the institutional embodiment of the human need for strong forms of common life in circumstances of substantial cultural diversity. The pluralist standpoint which is here defended aims to answer the question: how may peace and common life be achieved, in historical milieux of great cultural diversity, such as our own?

This pluralist view has in common with the post-liberal position, for which I have hitherto argued, that it takes as a point of departure that the recent liberal ideal of the neutral state is indefensible. It is indefensible, partly because – as Raz has shown[11] – the ideal of neutrality with respect to rival conceptions of the good is itself incoherent. It is indefensible for another reason. The pluralism of values which is invoked, in Rawls and other recent liberal writers, to support the liberal ideal of neutrality, is the attenuated species of pluralism arising from diverse individual life-plans informed by personal conceptions of the good that may be rationally incommensurable. The variety of value-pluralism that is most salient in the context of the world today is not of this diluted and individualistic variety, but arises from the plurality of whole ways of life, with their associated moralities and often exclusionary allegiances. The liberal ideal of neutrality is a wholly inadequate response to this form of value-pluralism – the most important and challenging in current circumstances – because the conceptions of the good in which it is expressed resist legal privatization – that relegation to the private sphere of voluntary association which would be their fate in the neutral state envisaged in liberal theory. The liberal ideal of neutrality is, in fact, a demand for the legal disestablishment of cultural traditions, which is to say, a denial of legal recognition to distinctive ways of life. To respond with liberal neutrality to rival demands for legal recognition from different ways of life is a classic example of liberal legalism. Legal pluralism seeks to meet this demand by the creation of a diversity of jurisdictions for the various communities, which – unlike the chimera of a neutral liberal state – is an achievable objective with numerous historical antecedents.

Though it has in common with it a rejection of the liberal legalist utopia of a neutral state, the pluralist view here advocated differs from the post-liberal position in that it does not presuppose, or entail, endorsement of the central institutions of Western civil society. A pluralist regime could exhibit the virtue of toleration with regard to different religions and world-views, according them full legal recognition, and yet be a *weltanschauung*-state. The Moorish kingdoms of medieval Spain and the contemporary Malaysian state are each of them Islamic polities, yet they practise toleration and indeed pluralism in religious matters. The United Kingdom retains (for the while) an established Anglican church, yet few societies are as latitudinarian as contemporary Britain. Both the Roman and the Ottoman empires were exemplars of legal and religious pluralism, with the Ottoman *millet* system institutionalizing legal recognition of the different religious communities, but in each there was an established faith or state cult. Of course, pluralist political orders will resemble civil societies far more than totalitarian states or fundamentalist regimes, in that, though they may be *weltanschauung*-states, they will not be animated by an overriding project of propagating a religion or ideology: any such objective will be subordinated to, or at the very least constrained by, concern for peace and common life among and within the various ways of life the pluralist order contains.

In earlier work, the conception of civil society which I developed was developed, in part, contrastively, by reference to regimes – totalitarian and fundamentalist regimes, for example – in which the distinction between the state and society has been obliterated. This contrastive understanding of civil society remains valid, but it is far from exhaustive of the varieties of regime we find in the world. Both civil society and totalitarianism are Western categories which capture Western-derived regimes;[12] and fundamentalism is best understood, in many contexts, as a reactive phenomenon, responsive to Westernization. As the Occidental ideologies continue to wane, and non-Occidental cultures assert themselves in political terms, we may reasonably expect, as in earlier periods of history, to see a far wider range of regimes than can be captured in the Western category of civil society and its contraries. The forms in which the institution of property develops, and in which law develops – to take two further constitutive practices of Western civil society – may be expected to be various, and to be different in some important respects from their exemplars in Western civil societies. It is this diversity that the pluralist view aims to theorize.

The pluralist view takes deep cultural diversity to be a common historical occurrence and an ineradicable feature of many, indeed most contemporary societies. This brings out a decisive point of difference between the pluralist view of political order and that maintained by traditionalist or reactionary critics of liberalism. Such conservative critics of liberalism see political order as serving the Old Right project of restoring, or instituting, an 'integral' or 'organic' culture, and their policy with regard to cultural minorities is one that forces on them alternatives of assimilation or exclusion from the political order. It is unclear if such a contemporary theorist of the Old Right as Roger Scruton would accept this characterization of his standpoint, but that it has points of affinity with Maurrasian integralist nationalism, say, seems undeniable.[13] Pluralists reject this Old Right project for the same reason that they reject the Enlightenment project. Both seek to roll back the reality of cultural diversity for the sake of an imaginary condition of cultural unity – whether that be found in a lost past or in a supposed future condition of the species in which cultural difference has been marginalized in a universal civilization. Both perspectives are alien to that of the pluralist, which takes the reality of cultural difference as a datum of political order.

A pluralist political order may nevertheless deviate from the central institutions of a liberal civil society at crucial points. It need not, and often will not possess an individualist legal order in which persons are the primary rights-bearers. The principal bearers of rights (and duties) in a pluralist political order will be communities, or ways of life, not individuals. Of course, many pluralist political orders will possess mixed legal systems, and legitimately so: the legal system of contemporary India, for example, is partly the individualist, secular one inherited from the British, partly Islamic and partly Hindu, with the differences focusing, not unnaturally, in the law of marriage and the family, and conflicts of jurisdiction not uncommon. That there should be such mixed systems, which stop short of full legal pluralism, is unavoidable and in many contexts desirable on pluralist grounds. Equally – anticipating a familiar liberal objection – there will sometimes be a good question as to how ways of life are to be individuated so as to make their legal recognition workable. This will plainly be an issue where intermarriage is common between members of different cultural groups, and where plural inheritances are otherwise common. It will also be a question where, in a society divided on religious lines, one or more of the religions permits or encourages conversion, as with Islam in contemporary India (where there is significant conversion from the Hindu caste of untouchables). In most, if not all pluralist political orders, there has been legal provision for migration from community to community, and for those with plural inheritances. There remains still a fundamental difference between liberal civil societies in which individuals are the primary rights-bearers and pluralist orders which vest most rights and duties in communities.

It is important to note that, from the standpoint of pluralist theory, whether a pluralist political order is appropriate is itself a matter of time, place and circumstance. It is far from being a consequence of pluralist theory that pluralist political orders are everywhere legitimate, necessary or desirable. In societies with strong individualist traditions and very high levels of interpenetration of cultural traditions, such as the United States, a liberal civil society, whatever its social costs and however reformed, is the only real historical option, no matter what radical communitarians may wish. Equally, liberal civil institutions are clearly appropriate in a society, such as contemporary France, which is multi-ethnic but (unlike the United States) successfully monocultural, or (like contemporary Australia, but again unlike the United States) which is successfully multicultural. In the countries of the European Union, as presently constituted, the institutions of a liberal civil society accord both with long-standing cultural traditions and with contemporary needs. The central proposition of pluralist political theory, which is that different legal and political institutions are desirable and legitimate in different cultural and historical milieux, itself entails that liberal regimes should sometimes be legitimate.

The unit and constitution of a pluralist political order will also properly vary with time, place and circumstance, according to the pluralist view. In contexts in which a viable national political culture exists and has allowed at least a partial transcendence of ethnic allegiances, the appropriate unit may be the sovereign nation-state, with many functions devolved to regional and local levels. Where commonalities of cultural tradition and economic development are present, supranational associations of such sovereign states may come into being – though we may be sure that such projects as that of a federal superstate in Europe will remain utopian owing to the lack, in any future that is foreseeable or even imaginable, of a transnational European political culture. Where ethnic allegiances prove stronger than a shallow or deformed national culture, and where the non-territorial jurisdictions of legal pluralism are not acceptable to peoples whose mutual relations are ruled by suspicion or enmity, as in former Yugoslavia, there may be no realistic alternative to the construction of ethnically based sovereign states. In this last case, the worst from both a liberal and a pluralist perspective, political practice is likely to give way to war as it becomes increasingly clear that the terms of a political settlement will themselves be substantially determined by the military balance of forces. In some contexts, such as that of the Russian Federation, it is at least arguable that the human costs – in terms of the brutalities of war and the atrocities of 'ethnic cleansing' – of setting up sovereign nation-states in territories of long commingled human populations which have never known nationhood may be so vast and terrible as to mandate a neo-imperial regime in which a Hobbesian peace is kept among the rivalrous peoples. The vital point here is that pluralist theory is open as to the form of state organization – sovereign nation-state, confederal or federal union, or empire – best able in any given historical context to embody the pluralist regime of a peaceful *modus vivendi* among different cultural traditions, ways of life and peoples.

The pluralist view is permissive and open, also, about the internal constitution of an acceptable regime. It need not contain democratic institutions, nor the institutions of a Western-style civil society. As I understand it, the project currently underway in China is that of developing market institutions, having many features that distinguish them from Western exemplars, *without* the apparatus of democracy or a Western-style civil society. This project may fail; but, if it does, it will be as a result of historically familiar problems of state disintegration in China, not because all polities are fated to converge on Western norms of democracy or civil society. Contrary to the ideologues of the New Right, nothing in the project of constructing or developing market institutions commits anyone to the adoption of the institutions of democracy or civil society.[14] Whether democratic institutions are mandated is, on the pluralist view, a matter of time, place and circumstance, not of universally authoritative principle. The pluralist standard of assessment of any regime is whether it enables its subjects to coexist in a Hobbesian peace while renewing their distinctive forms of common life. By this standard, the current regime in China might well be criticized for its policies in Tibet; but such a criticism would invoke the intrinsic value of the communities and cultural forms now being destroyed in Tibet, not universalist conceptions of human rights or democracy. The practical and political implications of such a criticism, though they might be radical, would still be very different from those, commonplace in Western countries, which attack the current Chinese regime because it refuses – rightly, in my view – to accept Western norms and practices as authoritative in China. On the pluralist view, there is no democratic project that has authority for all peoples and all circumstances. Like other political institutions, democracy is a convenient device, whose usefulness turns on its contribution to peace and the renewal of valuable forms of common life.

The pluralist view defended here involves the abandonment, not only of any democratic project, but also of the liberal project, even as that is found in such agonistic liberal theorists as Berlin and Raz. The liberal project of stating, and enforcing, universal limits on governmental power, especially when it is coercive, amounts to the prescription that a single form of political order be everywhere installed regardless of the cultural traditions and ways of life of its subjects. That political orders should be vessels for the transmission of ways of life across the generations, and that the forms of government may legitimately vary according to the cultures of the peoples they serve, are propositions rejected by all liberals, new and old. Yet they are implied by strong value-pluralism – especially by its deepest version, in which the most radical form of value-conflict is not the competitive moral pluralism which arises when individual life-plans or conceptions of the good express incommensurable values, but rather that which occurs in conflicts between whole ways of life, each with their characteristic, and often exclusionary excellences, virtues and goods. The pluralist position I have sketched here is, in part, merely a spelling-out of one of the implications of this value-pluralist insight – namely, the implication that, if there are ways of life embodying genuine forms of human flourishing that require as their matrices non-liberal social and political structures, then a pluralist moral theory which recognizes such forms of human flourishing must be complemented by a pluralist political theory, which recognizes as legitimate forms of political order that are not, and will never become, liberal. Standard or conventional liberal thought, as it is found prototypically in the work of Rawls, resists this result, because in it value-pluralism is trivialized and banalized. In its conventional liberal uses, the pluralism of values refers to incommensurabilities arising among and within individual plans of life and personal conceptions of the good, but not to those which arise in the relations of whole ways of life, and liberal principles themselves are supposedly insulated from incommensurabilities arising within and among personal conceptions of the good. If, on the other hand, value-pluralism is not so banalized and trivialized, if it is seen as applying to whole ways of life and as infecting (and disabling) the so-called principles that are articulated in liberal political philosophy, then liberalism itself is undermined. In short, to follow through on the implications of strong value-pluralism inexorably entails relinquishing the liberal project.

Even non-standard or agonistic liberalism is not immune to the subversive force of value-pluralism. There is a tension in the agonistic liberalisms of Berlin and Raz, in so far as they aim to give reasons for according a universal or general priority over other political goods to their differing conceptions of freedom. Berlin's claim that collective well-being, equality and liberty, for example are irreducible and incommensurable values is not easily reconciled with the claim he sometimes also makes that freedom – in his preferred conception of negative liberty – is to be accorded a general, though never absolute priority over other ultimate values. In Raz the priority accorded to autonomy within Raz's perfectionist liberalism is thoroughly problematic. In Raz's account of it, autonomy derives its value from its status as an ingredient in human flourishing in certain definite social and cultural milieux – those, such as our own (according to Raz), which are characterized by high levels of social and occupational mobility, in which skills of choice-making are functionally indispensable. This is a functional explanation of the value of autonomy, which is nearly indistinguishable from a merely instrumental account;[15] and it is difficult to see how such a radically contextualized, and historicized, view of autonomy, in which autonomy is elevated to the central position in liberal political morality, can be squared with the universalist claims that go with traditional liberalism, or with the strong claims Raz makes for the role of a liberal state in promoting autonomy.[16] If the autonomous life is not in itself better than other forms of life – as Raz has himself rightly stressed[17] – and it makes a vital contribution to a distinct mode of human flourishing only in certain definite social milieux, then it seems reasonable to promote it only in so far as the benefits in terms of human well-being Raz claims for it are clear. Here the empirical record looks a good deal more equivocal than Raz allows. It is in particular far from clear that Asian immigrants, whose cultural traditions do not valorize autonomy, do worse – from the standpoint of individual well-being – than representative members of liberal societies which do so valorize it. Indeed the opposite case could be made, from the available evidences, with equal, or greater conviction: that such cultural groups are doing as well, or better, than most in the liberal societies in which they have formed enclaves. There seems to be a tension, perhaps ineradicable in Raz's liberalism, between the radically historicized and contextualized account of autonomy he advances and the central and dominating role he wishes autonomy to have in political morality.

The upshot of the dominant role autonomy plays in Raz's liberalism – explicitly in his major work, if less unequivocally in later writings[18] – is that a liberal society must be a monocultural society, at least with respect to the mores required by autonomy. Here I think Raz has grasped a point of fundamental importance, perceived by Mill but not by Rawls – that a liberal state cannot be neutral with regard to illiberal forms of life coming within its jurisdiction. Or, to put the matter still more shortly, Raz is entirely correct in seeing liberalism itself as a whole way of life, and not merely a set of political principles or institutions. The trouble is that, if value-pluralism is true at the level of whole ways of life, then the liberal form of life can have no special or universal claim on reason. This is a difficulty that besets Berlin's liberalism also, even though it resists elevating autonomy to a central or dominating place in liberal morality, since it accords a parallel role to negative liberty. In both cases the liberal project, which is pursued *sotto voce* in their writings, is undermined by the value-pluralism which they also espouse.

The pluralist view here defended cannot but be anathema to fundamentalist or doctrinal liberals. It must be so, in that it repudiates the universalist pretensions of liberal theory, together with the Enlightenment philosophy of history – of the desirability of ultimate cultural convergence on a universal civilization – on which liberal universalism reposes. It must be so, again, in that the forms a pluralist *modus vivendi* may legitimately assume are not dictated by pluralist theory, but are settled – if at all – in political practice. Agonistic liberal theory, as I understand it, seeks to show that the liberal form of life has a superior claim on reason arising from its supposed tolerance of value-pluralism. This was the view I myself held, and termed post-liberal.

The present discussion has aimed to take our inquiry one step further – from an agonistic liberal, or post-liberal position, in which liberal institutions and practices are commended for their hospitality to forms of moral diversity marked in value-pluralism, to a pluralist view, in which liberal forms of life enjoy no special privileges of any kind.

10

ENLIGHTENMENT'S WAKE

So far as we can wean ourselves from willing, we contribute to the awakening of releasement.

M. Heidegger, *Gelassenheit*[1]

ENLIGHTENMENT AND DISENCHANTMENT

In the late modern period in which we live, the Enlightenment project is affirmed chiefly for fear of the consequences of abandoning it. Except in the United States, where it has the status of a civil religion, it carries little positive conviction. Yet much professional philosophy is devoted to anxious apologies for the Enlightenment's central enterprises, such as the rational reconstruction of morality, and the assertion by science of authority over all other forms of knowledge. Further, enfeebled though it has become in most of the Western cultures in which it originated, the Enlightenment project continues to inform many areas of thought and discourse aside from the increasingly culturally marginal activity of academic philosophy. In the rhetoric, and even in some measure in the practice of international relations, for example, conceptions – such as doctrines of universal human rights – whose provenance is manifestly that of the Enlightenment enjoy an anachronistic authority which derives partly, in all likelihood, from the manifest absence of any coherent alternative. Ours are enlightenment cultures not from conviction but by default.

Within political thought, the hegemony of liberalism has gone with an apologetic mode of theorizing. The tacit or declared objective of philosophical inquiry has been the delivery of a rational justification of liberal political morality – a transcendental deduction, that is to say, of *ourselves*. More than any other branch of philosophical inquiry, recent political philosophy has been what Wittgenstein called 'bourgeois' philosophy – philosophy devoted to the search for 'foundations' for the practices of particular communities. In its fearful and defensive tone, and in the dread it expresses of the dire consequences of shedding cherished convictions, liberal political philosophy resembles nothing so much as the Christian apologetic theology of a generation or so ago, when it was already apparent that Christianity had ceased to be the prime animating force in the culture of most Western societies, but when fear still inhibited clear thought about the nature and possibilities of a post-Christian culture.

We live today amid the dim ruins of the Enlightenment project, which was the ruling project of the modern period. If, as I believe, the Enlightenment project has proved to be self-destroying, then that fact signals the close of the modern period, of which we are the heirs. Our patrimony is the disenchantment which the Enlightenment has bequeathed to us – a disenchantment all the more profound since it encompasses the central illusions of the Enlightenment itself. Contrary to the hopes which buoyed up Enlightenment thinkers throughout the modern period, we find at the close of the modern age a renaissance of particularisms, ethnic and religious. In the post-communist world, where the disintegration of the Soviet state has inaugurated a period of upheaval and convulsion fully comparable with that which followed the fall of the Roman Empire, the collapse of the Enlightenment ideology of Marxism has not, as Western triumphalist conservatives and liberals supposed, issued in a globalization of Western civil society, but instead in a recurrence to pre-communist traditions, with all their historic enmities, and in varieties of anarchy and tyranny. The fate of those parts of the post-communist world whose cultural inheritance is European is likely to be a hard one, since the extension to them of Western market institutions is occurring during just the historical moment in which Western cultures, and therefore Western market institutions, are beset by a crisis of legitimacy. For, within Western cultures, the Enlightenment project of promoting autonomous human reason and of according to science a privileged status in relation to all other forms of understanding has successfully eroded and destroyed local and traditional forms of moral and social knowledge; it has not issued in anything resembling a new civilization, however, but instead in nihilism. (The United States is, as ever, an exception in this regard, since in it both fundamentalist religion and fundamentalist affirmations of the Enlightenment project remain strong. The collapse of these fundamentalisms in the United States, however, were it to occur, would likely be accompanied by an outbreak of nihilism of a violence and intensity unknown in other Western countries; such an outcome is prefigured in much contemporary North American art, literature and popular entertainment.) The Western humanist and modernist project of subjugating nature, which in its Soviet version wrought ecological catastrophe on an almost apocalyptic scale, is now being pursued with Weberian rationality through the development of capitalist institutions in the post-communist societies, and in the so-called emerging countries; but throughout the world the market institutions through which the natural world is exploited, themselves increasingly disembedded from any community or cultural tradition, are ever more chaotic, and elude any form of human accountability or control. The legacy of the Enlightenment project – which is also the legacy of Westernization – is a world ruled by calculation and wilfulness which is humanly unintelligible and destructively purposeless.

Wherever the Enlightenment project has animated a culture or a polity, it has evoked counter-projects of re-enchantment of the world, via fundamentalist religion or a reversion to premodern forms of thought or community. Where traditional cultural forms remain intact, it is sensible to seek to nurture them, to shelter them from modern technologies which would rend them, and to develop new technologies which serve human needs while preserving traditional communities and cultural forms. Where modernization has been achieved without the destruction of the traditional culture, and without the incursion of the illusions of the Enlightenment – as in Japan and Singapore, Malaysia and potentially perhaps in China, despite its Marxist inheritances – it is reasonable, and in fact imperative, to resist Western demands for the development of social and economic institutions on a bankrupt Western model. Even in those non-Occidental cultures which have preserved themselves substantially intact, and which have modernized without Westernizing their social forms and structures, the impact of the revolutionary nihilism of Westernization has been to disrupt traditional conceptions of the human relationship with the earth, and to supplant them by humanist and Baconian instrumentalist understandings, in which nature is no more than an object of human purposes. In those non-Occidental cultures which have remained substantially intact, there may nevertheless be a possibility of a recovery of their traditional conceptions, such that they might successfully integrate Western technology without thereby succumbing wholly to Western humanism and nihilism.

In the Western cultures themselves, by contrast, the Enlightenment project has irrecoverably displaced traditional forms of knowledge and self-understanding, and it is continuous with far older, religious and intellectual traditions, whose ruin is now manifest. The self-undermining of the Enlightenment project, as I shall interpret it, encompasses the dissolution of elements of the Western tradition – such as the humanism of the Christian tradition and the logocentrism of Greek philosophy – which are foundational and primordial in that tradition. It is with the predicament of these Western enlightenment cultures that I am here concerned. On the argument I shall present, there can for these cultures be no re-enchantment of the world, and no recovery of the Enlightenment project. For us, the post-modern condition of fractured perspectives and groundless practices is an historical fate, which we are wise to make the best of. At the same time, the post-modernist stance is typically one which rejects Enlightenment reason while (like the Romantic move-ment) retaining its commitment to a humanist emancipatory project – a shallow and ultimately incoherent perspective. In truth, neither a return to a pre-modern world-view nor the post-modern affirmation of a distinctively modernist project are viable historical options for us. We need to consider how to think and act in a culture that has been transformed irreversibly by an Enlightenment project that has shown itself to be self-consuming. I shall develop this view, in part, by taking as foils for my argument the anti-modernist analysis of contemporary intel-lectual life of Alasdair MacIntyre, and the anti-foundationalist, post-modern liberalism of Richard Rorty. Against both, I shall argue that the Enlightenment project has irreversibly trans-formed Western cultures, and that its failure – or, as I prefer to say, its self-undermining – carries with it the rupture of the central intellectual traditions of the West, and marks for that reason a major discontinuity in Western cultural history. And, whereas I shall maintain against MacIntyre that there can be no revival of pre-modern modes of thought, I shall argue against Rorty that the foundering of the Enlightenment is bound to alter liberal forms of life even when these are received as inheritances of historical practice rather than as the embodiment of a rationalist project. Contrary to Rorty, whose post-modernism – like most post-modernism – is the modern humanist project without its foundationalist matrix, the dissolution of the Enlightenment project carries with it the ruin of the distinctive modern project of emancipation in a universal civilization.

What was the Enlightenment project? Alasdair MacIntyre identifies correctly its central thrust, and its relevance to intellectual and cultural life in our own time, when in his *After Virtue* (1981) he refers to 'the project of an independent rational justification of morality' and observes, again correctly, that 'the breakdown of this project provided the historical background against which the predicaments of our own culture become intelligible.' It is, in MacIntyre's view, against the background of the failure of the Enlightenment project to give a rational grounding to morality that 'the distinctively modern standpoint appears in something like fully-fledged form' – that distinctively modern standpoint 'which envisages moral debate in terms of a confrontation between incompatible and incommensurable premises and moral commitment as the criterionless choice between such premises, a type of choice for which no rational justification can be given'.[2]

The Enlightenment thinkers who proposed the project of a rational refounding of morality were at one, whatever their many differences of view on other topics, both in their views as to the content of morality and in their conception of the structure or form of rational justification which morality requires. As MacIntyre puts it,

Consider certain beliefs shared by all the contributors to the project. All of them ... agree to a surprising degree on the content and character of the precepts which constitute genuine morality. Marriage and the family are *au fond* unquestioned by Diderot's rationalist *philosophe* as they are by Kierkegaard's Judge Wilhelm; promise-keeping and justice are as inviolable for Hume as they are for Kant. Whence did they inherit these shared beliefs? Obviously from their shared Christian past compared with which the divergences between Kant's and Kierkegaard's Lutheran, Hume's Presbyterian and Diderot's Jansenist-influenced Catholic background are relatively unimportant. At the same time as they agree largely on the character of morality, they agree also upon what a rational justification of morality would have to be. Its key premises would characterise some feature or features of human nature; and the rules of morality would then be explained and justified as being those rules which a being possessing just such a human nature could be expected to accept.[3]

The failure of this Enlightenment project, which MacIntyre rightly sees as inevitable, gives rise to the central dilemmas of modern moral theory.

On the one hand the individual moral agent, freed from hierarchy and teleology, conceives of himself and is conceived by moral philosophers as sovereign in his moral authority. On the other hand the inherited, if partially transformed rules of morality have to be found some new status, deprived as they have been of their older teleological character and their even more ancient categorical character as expressions of ultimately divine law.[4]

The collapse of the Enlightenment project also gives contemporary moral discourse its distinctive character of emotivism or subjectivism, in which moral judgements are in the end assimilated to preferences, and of deep incoherence. A feature of our current circumstance stressed by MacIntyre – entirely rightly, in my view – is that we no longer possess anything like a coherent moral vocabulary, any specification of the human good or of the virtues in terms of which moral reasoning can proceed. We live rather among the fragments of archaic moral vocabularies, whose undergirding structure of metaphysical and religious beliefs has long since collapsed. Our moral notions are in many ways like the *taboos* of which Captain Cook writes in the journal of his third voyage to Polynesia – taboos which were abolished, with extraordinary ease and without any significant social consequences, by Kamehameha II in 1819. As MacIntyre asks, 'Why should we think about our modern uses of *good, right* and obligatory in any different way from that in which we think about late eighteenth century uses of taboo? And why should we not think of Nietzsche as the Kamehameha II of the European tradition?'[5] On the view I shall myself defend, the answer to this, perhaps rhetorical, question of MacIntyre's is that the moral vocabulary of the late modern age is as archaic and incoherent as Nietzsche suggested, and in that regard is indeed closely akin to the late-eighteenth-century Polynesian discourse and practice of taboo.

For MacIntyre, in *After Virtue*, the breakdown of the Enlightenment project was inevitable because it was, from the first, misconceived; and the collapse of this modern project establishes Nietzsche as the modern moral theorist 'if the only alternatives to Nietzsche's moral philosophy turn out to be those formulated by the philosophers of the Enlightenment and their successors'.[6] These are not for MacIntyre, however, the only alternatives to Nietzsche's moral philosophy; a systematic alternative is available in 'the most powerful of pre-modern modes of moral thought', which is the moral philosophy of Aristotle. MacIntyre's argument is that

either one must follow through the aspirations and the collapse of the different versions of the Enlightenment project until there remains only the Nietzschean diagnosis and the Nietzschean problematic *or* one must hold that the Enlightenment project was not only mistaken, but should never have been commenced in the first place.[7]

MacIntyre's conclusion is that, if the problematic of Nietzsche's moral theory is to be avoided, then we must retrace our steps, and revive the moral theory that Nietzsche, together with all other moral philosophers of modernity, was steadfast in rejecting. We must step back altogether from the moral theory of modernity, and return to that of Aristotle.

In his subsequent writings, MacIntyre has reaffirmed the central argument of *After Virtue*, and given the reader a sketch of what a revived Aristotelian moral theory, as presented in the context of contemporary philosophy, might look like. He has insisted that the Enlightenment project, though it was an episode in the history of philosophy, was far more than that: it, and its failure, are events in the history of modern culture. More specifically, in his *Whose Justice? Which Rationality?* (1988) MacIntyre insists that

. . . it is of the first importance to remember that the project of founding a social order in which individuals could emancipate themselves from the contingency and particularity of tradition by appealing to genuinely universal, tradition independent norms was and is not only, and not principally, a project of philosophers. It was and is the project of liberal, individualist society, and the most cogent reasons we have for believing that the hope of a tradition-independent rational universality is an illusion derive from the history of that project. For in the course of that history liberalism, which began as an appeal to alleged principles of shared rationality against what was felt to be the tyranny of tradition, has itself been transformed into a tradition whose continuities are partly defined by the interminability of the debate over such principles.[8]

The modern project, which is the Enlightenment project of refounding morality and society on universal, tradition-independent rational principles, has had several forms, including notably Marxism; but, for MacIntyre – surely rightly – it is in liberalism that the modern project is now historically and politically embodied. Indeed, for all the criticism that it encourages and institutionalizes, liberalism enjoys virtual hegemony in modern Western intellectual life. As MacIntyre puts it:

> The starting points of liberal theorizing are never neutral between conceptions of the human good; they are always liberal starting points. And the inconclusiveness of debates within liberalism as to the fundamental principles of liberal justice . . . reinforces the view that liberal theory is best understood, not at all as an attempt to find a rationality independent of tradition, but as itself an articulation of an historically developed and developing set of social institutions and forms of activity, that is, as the voice of a tradition.[9]

One might even say that, with the transformation of liberalism into a tradition, the failure of the Enlightenment project is itself institutionalized. The work of John Rawls, and the canonical (or, better, iconic) role that that work has in liberal theorizing, is perhaps a good example of the hegemony that liberalism has achieved within modern intellectual life, and of the irony that it has achieved the status of an almost unchallenged tradition by institutionalizing the failure of the Enlightenment project of rationally refounding morality to which liberalism as a doctrine was, in all of its varieties, unreservedly committed.

With MacIntyre, I think that the Enlightenment project was the defining modern project and that the failure of the Enlightenment project, arising as it did from incoherences in its central commitments and beliefs, was inevitable. Again with MacIntyre, I believe that, especially since the theoretical and political collapse of Marxism, it is in liberalism that the Enlightenment project is now most powerfully, and certainly most pervasively, embodied; and this project is not only, or even mainly, a project of philosophers, but also, and chiefly, the project of modern liberal individualist society – and above all, I would add, of US individualist society. Finally, I share with MacIntyre the conviction that the end-result of the Enlightenment project, what I wish to term its self-undermining effect, is best expressed in the thought of Nietzsche, at least in so far as that is successfully critical and subversive rather than – in my view, as in MacIntyre's – unsuccessfully mythopeic and constructive. What I call the self-undermining effect of the Enlightenment is well summarized by MacIntyre, when in his most recent study, *Three Rival Versions of Moral Inquiry: Encyclopaedia, Genealogy and Tradition* (1990), he observes:

> . . . whereas it was a tenet of Enlightenment cultures that every point of view, whatever its source, could be brought into rational debate with every other, this tenet had as its counterpart a belief that such rational debate could always, if adequately conducted, have a conclusive outcome. The point and purpose of rational debate was to establish truths and only those methods were acceptable which led to the conclusive refutation of error and vindication of truth. The contrast with contemporary academic practice could not be sharper. For with rare exceptions the outcomes of rational debate on fundamental issues are systematically inconclusive. . . . We can thus contrast the various Enlightenment's strong conceptions of rationality with this weak conception. . . . What would be required, on this contemporary view, for a conclusive termination of rational debate would be appeal to a standard or set of standards such that no adequately rational person could fail to acknowledge its authority. But such a standard or standards, since it would have to provide criteria for the rational acceptability or otherwise of any theoretical or conceptual scheme, would itself have to be

formulable and defensible independently of any such scheme. But – and it is here that contemporary academic practice breaks radically with its Enlightenment predecessors – there can be no such standard; any standard adequate to discharge such functions will itself be embedded in, supported by, and articulated in terms of some set of theoretical and conceptual schemes. Thus since, so far as large-scale theoretical and conceptual structures are concerned, each rival theoretical standpoint provides from within itself and in its own terms the standards by which, so its adherents claim, it should be evaluated, rivalry between such contending standpoints includes rivalry over standards. There is no theoretically neutral, pre-theoretical ground from which the adjudication of competing claims can proceed. It is all too easy to conclude further that therefore, when one large-scale theoretical and conceptual standpoint is systematically at odds with another, there can be no rational way of settling the differences between them. And Nietzsche's genealogical heirs do so conclude, for this as well as for other reasons.[10]

Against the Nietzschean genealogical view of inquiry as disclosing incommensurability and undecidability among a plurality of moral and other perspectives, MacIntyre affirms a conception of inquiry, avowedly Thomistic in origin and inspiration, that is explicitly tradition-dependent but whose superior rationality is exemplified in its resolution of difficulties generated by, but unsoluble in the terms of, other rival traditions.

For MacIntyre, as for myself, the Enlightenment was a self-defeating project, in both intellectual and political terms, and its self-destruction was consummated in the thought of Nietzsche. The self-defeatingness of the Enlightenment project, which is the self-undermining effect of modernity in inexorably disclosing its own groundlessness, is for MacIntyre reason to step back from the greatest moral theorist of modernity, Nietzsche, in order to vindicate in terms adequate to contemporary philosophical inquiry the pre-modern intellectual tradition of Aristotelianism, particularly in its central Thomistic version. For me, by contrast, the self-defeat of the Enlightenment project, particularly as that is expressed in the thought of Nietzsche, is the end-point of that larger and longer Western intellectual tradition of which Thomism was one of the most powerful syntheses. There can, in my view, be no rolling back the central project of modernity, which is the Enlightenment project, with all its consequences in terms of disenchantment and ultimate groundlessness. The modernist project of Enlightenment, though it broke with pre-modern, classical and medieval, thought at many points, was also continuous with it in its universalism and its foundationalist and representationalist rationalism. The pre-modern world-view, as that is found in both Aristotle and Aquinas, is that in which human moral categories are taken to track the structure of things in the world, and in which human reason reflects in microcosm the order of the cosmos. The modern world-view takes over from the classical Western tradition the conception of thought in which it mirrors or represents the world and in which its rationality is a matter of resting on universal foundations. It is this conception of thought that is exemplified in both classical Western philosophy and in Christianity until modern times.

One may interpret the modern period as that in which the metaphysical and religious beliefs of the classical and Christian periods are shed or marginalized, but in which the moral categories and hopes which they supported are secularized or naturalized in humanist doctrines of autonomous reason, historical progress, romantic self-creation and similar ideas. Nietzsche's insight was, in effect, that this modern world-view was transitional, a half-way house between the central, classical beliefs of the West and an as-yet-unborn culture in which those commitments had been shed. For Nietzsche, as for myself, there is no way back from the Enlightenment and its disenchantments through a revival of any pre-modern scheme of thought, if only because the Enlightenment was itself an authentic development of a central Western tradition going back to Socrates, and indeed beyond, to the pre-Socratics, such as Parmenides and Heraclitus, in whose fragments the fundamental commitments of Greek logocentrism – which I understand as the conception in which human reason mirrors the structure of the world – are affirmed. For this reason, the thought of Nietzsche, especially but not exclusively his thinking about morality, is unavoidably and rightly the starting-point of serious reflection for us, at the close of the modern age which the Enlightenment project, in all its diversity, inaugurated. The dissolution of morality, as that was conceived in both classical and Christian terms, and the fracturing of the inherited Western world-view into a diversity of incommensurable perspectives, which is accomplished in Nietzsche's thought, are irreparable, and any cultural losses they may entail are irretrievable. We shall make the best of the opportunities this cultural mutation affords if we relinquish the search for grounds – metaphysical, transcendental or rational – on which we have run aground in nihilism. Instead, abandoning the spirit of seriousness that has animated Western philosophy from its founding, we may then come to regard the world-views intimated in our culture lightly and playfully, as evanescent art forms rather than weighty representations of truth.

The post-modern condition of plural and provisional perspectives, lacking any rational or transcendental ground or unifying world-view, is our own, given to us as an historical fate, and it is idle to pretend otherwise. Yet it is just such a self-deception that is implicit in all those contemporary apologies for liberalism – including Rorty's – which trade on the central beliefs and commitments of the Enlightenment. It is no less idle to try to wish this condition away, by seeking – as MacIntyre does – to roll back the experience of modernity from which it arises. We are better occupied in considering how it came about that we should be in this condition, and how best we can cope with it. And, to summarize here the results of the complicated and lengthy inquiry into which I enter below, we shall turn to our best advantage the opportunities our present historical circumstances allow us, and suffer least from the disadvantages that unavoidably go with it, if we relinquish the liberalisms and the humanisms by which the Enlightenment cultures were, and continue to be, animated. We find hints and intimations as to the mode of thinking which best responds to our present condition, I shall suggest, in the later thought of Heidegger, and most particularly in the mode he calls *Gelassenheit*, which is the mode of 'releasement' in which we let things be rather than aiming wilfully to transform them or subject them to our purposes. It is in reaching a new relationship with our natural environment, with the earth and the other living things with which we share the earth, in which human subjectivity is not taken to be the measure of all things, that a turn in our inherited traditions of thought is accomplished, which opens up the possibility of profoundly different forms of human community dwelling together on the earth in peace. But in entering this mode of *Gelassenheit* we need to rid ourselves entirely of the nostalgias – for Being, and for a form of pre-reflective rootedness – which haunted Heidegger's thought throughout its several turns, and which – more than Heidegger's undoubted combination of political ignorance with ruthless opportunism – account for his deep and never-renounced engagement with Nazism.[11]

The political forms which arise from a renunciation of liberalism and humanism, in our historical context of trailing in Enlightenment's wake, may yet prove to be mostly destructive and harmful, as Heidegger's own history and the examples in recent decades of fundamentalist regimes, of ethnic wars, tyrannies and anarchies, unfortunately suggest. If these frenzied and repellent movements do turn out to be the principal political embodiments of the undermining and overthrow of the modern project, this will in my view be a fate arising from our inability either to overcome or to accept the central consequences of modernity, most especially from our incapacity to tolerate the disenchantment that accompanies it. For both Nazism and fundamentalism are intelligible as distinctively, and indeed peculiarly, *modern* phenomena, precisely in virtue of their reactive character as movements arising, dialectically, *against* the constitutive institutions and forms of life of modernity. (Italian Fascism was, at least in its inception, a fully-fledged modernist movement, rather than a reaction against modernity. Its differences from German National Socialism are, in this as in other respects, more compelling than its similarities.[12] At the same time, it is important to grasp that all forms of twentieth-century totalitarianism, Soviet and Maoist as well as Nazi, are at once uniquely Western, and distinctively modern, in their cultural origins.) No less distinctively modern, and no less reactive in character was the Romantic Movement, which together with assorted reactionary thinkers such as de Maistre mounted from the early nineteenth century onwards a consistent challenge to most of the central beliefs and projects of the Enlightenment. In the work of some thinkers of what Isaiah Berlin has illuminatingly called the Counter-Enlightenment,[13] and in the thought of J. G. Herder especially, there are some incisive criticisms of the philosophical anthropology, the philosophy of history and the conceptions of political order advanced by the Enlightenment thinkers. If the thinkers of the Counter-Enlightenment had any single concern in common, however, it was that the disenchantment produced by Enlightenment rationalism be resisted and indeed reversed by the exercise of human creative and imaginative faculties, as these were conceived by the Romantics and by modern critics of rationalism such as Pascal and Kierkegaard. These Romantic and irrationalist thinkers of the Counter-Enlightenment were modernists in the central role they accorded in their thought to human imagination – in the case of the Romantics, to self-creation – and to will. They differed from the Enlightenment thinkers in their perception of the Enlightenment project as one which brought disenchantment in its wake and in their more or less conscious attempt at a re-enchantment of the world via religious faith or human creativity.

On the view advanced here, by contrast, the disenchantment that trails in Enlightenment's wake is a fate that can perhaps be tempered, but not overcome. It may be tempered by an understanding that the Enlightenment's ascription to science of a prescriptive authority whereby other forms of knowledge can be humiliated is itself an illusion – the illusion that the diverse forms of human knowledge, or even of scientific knowledge, can be unified in a single system or brought under the discipline of a single method. The idea that there is such a thing as a unitary scientific method, even a scientific world-view, is merely one of the many superstitions of Enlightenment cultures. Science – unlike religion, and certainly unlike philosophy – remains in modern Western cultures a massively powerful social institution, deeply protective of its interests and dogmas. If the passion of doubt has a home in the Western cultures in our time, it is not in the sciences, but among the shrinking congregations of the religious, and in the humanities. The pretensions of science to contain a rationally privileged world-view should be, and can be humbled; but the pre-modern Western view of the world as inherently supportive of human values cannot be revived. Nor can the forms of 'organic' social order which supposedly existed prior to the disruptive growth of modern consciousness be restored. The history of the anti-modernist political movements of our time, such as fundamentalism and Nazism, shows the delusive and destructive character of any political project of rolling back modernity. The historical record of such movements, however, is no assurance that the anti-modernist project they embody will not be attempted again.

In a more modest but also a more hopeful prospect than those promised by movements which express a revolt against modernity, the political forms which may arise in truly post-Enlightenment cultures will be those that shelter and express diversity – that enable different cultures, some but by no means all or even most of which are dominated by liberal forms of life, different world-views and ways of life, to coexist in peace and harmony. For this development to be a real historical possibility, however, certain conceptions and commitments that have been constitutive, not merely of the Enlightenment and so of modernity, but also, and more fundamentally, of the central traditions of Western civilization, must be amended, or abandoned. Certain conceptions, not only of *morality* but also of *science*, that are central elements in Enlightenment cultures must be given up. Certain understandings of *religion*, long established in Western traditions, not as a vessel for a particular way of life but rather as the bearer of truths possessing universal authority, must be relinquished. The most fundamental Western commitment, the *humanist* conception of humankind as a privileged site of truth, which is expressed in Socratic inquiry and in Christian revelation, and which re-emerges in secular and naturalistic form in the Enlightenment project of human self-emancipation through the growth of knowledge, must be given up. The mutation in the dominant Western self-conception which these alterations in belief carry with them is not inconsiderable; its effects are unlikely to be confined to the dwindling and peripheral practitioners of philosophy as an academic discipline. On the contrary, it is reasonable to expect much else in the culture we inherit to be altered by the general recognition, should it occur, of the failure of the Enlightenment project, and of the sources of that failure in certain deeper, and much older, features of the central Western tradition.

Against Rorty, for example, I shall maintain that it is unreasonable to expect the institutions and practices of liberal society to survive unaltered the cultural mutation encompassed in abandoning the Enlightenment project. More plausibly, pluralist forms will emerge, animated by the goal of facilitating a *modus vivendi*, not only or primarily among different personal life-plans or conceptions of the good, but first and foremost among different communities and their associated cultural traditions. Such pluralist institutions may reasonably adopt elements of liberal practice where that is a living historical inheritance which meets contemporary human needs; but the pretensions of liberal societies to be germs of a universal civilization must be forgone. Liberal states must learn to live with non-liberal states, liberal cultural forms with non-liberal ones, in peace and harmony. Further, and perhaps decisively, once liberal practice is released from the hallucinatory perspective of liberal theory, it will be seen for what it always was – not a seamless garment, but a patchwork quilt, stitched together and restitched in response to the flux of circumstance. Nothing in liberal practice is then central, foundational or indispensable; there is nothing in liberal forms of life that is fixed or exempt from questioning. Particular liberal policies and projects – such as the policy of global free trade embodied in the GATT project – must be reconsidered and rejected, in so far as they amount to the attempted dissolution of distinctive ways of life animated by incommensurable cultures in the all-consuming commensurability and homogeneity of the global market. Liberal practice, inasmuch as it exemplifies the ideal of a single system of liberties or rights that is authoritative for all regardless of their cultural traditions or community memberships, must be abridged or modified. In this, and several other respects, liberal practice requires criticism and amendment – not acceptance as a self-justifying form of life.

The form of criticism which liberal practice demands is not one that invokes rational 'principles', or the universal requirements of 'human nature' – though a prelude to such criticism may be a critique of the rationalist conception of reason and the absurd philosophical anthropology presupposed in liberal theory. Rather it is a criticism in terms of the human needs of particular human beings, members of concrete historic communities and practitioners of specific cultural traditions. It seems to me to be thoroughly unreasonable to suppose that liberal practices, or the liberal form of life, will emerge unamended from such practical criticism by exponents of other ways of life. On the contrary, we may reasonably anticipate that liberal practices will be reformed, or abandoned, when it becomes manifest that they do not best facilitate the satisfaction of human needs in the late modern context of deep cultural diversity. If, as I believe, liberal practice is best conceived as a miscellany of ad-hoc improvisations, made over the generations in the pursuit of a modus vivendi, then no part of it can be regarded as sacrosanct; it can, and should, be rewoven, or unravelled, as circumstances and changing human needs dictate. Indeed the very idea that there is such a thing as the liberal form of life that it makes sense to attack or defend may come rightly to be seen as a relic of Enlightenment rationalism.

For my present purposes, I shall employ 'liberal' and its associated forms nominalistically, as a term of art, in the belief that my meaning will be commonly understood; but my underlying view will be throughout that liberal societies are miscellanies of conventions and practices, not exemplars of any ideal type. The upshot of my inquiry is that, in the context of emerging post-modernity, liberal practice can have no special authority even for those cultures in which it is an historic inheritance. For this reason, neither Rorty's post-modern bourgeois liberalism,[14] nor the post-modern liberal conservatism I have myself argued for in the past,[15] takes the full measure of the cultural metamorphosis that the passing of the Enlightenment project comprehends – a transformation comparable in scale and depth with the passing of Christianity as a unifying world-view. Contrary to the post-modernist stance which seeks to affirm a modern project of self-creation through the strategy of deconstruction, and which aims to make the cultural fragmentation of the West a universal condition, we need to recognize the passing of the Enlightenment project as an episode in *Western* culture – albeit one with global repercussions. Once we cease to be captivated by the Enlightenment project of a universal civilization animated by a unified world-view, and begin to regard that project from a standpoint of historical distance, we may come to think of the plural inheritance of incommensurable perspectives which is our unalterable condition in Western cultures as an historical gift to be enjoyed rather than merely as a fate to be accepted or endured.

MODERNITY IN RETROSPECT

> *Thinking is the most precursory of all precursory activities of man in this era, when Europe's modern age is just beginning to spread over the earth and be consummated. Moreover, it is not just a surface matter of nomenclature whether we look on the present age as the end of modern times, or whether we discern that today the perhaps protracted process of the consummation of modern times is just starting.*
>
> M. Heidegger, *What is Called Thinking?*[16]

To attempt a diagnosis of the modern period may well appear untimely and ill-conceived, given that we ourselves belong to it. As John Lukacs has pointed out,[17] the term 'Middle Ages' came into use only around two centuries after the waning of the Middle Ages had unmistakably set in. With us, to be sure, the passing of the modern age and the awareness that we are on the brink of a post-modern epoch are so nearly simultaneous as to be hardly distinguishable; the risk is indeed that pronouncements of the end of the modern period will prove to be merely further symptoms of modernity, and so self-refuting. Nevertheless, an attempt at understanding modernity is a task virtually imposed upon us by our current circumstances, and the evidences that we are near the close of the modern period are many and compelling. What then *was* modernity, and how was it related to the Enlightenment project which is the subject matter of my present inquiry? 'Modernism' is a term of art in many forms of discourse: but my concern here is with the world-view, or system of beliefs, which most distinctively characterizes the modern period. The elements of this world-view are found in a variety of forms, and they are not connected with one another, as links in a chain of reasoning, by relations of mutual entailment or strict implication. Yet they hang together to compose a coherent and recognizable modernist outlook, which functions as the matrix of the Enlightenment project of refounding morality and social life on universal and rationally compelling principles.

One of the central elements of this modernist world-view is a conception of *science* as the supremely privileged form of knowledge – that form of understanding the natural world which yields control and mastery of it. This conception of science was expressed by Francis Bacon, in the early seventeenth century, when in *The New Atlantis* he wrote of 'the knowledge of causes and secret motions of things, and the enlarging of bounds of human empire, to the effecting of all things possible'.[18] The conception of the natural world as an object of human exploitation, and of humankind as the master of nature, which informs Bacon's writings, is one of the most vital and enduring elements of the modern world-view, and the one which Westernization has most lastingly and destructively transmitted to non-Western cultures. Its roots are old and tangled, but centrally important among them is the Christian conception of the unique status of human beings as loci of infinite worth, immortal souls in a perishable world created by God for human use. This is a conception which contrasts sharply with the ancient, pre-philosophical Greek conception of human beings as mortals in an everlasting world, but which is informed by Greek ideas of *logos*, and of humans as the animal whose nature partakes of divine rationality, as these were assimilated into Christianity. In Christian theism, value is an emanation of personality, human or divine; human beings have infinite worth because they partake of the divine personality that created them; and a world without personality, if such there could be, could not but be worthless. Denuded of its theistic framework and content, the idea of the human species as the source of value in the world, and of human relations with nature being instrumental ones in which human activities alone are value-creating, emerges in modern times as secular humanism, which from the Renaissance onwards is a defining element in the modern world-view. It is integral to the humanist conception of humankind and of its relations with nature, as this figures in the Enlightenment project and in its predecessor Christian world-view, that in the absence of human beings the natural world – of animals and ecosystems, for example – is destitute of value; and the proper relations of humans with the natural world are relations of domination and exploitation.

This humanist conception need not, and often did not, comprehend the historical philosophy of progress, and the project of emancipating the species as a whole from ignorance and servitude, with which it was associated in the Enlightenment project. Indeed one of my central arguments is that modern Enlightenment humanism is continuous with and in large measure a modification of Christian humanist conceptions of humankind and the world. The pre-modern world-view, as it existed in Europe, was defined by the conviction that the world was pervaded by personality, with the ultimate guarantor of human values being a divine personality. Modern thought, as it emerged from the dissolution of the medieval world, represents the progressive secularization of the Christian conception of personality as the originator of value in the world. Enlightenment historiography, which is the project of writing a universal history, is in effect the history of the human species conceived as a single person. This Enlightenment project of a universal human narrative may be, and often is, associated with the idea of historical progress, as when Edward Gibbon writes in his chapter 'General Observations on the Fall of the Roman Empire in the West': 'We may therefore acquiesce in the pleasing conclusion that every age of the world has increased, and still increases, the real wealth, the happiness, the knowledge, and perhaps the virtue, of the human race'. The Enlightenment conception of a single universal human narrative, however, by no means requires, or presupposes, any such conception of progress.

In the thought of Thomas Hobbes, for example, the Enlightenment project is given an early and stark articulation which contains nothing akin to a theory of progress. In Hobbes, a materialist metaphysics, the inertial conception of motion of early modern science and an uncompromisingly subjectivist account of value as created solely by human desiring and willing are combined to yield a conception of humankind and the world in which the horizon of improvement of the human lot is low and clouded. Hobbes is nevertheless a prototypically modern, and indeed a proto-Enlightenment thinker, partly in virtue of the humanist conception of humanity he takes from Christianity, and partly in virtue of the rationalist conception of reason he takes from Descartes. This latter conception, in which only that which survives systematic doubt has rational justification, is deployed by Hobbes in the project of reconstructing moral reasoning in the axiomatic form of a moral geometry. It is further allied with Hobbes's subjectivist conception of value to yield an account of political allegiance in terms of the rational choice of representative human subjects, considered in abstraction from the cultural traditions and historical narratives in terms of which human identities are in practice constituted. Aside from his particular account of human motivation in terms of death-avoidance, and his distinctive conception of reasoning as a reckoning of prudential consequences mediated through laws of nature,

Hobbes's model of political order as being generated by the rational choices of universal human subjects was a paradigm for all Enlightenment political thought. The same model of political order, more explicitly dependent on the moral premises of Christian theism, recurs in Locke's thought, and, underpinned by a very different conception of practical reasoning, in Kant.

A commitment to rationalism – whether it was made in the form of the project of a rational or natural religion, or aspired to a wholly secular content – is one of the defining elements of the modernist world-view of which the Enlightenment project is the most powerful expression. In this, as in other decisive respects, the Enlightenment is at once continuous and discontinuous with the central Western tradition which preceded it and which in modified form it continues to exemplify. Despite dissenters who recur throughout Western intellectual history – such as the Sophists and the many varieties of fideist, from Tertullian to Kierkegaard and Shestov – the central intellectual tradition of Western culture was and remains foundationalist and representationalist. (By contrast with fideism, scepticism, in both its classical and modern varieties, is best thought of as a variation on the central Western tradition, in which the representationalist and foundationalist project is perceived to have foundered, but is not therefore abandoned.) In it human thought tracks or mirrors the contours of a single independent reality, and does so from a ground of truths, even if they be only the sense-impressions of naive empiricism. The dominant modern conception of reason is that which Charles Taylor summarizes, when he refers to

> the picture of an agent who in perceiving the world takes in 'bits' of information from his or her surroundings, and then 'processes' them in some fashion, in order to emerge with the 'picture' of the world he or she has; who then acts on the basis of this picture to fulfill his or her goals, through a 'calculus' of means and ends.[19]

Taylor notes that modern reason, so conceived, expresses to some extent the common sense of our civilization, and has its roots in pre-modern conceptions. In its project of developing a non-perspectival representation of things, a 'view from nowhere' – whether through Descartes's clear and distinct ideas, Locke's rules of evidence or the methodological conventions of Popper – modern reason is at one with ancient rationalism. The conception of intellectual inquiry as tending to convergence on an absolute conception of the world is what unites rationalism in all its forms – including pragmatism, as it is found in the thought of C. S. Peirce and many others. The rationalisms of the Enlightenment were critical and contestatory of their cultural inheritance, but they were none the less developments of its founding projects in pre-Socratic logocentrism and in Socratic inquiry, with the latter's categorical distinction between truth and opinion, and its unshakeable conviction of the identity of knowledge, virtue and emancipation, in human life. Of course, in late medieval times, following the rediscovery of Aristotle, rationalist conceptions were yoked to Christian purposes in the synthesis of Greek and Hebraic traditions attempted in the thought of Aquinas; and Plato's rationalism had long been incorporated in Christian Neo-Platonism. In the thinkers of the Enlightenment, religious beliefs are retained, if at all, only in a naturalized form, as part of a Deist rational theology. What is most distinctive of the rationalisms of the Enlightenment, however, is the identification of the growth of knowledge with the practice of science. It is this step which marks the difference of modern from ancient or medieval rationalism.

It is not so much the Enlightenment's conviction that intellectual inquiry can disclose the structure of things to humankind as its affirmation that experimental science is the supremely authoritative source of human knowledge that gives Enlightenment rationalism its distinctive flavour. Similarly, from the founding period of Greek philosophy onward, Western culture had harboured the project of giving moral life a foundation in reason. But, whereas pre-modern rationalism had sought a ground for morality in an order of things that was independent of humankind – in Aristotle's metaphysical biology and cosmology, in Plato's conception of the timeless and changeless Forms, in Aquinas's theistic restatement of the Aristotelian conception of natural law – the project of the Enlightenment was the bolder, and more hubristic one of founding a reconstructed morality on autonomous human reasoning alone. Despite their very different views of the relations of reason with the passions, Hume and Kant were at one in affirming that morality must be grounded solely in the autonomous activity of the human species, and depended at no point on the truths of religion or on appeal to any extra-human reality. If, in Kant, the content of morality was guaranteed by covert – and, from the standpoint of Kant's official philosophy, illicit – reliance on a teleological view of the world whose provenance was that of Christian theism, in Hume it was under-written by a doctrine of the constancy of human nature to which the experimental method which he advocated in the moral or social sciences lent little support. The central objection to the Enlightenment project of reconstituting morality as a construction of the human reason – even if, as in Hume, it be a highly conservative reconstruction which depends decisively on claims about human passions and social conventions – is that neither the experimental or empirical method which the thinkers of the Enlightenment revered in the sciences nor any other mode of rational inquiry will yield the morality on whose content they are all agreed. What empirical inquiry – anthropological, historical, sociological – discloses is an irreducible diversity of cultural forms, in which both the contents of morality, and the conception of morality itself, vary widely. And, contrary to the claims of Enlightenment thinkers to this day, there is no form of reasoning whereby this manifest diversity of moral cultures can be corralled within the ring-fence of a single universal civilization.

This was one of Nietzsche's central arguments against the Enlightenment project – that the evidences of history and our knowledge of other cultures offer no support for the Enlightenment idea (frequently affirmed by Hume) of a universal consensus on the essential content of morality. Nietzsche's critique of the Enlightenment project of a universal rational morality had other sources, of course: most particularly, his suspicion of the classical and Christian conception of the unity of the virtues. As Alexander Nehamas puts it, in the best recent study of Nietzsche's thought, Nietzsche held that 'evil features are not simply ineliminable but actually necessary if any good features are to be possessed at all'.[20] This is not only a denial of the claim, common to Aristotle and Aquinas, that having one virtue entails having all the others, but also the counter-claim that possessing one virtue, or good quality, may presuppose having another quality or attribute that is vicious or evil. This counter-claim is only a statement, in the context of moral psychology, of one of Nietzsche's central insights – that the goods specified by morality often have among their necessary conditions things specified by morality as evil. In political contexts, as Nietzsche often observes, this dependency of the good upon the evil arises when states, with their systems of law and justice, are founded by acts of lawlessness, injustice and usurpation. This Machiavellian and Nietzschean insight is still far from having been absorbed by contemporary political thought. Still less understood is the most radical result of the Nietzschean critique – that not only the content but also the authority of morality must shift once it has been thoroughly naturalized. The Kantian-Christian conception of morality as a peculiar institution,[21] having unique authority in practical life over all other sources of value, is destroyed by the Nietzschean insight that conditions which morality specifies as immoral are necessary to the existence of morality itself.

In its most general terms, the upshot of the Nietzschean critique is that all valuation is perspectival. There is no view from nowhere which is 'the moral point of view'; there are only diverse moralities and value-perspectives.[22] The priority of 'morality' among value-perspectives is a mere prejudice, arising, partly, no doubt, from the illusion that there is a uniquely, and presumably immutable, moral viewpoint, that has authority for all human beings. Nietzsche's argument, however, is that few things in human life are more changeable or more variable than moral judgements. Indeed, our current conception of morality is itself a modern coinage: among the Greeks, *ethics* did not demarcate any peculiar sphere of uniquely weighty considerations, but rather the process of practical deliberation in which we come to a decision as to what we have best reason to do. According to Nietzsche, with the waning of Christianity – which is a development in Western cultural history, already far advanced, not a thesis in philosophical atheism – the conception of morality as a uniquely authoritative sphere of valuation and practical reasoning whose principles are binding upon all is bound to lose credibility and, ultimately, coherence. In this Nietzschean perspective, the Enlightenment project of unifying all values under the aegis of a rational reconstruction of morality is merely a long shadow cast in the slow eclipse of Christian transcendental faith.

For Nietzsche, of course, the project of a rational morality is at least as old as Socrates, and is coterminous with the practice of 'philosophy'. In such a Nietzschean perspective, the Enlightenment was an attempted synthesis of the Socratic identification of knowledge with virtue with a morality whose content derived principally from Christianity: the Enlightenment project was for modernity what Thomism was for the medieval world. The Enlightenment project failed because the radical empiricism of modern science, when applied to the history and sociology of morals, revealed no human consensus but instead an ultimate diversity of moral perspectives. As Horkheimer and Adorno put it in their book, *Dialectic of Enlightenment*: 'Ultimately the Enlightenment consumed not just the symbols (of social union) but their successors, universal concepts, and spared no remnant of metaphysics'.[23] It was bound to fail for another and larger reason. Modern science, in so far as it is more than a Baconian instrument for the mastery of nature, depends on a faith in an ultimate scheme of things that is ultimately metaphysical and, according to Nietzsche, Platonistic. This metaphysical faith ceases to be available to us as the transcendental affirmations of Christianity become ever fainter traces in Western culture. In consequence, science becomes perceived to be itself perspectival in character; it is that perspective whose objects are the pragmatic ones of predictability and control of nature. For Nietzsche, this transformation in the cultural role of science occurs not as an effect of any development in philosophy, but in tandem with the cultural decline of Western religion. Epistemological realism in the philosophy of science – the Platonistic idea of science as the quest for truth – ceases to be credible because metaphysical realism has ceased to be a live cultural option. Just as one may speak of Nietzsche's atheism as methodological, so one may term his view of science as that of a methodological pragmatist.

In this ironical development – as yet far from being completed – scientific inquiry, whose roots are in a Platonistic and Christian metaphysical faith, produces a disenchantment of the world which issues in a view of science as merely that human practice whose goal is control of nature. Nietzsche may hold to a position in the theory of knowledge that can properly be called *perspectivist* or *irrealist*; if so, this position may be worth exploring in the theory of value also, since it may offer a refreshing alternative to the old dichotomies of subject and object, fact and value, which have dominated discourse about both morality and science. As I interpret him, however, Nietzsche is not primarily concerned to advance any thesis in philosophy, but rather to offer a diagnosis of our culture. His thesis is that the permeation of Western culture by the critical Socratic spirit and by the radically experimental methodology of science has displaced all transcendental faiths, including that which animated science itself, and removed the very idea of an absolute point of view on things from the cultural lexicon. The emergence of science as the supreme epistemic authority reaches its apogee in the fracturing of any unitary world-view into a plurality of incommensurable perspectives, with science itself expressing an instrumentalist perspective on nature. Just as the Kantian-Christian conception of morality's unique authority over all forms of valuation is destroyed by Nietzsche's insight into the immoral preconditions of morality, so the Platonistic-Christian conception of science as the quest for an absolute point of view on the world is destroyed as the metaphysical faith which it expresses is undermined by scientific empiricism. As I understand it, the hollowing out of the public culture of modern Western societies of their animating conceptions of science and morality is at least part of what Nietzsche means by 'nihilism'. This self-evacuation of modern Western cultures and their consequent permeation by nihilism also captures Nietzsche's view on why the Enlightenment project – in which science was taken to be normative for all spheres of thought, including morality – could not but be self-defeating.

It is in Nietzsche, who inherited and completed the critical rationalism of the Enlightenment, rather than in the excesses of the reactionaries and romantics of the Counter-Enlightenment, that the definitive critique of the Enlightenment project is to be found. In a reactionary thinker such as Joseph de Maistre we are impressed by a modernity and a lucidity that a mere polemicist of tradition like Edmund Burke could never achieve; yet the reactive character of de Maistre's thought confines it within the conventions of thought which governed the Enlightenment itself. One of these assumptions, eminently Christian in origin, was that of the meaningfulness of human history, of which E. M. Cioran writes, in his notable essay on de Maistre:

> To attribute a meaning to the historical process, even one derived from a logic immanent to the future, is to subscribe, more or less explicitly, to a form of Providence. Bossuet, Hegel, and Marx, by the very fact that they assign a meaning to events, belong to the same family or at least do not essentially differ from each other. . . . To turn from a theological or metaphysical conception to historical materialism is simply to change providentialisms.[24]

The same insight is expressed by Max Horkheimer, in his celebrated essay on 'Schopenhauer Today':

> A new vision of the future world replaced the old: a universal rational society. From St. Augustine to Bossuet history had been understood as progress, as the history of salvation, in which the messianic kingdom was the necessary goal. Translating this into the secular sphere, Holbach and Condorcet saw social history as the path to earthly fulfillment. . . . The one thing which the empiricism of the European Enlightenment had in common with the rationalism it superseded was that the image of the future was couched in concepts which were as if innate and could dispense with empirical verification: liberty, equality before the law, protection of the individual, property.[25]

The idea of a universal human narrative, particularly one informed by moral categories of suffering and redemption, belongs in the Enlightenment because it belongs to the Christian civilization whence the Enlightenment came. It is an idea that neither Burke nor even de Maistre, or any of the Enlightenment's reactionary critics, were able to challenge. The idea of a universal history was unavoidable for them, as part of their unquestioned cultural inheritance, and remained so in Europe until Herder and his followers advanced an alternative conception of human history as an exfoliation of incommensurable cultures. This idea – though it was combined in Herder's own thought with an idiosyncratic version of providentialism – struck at the roots of the Enlightenment philosophy of history because it also undermined the Christian conception of the universal history of the species. Yet the Romantic thinkers whom Herder inspired shared with the Enlightenment a humanist anthropology, which is a central element in any modernist world-view. In truth, the Enlightenment and the Counter-Enlightenment were currents of thought watered by the same stream of humanism, which flowed into and strengthened one another. If, for example, Hume's scepticism about natural necessity fed modern irrationalism by its influence on J. G. Hamman and thereby upon Hamman's great disciple Kierkegaard,[26] it is no less true that Kant's idea of the autonomy of the will, severed from its rationalist matrix, and transformed into a radical humanist doctrine of self-creation, informed Romantic thought. Indeed, as Heidegger has correctly argued, the thought of Nietzsche himself is moulded by humanist assumptions. However, as we shall see in the last section of this inquiry, Heidegger's own thought is not wholly free of traces of humanism.

Nietzsche's thought represents at once the culmination and the self-overthrow of the Enlightenment because in it a humanist affirmation of humankind's self-creation, and of the subordination of the non-human world to human will and valuation, that is expressive of the Enlightenment at its most radical, is advanced without the undergirding theory of knowledge or philosophy of history which supported humanism in the Enlightenment project. To be sure, Nietzsche's radical humanism owes much to Christian traditions, and is scarcely conceivable in other cultural contexts, such as those of Hinduism or Buddhism, Taoism or Shinto, the ancient Greek culture captured in the *Iliad*, or the traditions of Judaism: probably only someone steeped in Christian sensibility could have envisaged such an absurdity as the *Übermensch*. This is only to underscore the debts of Enlightenment humanism to Christianity. Nietzsche's thought accomplishes the dissolution of the Enlightenment project, because in it the apotheosis of human subjectivity is combined with a subversive critical reason and only the will-to-power remains. Without endorsing Heidegger's own interpretation of Western history, in which the history of philosophy and the history of Western peoples are conflated, and the thought and cultures of some Western peoples are accorded an arbitrary priority in a suspect historical metanarrative, we can recognize a Heideggerian insight of great power in the claim that in the modern world Westernization means the triumph of instrumental reason. In the late modern period, as Nietzsche anticipated, instrumental reason would no longer be guided by an Enlightenment project that the self-consuming activity of critical reason had destroyed, but would express merely will-to-power in the technological domination of the earth.

It is this historical development of Enlightenment and Christian humanism that Heidegger finds most starkly expressed in Nietzsche's thought, and which Heidegger rightly sees as issuing in nihilism. As Heidegger puts it, in his great essay, 'The Word of Nietzsche':

> Nihilism, thought in its essence, is ... the fundamental movement of the history of the West. It shows such great profundity that its unfolding can have nothing but world catastrophes as its consequence. Nihilism is the world-historical movement of the peoples of the earth who have been drawn into the power realm of the modern age.[27]

As Heidegger goes on to explain, this world-historical movement of Western nihilism is expressed in the humanist project of subjugating and exploiting the earth that has now become global in its reach:

Man enters into insurrection. The world changes into object. . . . The earth itself can show itself only as the object of assault that, in human willing, establishes itself as unconditional objectification. Nature appears everywhere . . . as the object of technology.[28]

It is in the global reach of this Western nihilism, as mediated through the technology whereby Western people have sought to appropriate the non-human world, that the last phase of the modern age is accomplished. In this last period of modernity, Western instrumental reason becomes globalized at just the historic moment when its groundlessness is manifest. The embodiment of instrumental reason in modern technology acquires a planetary reach precisely when the animating humanist project which guided it is overthrown. Nothing remains of this project but the expansion of human productive powers through the technological domination of the earth. It is this conjunction of the global spread of the Western humanist project with the self-undermining of its most powerful modern embodiment in the Enlightenment that warrants the claim that we find ourselves now at the close of the modern age.

POST-MODERNISM AND ILLUSION

As a response, thinking . . . is a highly errant and in addition a very destitute matter. Thinking is perhaps, after all, an unavoidable path, which refuses to be a path of salvation and brings no new wisdom. The path is at most a field path, a path across fields, which does not just speak of renunciation but already has renounced, namely, renounced the claim to a binding doctrine and a valid cultural achievement or a deed of the spirit.

M. Heidegger, 'A Letter to a Young Student'[29]

Though there are modern and even Enlightenment thinkers who do not subscribe to any doctrine of progress, such as Hobbes and Hume, an historical philosophy which incorporates the idea of progress towards a universal civilization is integral to the Enlightenment project and central in the self-image of the modern age. Even now, towards the close of the modern period, when most of the elements of this modern self-image have been effaced or destroyed on the terrain of history, it remains common to identify modernization itself with the replication across the world of the original Western exemplars of modernity. Thus, modernization is equated with Westernization in the sense of secularization or liberalization, the spread of the institutions of Western civil society, the adoption by other cultures of Western morality, of individualism, or of the idea of progress itself. The notion that modernization means repeating the Western experience of modernity, and so of converging upon Western institutions and cultural forms, is itself one of the principal illusions of the modern age, subverted by many of the most decisive developments in modern history. At the same time, this deceptive self-image of modernity passes over and leaves unremarked the one sense in which modernization has meant Westernization – namely, the adoption by other cultures of an instrumental perspective on the earth which is ultimately nihilistic. Before this can be clarified, however, it may be useful to consider how the established self-image of the modern age is deceptive, and how it informs the work of many of those who think of themselves as post-modernists. Among the latter is Richard Rorty, whose provocative and instructive attempt at a post-modern liberalism reveals the dependency of much post-modern discourse on an interpretation of modern history that belongs integrally with the Enlightenment project.

For the historical philosophy which the Enlightenment project incorporates, in which cultural difference must in the end yield to rationality and generic humanity as these are embodied in a universal human civilization, modernization and Westernization are and must be one and the same thing. Whether the model for the universal civilization be American, as typically it is in our time, or (as it was for the most part in the eighteenth century) French, it is presupposed that the modernization of any culture inescapably involves shedding its indigenous cultural traditions and adopting those of the West. It is difficult to see how this presupposition survives the example of Japan's modernization during the Meiji period, in which Japan grafted industrialization and modern technology (including military, and especially naval technology) on to the intact stem of a wholly non-Occidental social structure and cultural tradition. It is fair to say that, whereas the technologies of the European Enlightenment were adopted wholeheartedly by Japan in its determination to avoid the fate of other Asian peoples who had suffered colonization by European powers, particularly those of China and India, the constitutive beliefs, or illusions, of the Enlightenment project were never accepted by any significant body of opinion in Japan, which remained as little culturally touched by these beliefs as it had been, earlier in its history, by Christianity. Western individualist moral culture, legalism, the belief in the meaningfulness of history and the universalist principles in terms of which Western cultural imperialism in Asia and elsewhere was given a philosophical rationale were rejected, or not taken seriously, in Japan during the period of its most intensive modernization. Elsewhere in Asia, and particularly in China, modernization entailed a breach, or an attempted breach, with indigenous cultural traditions, but not in Japan, where – as the destruction by Japan of the Russian Imperial Navy at Tsushima Straits in 1904, a 'brief sanguinary triumph'[30] over the West which triggered anti-colonialist movements all over Asia, suggests – it was most successful.

The modernization of Japan cannot without violence to historical reality be squared with the Enlightenment historical philosophy which equates it with Westernization. Nor can the modernization of Islamic cultures be assimilated to Western models in which it is accompanied by secularization. As Gellner has argued,[31] the distinctive characteristics of Islam are such that modernization works against secularization in most Muslim countries. It does so, in part, because the urban, literacy-based culture that goes with modernization strengthens the social position of Islamic scholars – a decisive social group in a scripturalist and legalist religion such as Islam. Further, and as a consequence, modernization promotes Islamic fundamentalism, not only as a reactive response to the perceived threat of Westernization, but also internally, as the stronger scripturalist traditions seek to purify religious practice of recent accretions. The idea that modernization and secularization go together, necessarily or typically, may be sustainable in respect of Christian countries, though the history of the United States provides a powerful counter-example, and it is not at all obvious that the development of societies whose religious traditions are those of Christian Orthodoxy will follow the same pattern. Even if, implausibly, such a generalization could be sustained in respect of all Christian cultures, it is wholly illegitimate to extend it – as European social theorists in the Enlightenment tradition from Marx onwards extended it – to other cultures and their religions. In fact, we have no reason to suppose that modernity and secularization are aspects, inseparably connected, of a single historical transformation. To make this supposition is like reasoning from the emergence of capitalist market institutions in England and parts of Northern Europe to the conclusion that flourishing market institutions go with, or even depend on, an individualist moral culture. This is a conclusion which it may have been reasonable for Marx to reach, given the evidences available to him, but it has been decisively overturned by the late-twentieth-century histories of the East Asian countries, the phenomenal success of whose market institutions seems to be accounted for partly by the background moral culture which is not individualist. In each case the mistake – which forms an integral part of the self-image of enlightened cultures – is to think that modernization means repeating the pattern of development of the European cultures, and ending up indistinguishable from them.

The historical reality is that fully modernized societies can come in many varieties: they need have none, or almost none, of the distinctive features of their original European exemplars. It may be true, for example, that the collapse of Soviet institutions, from 1989 onwards, is part of a global spreading of market institutions; but market institutions too come in many varieties, and it is a fundamental error to think that they are always, or even commonly, accompanied by the institutions of Western-style civil societies. This is yet another instance of the ruling error of the Enlightenment philosophy of history, which is the supposition that modernization compels the adoption of the cultural and political forms, generally secular and liberal, of the first European modern states and their successors. Without this Enlightenment historical philosophy, modern liberal cultures will appear in all their historical contingency, as singularities, which nothing in the nature of modernity itself underwrites. One of the central arguments I wish to defend here is that every defence of liberal practice as anything other than an aspect of the pursuit of a *modus vivendi* trades on a tacit philosophy of history of precisely this erroneous sort. Conversely, without the covert support it receives from such an historical philosophy, liberal practice has no special claim to be authoritative, even in societies in which it is long-standing, independently of the contingent contributions it makes to human well-being. The historical philosophy of the Enlightenment is a central element in the self-conception of enlightened liberal cultures; if they relinquish it, they cannot renew themselves as they were before, but must be transformed. This is to say that, even if they try to dispense with universalist claims, liberal cultures cannot do without a philosophy of history in which they are accorded a privileged status in modern history; but to say this is to say that liberal cultures depend on the Enlightenment project, and its illusions, for their very identity.

Richard Rorty has argued, skilfully and imaginatively, that liberal cultures have no need of the foundationalism expressed in the Enlightenment project, and have no reason to suppress awareness of their historical contingency. For Rorty, indeed, an ironical self-reflective awareness of the contingency of liberal discourse, subjecthood and community constitutes an enhancement of the liberal form of life, not a depletion of it. In this perspective, modern liberal cultures do not depend upon the distinctive illusions of modernity and of the Enlightenment, but are weakened by them. A post-modern liberalism would accept, even celebrate, the contingency of liberal culture, and would not see its foundationlessness as a lack: indeed, in Rorty's somewhat Nietzscheanized Deweyanism, the search for foundations itself betrays a lack of self-confidence on the part of liberal cultures. A post-modern liberal culture, accordingly, would be more recognizably, and more authentically liberal than its Enlightenment predecessor cultures, inasmuch as it would have extended critical reason and free discussion to the foundationalist project of the Enlightenment. The subjects of such a culture would find the absence of foundations for their practices no impediment to their solidarity; if anything, Rorty believes, giving up foundationalist projects and accepting the contingency of their practices and the fragility of liberal hopes would strengthen liberal ironists in their commitment to their form of life.

It is such an ironized form of liberal practice, detached from its historic matrix in the Enlightenment, that Rorty understands by post-modern liberalism. Rorty summarizes his project as the attempt:

> to reformulate the hopes of liberal society in a nonrationalist and nonuniversalist way – one which furthers their realization better than older descriptions of them do . . . in its ideal form,

the culture of liberalism would be one which was enlightened, secular, through and through. It would be one in which no trace of divinity remained, either in the form of a divinized world or a divinized self. . . . The process of de-divinization . . . would, ideally, culminate in our no longer being able to see any use for the notion that finite, mortal, contingently existing human beings might derive the meanings of their lives from anything except other finite, mortal, contingently existing human beings.[32]

Rorty contrasts his view – in which, he tells us, 'an ideal liberal society has no purpose except freedom',[33] and no justification for this devotion to freedom – with traditional liberalisms, and explains his meaning in calling his reformulated liberalism post-modern, as follows:

Hegelian defenders of liberal institutions are in the position of defending, on the basis of solidarity alone, a society which has traditionally asked to be based on something more than mere solidarity. Kantian criticism of the tradition that runs from Hegel through Marx and Nietzsche, a tradition which insists on thinking of morality as the interest of a historically conditioned community rather than 'the common interest of humanity', often insists that such a philosophical outlook is – if one values liberal practices and institutions – irresponsible. Such criticism rests on a prediction that such practices will not survive the removal of the traditional Kantian buttresses, buttresses which include an account of 'rationality' and 'morality' as transcultural and ahistorical. I shall call the Hegelian attempt to defend the institutions and practices of the rich North Atlantic democracies without using such buttresses 'post-modernist bourgeois liberalism'. I call it 'bourgeois' to emphasize that most of the people I am talking about would have no quarrel with the Marxist claim that a lot of those institutions and practices are possible and justifiable only in certain historical, and especially economic conditions. I want to contrast bourgeois liberalism, the attempt to fulfil the hopes of the North Atlantic bourgeoisies, with philosophical liberalism, a collection of Kantian principles thought to justify us in having those hopes. Hegelians think that these principles are useful for *summarizing* these hopes, but not for justifying them. I use 'post-modernist' in a sense given to this term by Jean-François Lyotard, who says that the post-modern attitude is that of 'distrust of metanarratives' . . . These metanarratives are stories which purport to justify loyalty to, or breaks with, certain contemporary communities, but which are neither historical narratives about what these or other communities have done in the past nor scenarios about what they might do in the future.[34]

Rorty's post-modern bourgeois liberalism is an historicist position inasmuch as it seeks to illuminate, and to improve, certain historical practices – those of liberal society – rather than to offer any foundation, or transcendental justification for them. It is also a pragmatist view, and an avowedly ethnocentric one, in that it takes matters of justification to be concerned with acceptability to particular communities, not with finding universally compelling foundations; and it embodies what he calls 'the American habit of giving democracy priority over philosophy'[35] in wishing to disengage public policy from philosophical inquiry. Rorty contrasts his own Deweyan position with Heidegger's by saying that Dewey's

'humanism' was not the power mania which Heidegger thought to be the only remaining possibility open to the West. On the contrary, it puts power in the service of love – technocratic manipulation in the service of a Whitmanesque sense that our democratic community is held together by nothing less fragile than social hope.[36]

In Rorty's post-modern liberalism, the disenchantment produced by the extension of critical reason to the foundationalist project of the Enlightenment is accepted, but is represented as the completion of that project, as giving rise to the possibility of a wholly secular, liberal and humanist culture, rather than – as Nietzsche conjectured, and as I myself believe – as signifying the self-undermining of that project.

Rorty's proposal for a post-modern liberalism is perhaps the most powerful attempt we are likely to see to reformulate liberalism in explicitly post-Enlightenment terms. It is nevertheless an exercise in illusion, since – like post-modernism generally – it seeks to shed the foundationalist claims of the modern humanist project while at the same time representing modernity on a Western model as a universal cultural condition. Rorty's post-modernism underestimates the role of the Enlightenment project in conferring a coherent identity on liberal cultures – particularly US liberal culture. It neglects the dependency of the public cultures of liberal societies on the historical philosophy of the Enlightenment – a dependency replicated, though at the same time repressed, in Rorty's own account of post-modern liberalism. And it vastly overestimates the degree to which contemporary liberal states harbour, and express, liberal cultures, where these are conceived as whole ways of life. These three features disable Rorty's post-modern liberalism fundamentally, since they impose on practitioners of liberal forms of life burdens of justification, not only with respect to those in other, non-liberal regimes but also in regard to those in liberal regimes who subscribe to non-liberal beliefs and practices, which post-modern liberalism cannot bear, but which it must address if – as I maintain – it is not a self-justifying form of life whose central elements are forced upon us as imperatives of modernity. As Rorty himself stresses, the requirements of justification are contextual or situational: what needs justifying to whom is a matter of the dialogic circumstance in which the demand for justification is made. In no modern state, not even the United States, is liberal culture so hegemonic as to have settled the agenda of justification on its own terms; in no modern state is liberal culture exposed only to immanent criticism. As a consequence, defenders of liberal practice have no option – not, to be sure, in virtue of any foundationalist conception of rationality, but instead because of their actual dialogic context – but to attempt to show its contribution to human well-being in terms that are not internal to liberal forms of life. To imagine that postmodern liberals are absolved of this responsibility is to suppose them to be beneficiaries of a cultural hegemony in their societies which exists in fact in none of them.

I have argued already that the idea that modernity necessitates convergence on the cultural forms of the English and North European exemplars of modernization is unhistorical and indefensible. Rorty's highly specific references to the cultures and political practices of the 'rich North Atlantic democracies' embody this unhistorical approach. The political cultures of France, Britain and the United States, say, have far less in common than lumping them together in the single category of 'North Atlantic democracies' reasonably implies. In France, powerful non-liberal political traditions have long existed, and continue to exist, as rivals to those which avow their paternity to the French Revolution; the idea of universal citizenship remains powerful, but there is a political consensus on monoculturalism; and the role of the distinctive discourse of the Enlightenment in the public culture is muted. In Britain, a powerful Hobbesian tradition has so far resisted incorporation into British institutions of anything akin to entrenched liberal rights or basic liberties; even the liberal conception of citizenship is not embodied in law or public discourse; and a pervasive scepticism, arising in part from the post-religious character of contemporary culture in Britain, and especially in England, makes the appeal of comprehensive ideology in any of its forms slight. In the United

States, liberal universalism is an ideology of undiminished strength, expressed in a legalist discourse of fundamental rights and in a commitment to multiculturalism which have no counterparts in any other modern state; profound popular Christianity and an Enlightenment commitment to world-improvement coexist and strengthen one another; and there is no tradition of thought or reflection, in the academy or in public life, that is not liberal. Assimilating the United States, France and Britain to a single category of 'North Atlantic democracies' is indefensible, given their large cultural and historical differences; indeed the category itself captures nothing deeply significant, but rather hypostatizes the alliances which emerged from the Second World War, and which are now dissolving, along with much else in the post-war settlement. It is indeed as an artefact of the post-war settlement, and not as anything deeper or more enduring, that we are bound to regard Rorty's allusions to 'the rich North Atlantic democracies'. (That they are no longer especially rich, by comparison with some of the East Asian countries, may be material to Rorty's argument, in so far as it seems to take for granted that liberal states will typically be among the most prosperous; but this is a point I shall pass over here.) In truth, the likelihood is that, now that the imperatives of the Cold War period are over, the European countries and the United States will increasingly decouple, not only strategically and economically, but also culturally, so that their cultural and political differences will become more, not less, decisive. It is difficult to believe that the forms of liberal culture will not diverge greatly, as a result of this likely decoupling, between the United States and the various European nations. Indeed, even as things stand now, Rorty's post-modern liberalism is an expression of American hopes, which are far from being shared by other liberal cultures, such as those in Europe.

That Rorty's paradigm for liberal culture is, in fact, Americocentric, is demonstrated by his endorsement of the core US liberal – and Enlightenment – projects of the political marginalization of culture and the development of a cosmopolitan world society. Thus Rorty writes that 'We can suggest that UNESCO think about cultural diversity on a world scale in the way our ancestors in the seventeenth and eighteenth centuries thought about religious diversity on an Atlantic scale: as something to be simply *ignored* for purposes of designing political institutions'.[37] And, in fleshing out his 'pragmatist utopia', Rorty tells us that:

> We see no reason why either recent social and political developments or recent philosophical thought should deter us from our attempt to build a cosmopolitan world-society – one which embodies the same sort of utopia which the Christian, Enlightenment, and Marxist metanarratives of emancipation ended.[38]

These and similar statements of Rorty's give the lie to a critic who argued in 1993 that 'Rorty's argument contains within itself an implicit defence of the world of nations, and thus a world of nationalisms'.[39] The very contrary is the case. Rorty *rejects* the central thesis of nationalism, which is that political order expresses, and presupposes, a common culture, and endorses the liberal Enlightenment project of privatizing culture, relegating it to the associational realm, and denying it embodiment in political institutions. He may be a US nationalist, but only in the all-too-familiar exceptionalist sense in which the United States is conceived, not as a nation in any historically recognizable sense, but instead as the model for liberal states everywhere, and indeed for all humankind. Rorty's post-modern liberalism differs from other forms of contemporary US liberalism in the candour and explicitness of its anti-foundationalism, but not in its content, which is an idealized version of the United States, conceived as the model for a 'cosmopolitan world-society', a universal civilization. This is an authentically Enlightenment liberalism, despite its post-modern self-description, because of its tacit philosophy of history – without which the US historical experience looks very much like an historical singularity. It is only if the US experience can plausibly be represented as more than a singularity that its practices can have more local authority. Rorty's historicist defence of liberal culture, like Hegel's and Dewey's, requires the support of general propositions about historical development, if it is to carry force for those – in the United States, let alone elsewhere – who are not already among its practitioners. For practitioners of non-liberal cultural forms, Rorty's defence of a liberal society that it 'has no purpose except freedom' will carry no weight, since they privilege other purposes and interests, such as the renewal of a valued way of life, over freedom. There may be and often are good Hobbesian reasons for compromise in a *modus vivendi*, but these are far from giving support to Rorty's American liberal project of politically disestablishing culture. Rorty's argument needs some such support, if it is even to carry weight with other liberals, such as John Stuart Mill and plausibly Isaiah Berlin, who believe that liberal institutions will be stable over a reasonable span of generations, only if they are embedded in particular national cultures, and who for that reason reject Rorty's Kantian and American liberal ideal in which cultural identity is privatized. Only a version of the Enlightenment philosophy of history in which the US model is hegemonic for all other societies, even liberal ones, would seem to assure this support.

The upshot is that a fullblooded acceptance of the contingency of liberal practices renders such practices merely incidents in the histories of particular cultures. Conversely, a fully postmodernist perspective will accord no special authority to liberal practice, and will certainly refrain from elevating one contemporary, and doubtless ephemeral element within it to the status of a 'pragmatist utopia' or a doctrine of 'social hope'. Post-modern perspectivism is bound to result in *Entzauberung*, or disenchantment, in regard to the local practices of liberal cultures, even more than those of others, precisely because the universalist claims of liberal philosophy have become embedded in the public culture of liberal societies. In removing from liberal practice the support of any universal narrative, disenchantment leaves liberal practices as particular practical expedients or strands in specific cultural traditions. In national cultures, such as those of France and the United Kingdom, of which liberal practice is only one element, the alteration produced by a genuine and comprehensive abandonment of the modern Enlightenment project may be expected to be significant but hardly dramatic; in the United States, where liberal culture comes closest to being hegemonic, it can scarcely be other than profound. More generally, Rorty's attempt to retain the cosmopolitan project of US liberalism parallels closely the attempt of some contemporary French thinkers to use post-modernist theory to buttress the traditional Left project of universal emancipation. In both cases, the relinquishment of the Enlightenment project undermines the liberal and Left project – though, as I shall argue, it lends no support to the Right project of cultural fundamentalism either. In other words, if Rorty is right in his belief, shared by Nietzsche, that the Enlightenment was a transitional and self-limiting episode in Western culture, and if he is mistaken in his apparent conviction that a version of the Enlightenment philosophy of history can survive the demise of the Enlightenment's foundationalist project, then Nietzsche's conclusion – that liberalism is the last casualty of the self-consuming critical reason celebrated in Enlightenment cultures – must be allowed to stand.

It may be useful at this point to sum up the criticisms I have made of Rorty's post-modern liberalism and connect them with my assessment of MacIntyre's project of reviving a pre-modern style of philosophical reasoning as a response to the incoherences of modernism. Rorty comments on MacIntyre's claim that contemporary moral discourse is incoherent by agreeing with it, but dissenting from MacIntyre's response: 'MacIntyre is right' he tells us,[40]

> in saying that contemporary moral discourse is a confusing and inconsistent mixture of notions that make sense only in an Aristotelian view of the world (e.g. 'reason', 'human nature', 'natural rights') with mechanistic, anti-Aristotelian notions that implicitly repudiate such a view. But whereas MacIntyre thinks we need to bring back Aristotelian ways of thinking to make our moral discourse coherent, I think we should do the opposite and make the discourse coherent by discarding the last vestiges of those ways of thinking.[41]

Here Rorty is undoubtedly on the right track in seeing that an Aristotelian reconstruction of morality presupposes an Aristotelian world-view of natural ends which has not been a viable cultural option since the rise of modern science. As Rorty puts his point, incisively:

> By dropping what he calls 'Aristotle's metaphysical biology', MacIntyre also drops the attempt to evaluate 'the claims of objectivity and authority' of 'the lost morality of the past'. For unless a knowledge of the function of the human species takes us beyond MacIntyre's Socratic claim that 'the good life for man is the life spent in seeking the good life for man', the idea of one narrative being more 'objective and authoritative' than another, as opposed to being more detailed and inclusive, goes by the board.[42]

Nor is Rorty's criticism blunted by MacIntyre's later work, which attempts to develop a somewhat relativistic Thomism by maintaining that the Thomist tradition resolves better than its Western rivals dilemmas which arise in all of them. It is not clear how the superiority of Thomism over its rivals is in MacIntyre's account to be established, if only because it is unclear which rivals he has in mind, and how much they have in common. Are non-Western intellectual traditions – the highly developed traditions of Mahayana Buddhism, as exemplified in the thought of Nagarjuna, say – to be judged wanting by standards internal to Thomism? And, if so, what has been shown by such a demonstration, if – as seems very plausible – the two traditions have too little in common to be comparable in the manner MacIntyre proposes? Such a result would seem to confirm their rational incommensurability rather than to overcome it. A neo-Thomistic attempt to rehabilitate a pre-modern style of philosophy, and thereby a pre-modern understanding of morality, by way of an account of tradition-dependent rationality must in any case fail, because – as Thomists themselves stress – Thomistic conceptions of the human good are inseparable from Thomistic metaphysics, if not from Thomistic theology. No such metaphysics is available to us today, however; indeed the very project of such a metaphysics is suspect, partly because, with the collapse of Aristotelianism, it could be sustained only with the support of theistic premises whose truth could not itself be – in a Thomistic or any traditional Christian perspective – tradition-dependent. Rorty's conclusion seems unassailable: however subtly pursued, MacIntyre's project of rehabilitating Aristotelianism is a hopeless one. It is true that rationality is tradition-dependent, and that in particular historical contexts some traditions emerge as more powerful than others in coping with problems which they have in common. In the historical context in which we find ourselves, which is that of the no man's land between the late modern age and early post-modernity, Aristotelianism is only one among a diversity of intellectual traditions, some non-Western, and some rationally incommensurable with it; but even in the more culturally parochial Western context in which comparative judgements of rationality are feasible, Aristotelianism must rank among the least promising traditions.

Rorty's own endorsement of a Baconian-Nietzschean position is revealing of the extent to which his own perspective is that of an unreconstructed modernist. He identifies Bacon's view with a mechanistic conception of nature and an instrumentalist conception of science, and rightly finds in Freudian accounts of the self a development of that Baconian view.[43] His preference for the later Wittgenstein's naturalistic and instrumentalist conception of language over that of the later Heidegger is further evidence of his modernism.[44] In the later Heidegger, language cannot be subordinated to human purposes or rendered transparent to human knowledge; even though it speaks through human beings, language often strains their understanding, whether because they cannot retrieve its sense, or because it is hinting at the unsayable.[45] Rorty's ultra-nominalist and instrumentalist conception of language as a set of tools for the achievement of human purposes is the direct successor to that of the Enlightenment, which (like Heidegger) Hamann and Herder incessantly, and rightly, criticized as expressing the modern humanist ideal of rational autonomy. It is partly because Rorty adopts this Enlightenment view of language, in which its expressive and constitutive role in relation to historic ways of life is devalued, that he is able to find his own pragmatist and cosmopolitan utopia unproblematic. It also makes possible his adherence to a Deweyan version of Nietzschean voluntarism, which is modern radical humanism allied to a thoroughly implausible American version of an Enlightenment philosophy of history.

Because its historical dependency on universalist claims has entered into its self-conception, if only by the back door of a tacit philosophy of history, liberalism cannot be transformed, easily and successfully, into a tradition. Like Christianity, to which it owes so much, liberalism must claim special status for itself – and does so, even in Rorty's ingenious attempt at a post-modern formulation of it. For liberalism to become merely one form of life among others would involve as profound a cultural metamorphosis as Christianity's ceasing to make any claim to unique and universal truth. Both would entail a mutation in the identity of the form of life as we have known it in historical practice. MacIntyre has observed perceptively that

> Like other traditions, liberalism has internal to it its own standards of rational justification. Like other traditions, liberalism has its own set of authoritative texts and its disputes over their interpretation. Like other traditions, liberalism expresses itself socially through a particular kind of hierarchy.[46]

There is this difference between liberalism and other, less hubristic traditions, however, that once its universalist claims are given up, liberal practice cannot avoid being humbled. Rorty's postmodern liberalism, once it is detached from its illicit modernist historiography, suffers a similar humiliation. In truth, liberalism is a tender blossom, which – like post-modernism – withers under the scorching glance of too much irony.

CONTINGENCY, DIVERSITY, AND MORTALITY

> *Releasement toward things and openness to the mystery belong together. They grant us the possibility of dwelling in the world in a totally different way. They promise us a new ground and foundation upon which we can stand and endure in the world of technology without being imperilled by it.*
>
> M. Heidegger, *Gelassenheit*[47]

Though the Enlightenment project of constructing a universal civilization has manifestly failed, the Westernizing impulse that it embodied has transmitted to nearly all cultures the radical modernist project of subjugating nature by deploying technology to exploit the earth for human purposes. This is, in fact, the real legacy of the Enlightenment project to humankind – the Baconian and Nietzschean, but also Christian and Marxian humanist project of turning nature into an object of human will. Emptied of its theistic and metaphysical content, and with the emancipatory promise of Enlightenment humanism manifestly illusory, Westernization impacts on the world's non-Occidental cultures in the late modern period as a form of revolutionary nihilism. Even those cultures, such as Japan, which have modernized without Westernizing, have been able to preserve their cultures and social structures from destruction by Westernization only by adopting conceptions and practices regarding the place of technology in cultural life and in respect of the relations of human activity with the earth that are prototypically Western. In this way, if in no other, the Enlightenment project of universal cultural homogenization has achieved its objectives.

At the same time, the Westernizing project of Enlightenment humanism has desolated traditional cultures in every part of the globe and visited devastation on their natural environments. The Soviet experience, in which an Enlightenment ideology wrecked the cultures of the Russian and many other peoples and a Western Promethean conception of human relations with the earth wrought irreversible damage to the environment on a vast scale, will likely go down in the longer perspective of history as merely a particularly dramatic episode in the world revolution of Westernization.[48] The Soviet collapse is probably best interpreted not, fortunately, as a victory for Western capitalism, but instead as a decisive moment in the global counter-movement against Westernization, now underway in many parts of the world, in which Occidental ideologies are repudiated and Western models of social life spurned; but there is no evidence, as yet, in the post-Soviet lands, in China or in Islamic countries, that the rejection of Western Enlightenment ideology is accompanied by resistance to the Western humanist project of the technological domination of the earth.

In the Western cultures, the foundations of Christian and Enlightenment humanism are now wholly eroded, but the universalist project which they animated is still far from being abandoned. The idea that Western civilization is simply one set of cultural forms among others remains as alien and unfamiliar as the idea that liberal regimes must expect to share the earth with others which will never adopt their institutions or political culture. In truth, the perception in the public cultures of Western societies that they in no sense constitute the germs of a universal civilization, if and when it comes to pass, will signify a major discontinuity in Western cultural history, since it will represent the acceptance that the West's foundationalist claims, on which its sense of privilege and superiority in respect of other cultures was grounded, are hollow. The foundering of the Enlightenment project is in this respect as threatening to the cultural fundamentalism of the Right in Western countries as it is to the emancipatory project of the Left. For in their anachronistic conviction that Western civilization is the paradigmatic cultural form for all humankind the vulgar epigones of cultural conservatism and the remaining *bien penseurs* of the Enlightenment are at one. It may be a shrewd instinct that has led Western conservatives in recent decades to throw in their lot with the paleo-liberal rationalism of the doctrinaires of the free market – the last form, perhaps, in which the Enlightenment project will find political embodiment. For the dissolution of the Enlightenment project cannot avoid carrying away much else in its wake, including some of the most primordial constitutive conceptions of Western civilization, to which Western conservatives are inextricably bound. For latter-day cultural conservatives, the Enlightenment may have been an unfortunate development in Western traditions, but it belongs authentically with these traditions; its overthrow cannot but be resisted, or denied, by them. Or, if it is accepted, it is only on the supposition that there are, or were, pre-Enlightenment Western traditions to which we can return. On the account developed here, by contrast, the consequences of the Enlightenment cannot be repaired by any retreat to tradition, since the same contradictions which brought to earth Enlightenment humanism also felled its predecessor, classical and Christian, cultures. The paradoxical situation in which we find ourselves now, in which Westernization has become in one decisive respect nearly universal at just the historical moment when the hollowing out of Western civilization by nihilism is virtually complete, and in which non-Occidental cultures are asserting themselves against the West while accepting its legacy of a nihilist relationship with technology and the earth, is one which no form of Western thought that is traditionalist or reactionary in its orientation can begin to grasp.

To attempt to prescribe for a recovery from Western nihilism is merely another form of Western humanist hubris. We can nevertheless discern a few of the steps we need to take, if we are to have any chance of opening a path through the ruins in whose shadows we presently live. The universalizing project of Western cultures, which in our historical context has become a nihilist expression of the will to power, must be surrendered, and replaced by a willingness to share the earth with radically different cultures. Such acceptance of diversity among human communities must not be a means of promoting ultimate convergence into sameness, but rather an expression of the openness to cultural difference. The acceptance of cultural diversity which is most needed is not the pluralism of plans and styles of life affirmed in Western liberal cultures, but a recognition of the reality of cultural diversity among whole ways of life. The political task is that of devising institutions in which communities and cultural traditions are given recognition and shelter, and in which their often conflicting claims are mediated and moderated.

In many parts of the world, such institutions can only be sovereign states which – unlike many existing nation-states – reflect an underlying national culture. The nation-state is not in this pluralist view a panacea, or – as in Wilsonian liberalism – a universal principle; it is an institutional device for the transmission of a common culture, which is appropriate to our circumstance in so far as it recognizes the contingency and the particularity of every common culture, and their irreducible diversity. Nation-building – which is the political task of the age, now that the unravelling of the post-war settlement is being followed by the fracturing of the nineteenth-century settlement, in Europe and throughout the world – will not always be possible, or desirable. In some circumstances – perhaps those of post-communist Russia, for example – the Hobbesian requirement of peace may mandate a neo-imperial framework of institutions; if so, it must, so far as it can, also satisfy the Herderian requirement that the common life of peoples or cultures be accorded recognition and protection. The animating project of pluralism is that different cultures should dwell on the earth in peace, without renouncing their differences. As is fitting in such a project, the institutions whereby they are enabled to do this will be diverse and variable, altering with circumstances and the needs of the communities concerned. For many Western countries, these institutions will be those of a liberal society, amended and reformed to reflect the contemporary reality of cultural diversity; but no universalist claims will be made on behalf of such experiments in *modus vivendi*.

Whatever its institutional forms, pluralism – by contrast with liberalism – expresses a surrender of the will to oneness and sameness which projects itself in Western universalism. (The Western will to universality need not be expressed in the terms of modern or Christian egalitarianism. Such a will was projected in the form of a hierarchy of domination in the racist *apartheid* regime of South Africa; it affirmed sameness through the assertion of difference.) In present circumstances, such a surrender implies resistance to such Western liberal projects as GATT – a project no less as radically hubristic, and as uniquely Western in inspiration as was Soviet communism – which aim to subject all human cultures and communities to the hegemony of unfettered technology and of global market institutions, as that is presently embodied in Western capitalism. In general, respect for the integrity of cultures, and for their differences, implies a view of political institutions in which they have the task of sheltering human settlements from the impoverishing cultural homogeneity that would otherwise be imposed upon them by the global imperatives of technology and of market institutions. Because of the historicity of human cultural forms, because human communities are constituted by narratives which span their generations, protecting them from impoverishment or destruction by global economic and technological forces means sheltering them from change; but it does not for that reason mean trying to recover any lost condition of unreflective rootedness. Resisting the hegemony of global technology and markets is a task that demands much skill and thought. Moreover, any community which attempts it is bound to confront the need to alter practices and institutions which have long expressed the nihilist relationship of human beings with the earth. It is legitimate, and indeed imperative, that we seek a form of rootedness which is sheltered from overthrow by technologies and market processes which, in achieving a global reach that is disembedded from any community or culture, cannot avoid desolating the earth's human settlements and its non-human environments. The form of rootedness that may thereby be achieved will be bound to differ from any that has existed hitherto, and it will be far from unreflective. It is part of the ironical dialectic of Enlightenment – like all true ironies, a fate to be endured, rather than a conundrum to be resolved – that protecting communities from its ravages will require all the resourceful rationality that disenchantment has engendered in us.

It is clear that local communities, by themselves, will be powerless in the face of these vast global forces. Indeed, in many contexts, the political institutions of single nations will be unequal to the tasks of constraining the workings of market institutions and limiting the invasive impacts of technology on their natural and cultural environments. Where this is so, regional institutions will be needed whereby the efficacy of national states can be enhanced; but such institutions properly work to tend and nurture distinctive cultures and communities, not – as has been the case with many transnational institutions thus far – to force on them an artefact of sameness. Such institutions, if they are to be able to counter the global forces of technology and of market institutions, rather than further entrenching them, must express and protect local and national cultures, by embodying and sheltering their distinctive practices. However, it is only if practices and understandings still exist other than those which embody the nihilist relationship with the earth that such political measures can assist in releasing us from nihilism. In somewhat Heideggerian terms,[49] we may say it is only if the 'earth' – the cultural ground of practices on which we live – is still fruitful that any such measures can be helpful in enabling us to dwell on the earth released from the imperative of the will to power which global technological and economic forces presently project. It is an open question whether the cultures of the Western peoples are still fertile in this sense.

The surrender of the will to power has its most important application in our relations with other forms of life, and with the earth. The project of subjecting the earth and its other life-forms to human will through technological domination is Western humanism in its final form. Its cultural ground, in a conception of the human species as a privileged site of truth, is pervasive in Western traditions; traces of it are present even in the thought of the later Heidegger, with its anthropocentric discourse of humankind as the clearing of Being.[50] It is difficult to envisage any path through the nihilism of contemporary Western culture which does not begin by clearing away the humanist conception of humankind's privileged place among other forms of life on the earth. Such a clearing is a necessary prelude to practices in which human beings seek to find harmony with the earth, rather than to master it, and devise technologies which assist them in this practice, instead of expressing their will to power. Here the mode of *Gelassenheit*, which Heidegger takes from the German mystics and particularly from Meister Eckhart,[51] in which we wean ourselves from willing and open ourselves to letting things be, is most needful in our circumstances. Contrary to much in even the later Heidegger, however, it is not openness to 'Being' that is needed, but instead an openness to beings, to the things of the earth, in all their contingency and mortality. Nor is entering the mode of releasement a matter of awaiting salvation by any god. It is true, and a vitally important truth, that the project of mastering technology, of subjecting it to human purposes, expresses a humanistic hubris, and ultimately a nihilism, that are themselves integral elements of the modern world-view.[52] To think that by wilfulness we can deliver ourselves from nihilism is itself a symptom of nihilism – indeed of nihilism in its most advanced form. But this is not to deny to human thought, or to human action, a vital preparatory role in making possible a turn in humankind's relation with the earth. Indeed the attitude which seems most consonant with *Gelassenheit* is that which is ready to exert human powers to the utmost in a vigilant guardianship over the things of the earth, but which leaves the event to 'the play of Being' – to the groundless contingency that makes and unmakes the world. Heidegger expresses such an attitude, perhaps, when he writes of language:

> This floundering in commonness which we have placed under the protection of so-called common sense, is not accidental, nor are we free to deprecate it. This floundering in commonness is part of the high and dangerous game and gamble in which, by the nature of language, we are the stakes.[53]

It is significant that, here and elsewhere, Heidegger speaks of a gamble and of play; his thought may be that, as in any wager, the upshot is not decidable by us, even though it is our very beings that are at stake. The sense of *Gelassenheit* which appears most consonant with our current situation in regard to the earth and the possibility of our dwelling in peace on it may be an application of this thought. By preparatory thought, and by well-judged action, including political action, we can open a path to the renewal of the 'earth' – of the cultural ground on which we stand; but we can no more bring about such a renewal by willing it than we can subject language to our purposes. We cannot even close off the possibility that the Western tradition cannot be renewed, such that its persistence is a danger to other cultural grounds which may yet be fruitful. In an idiom which partakes both of myth and science, it is a kindred thought which is expressed by theorists of Gaia, when they conjecture that the mortal earth may shake off the human species so as to gain for itself another lease on life.[54] The possibility that life on the earth may be preserved only by the expedient of catastrophe for the human species, like the possibility that the Western tradition cannot be renewed, is one to which any mode of thinking that is authentically free of humanism must open itself.

For giving up the humanism of the Enlightenment and its predecessor culture may not be a real possibility for modern Western cultures. The dissolution of the old moral forms, and of the old religions, with their humanist and universalist claims, which follows in the wake of the Enlightenment, may be a prelude to an irreversible – and, perhaps, not to be lamented – Western decline. The alteration in traditional conceptions of ethics and science, and indeed of thought, which comes with the abandonment of the central Western tradition of which the Enlightenment is the culmination and nihilism the result, may prove beyond the powers of Western cultures to absorb. It may be that the Western cultures are so deeply imbued with rationalism that they cannot tolerate a conception of ethics, for example, in which it is an aspect of the art of life, not to be distinguished categorically from prudence or aesthetics in its character, in which it shares with these practical arts a provisional character, and a local variability, which sits uncomfortably with both Socratic and Christian conceptions which are now elements in the common-sense self-understanding of our civilization. It may be that the status of science as the sole remaining accreditor of knowledge in Western cultures prevents them from perceiving the wholly pragmatic and instrumental practice it has now become. It may be that the humanist character of Christianity closes off for Western cultures any form of spirituality in which human hopes are not comforted and confirmed. And it may be that, though philosophy is so marginal an activity that it is redundant to speak of ending or transcending it, the calculative and representational mode of thinking which philosophy has privileged in modern times is now so hegemonic that the cultural space is lacking in which an alternative mode of thinking might occur. The present inquiry embodies the wager that another mode of thinking – found in some varieties of poetry and mysticism, for example – can assert itself against the domination of the forms of thought privileged by both science and philosophy in Western cultures. It is with these humiliated modes of thought that the prospect of cultural recovery – if there is such a prospect – lies. Only if the ground of Western cultures can renew itself through such modes of thought can any practical measure have lasting effect. The wager which this inquiry embodies, like that of the later Heidegger, at least in some of its aspects, turns on the chance that the power of calculative thought in contemporary Western culture is not irresistible. If, however, this wager proves to be a losing gamble, then the future for the Western cultures will be one of further hollowing out into nihilism, with eventual dissolution – or, worse, replication throughout the world as instruments of technological nihilism – being their fate.

In that event, any prospect of cultural recovery from the nihilism that the Enlightenment has spawned may lie with non-Occidental peoples,[55] whose task will then be in part that of protecting themselves from the debris cast up by Western shipwreck. Or it may be that even those non-Occidental cultures which have modernized without wholesale Westernization have nevertheless assimilated too much of the Western nihilist relationship with technology and the earth for a turning in man's relationship with the earth to be any longer a real possibility. If this were to be so, it would be consonant with the sense of releasement invoked in this inquiry, which encompasses an openness to ultimate danger, to the contingency and mortality not only of human cultures and of other living things, but also of the earth itself.

NOTES

1 AGAINST THE NEW LIBERALISM

1 Brian Barry, *Political Argument*, London: Routledge & Kegan Paul, 1965.
2 John Rawls, *A Theory of Justice*, Oxford: Oxford University Press, 1971.
3 Thomas Nagel, *Equality and Partiality*, Oxford: Oxford University Press, 1991.
4 Ibid., p. 177.
5 Stuart Hampshire, *Innocence and Experience*, London: Allen Lane The Penguin Press, 1989.
6 Allen Buchanan, *Secession*, Boulder, Colo.: Westview, 1991.
7 Robert Nozick, *Anarchy, State and Utopia*, Oxford: Basil Blackwell, 1974.
8 Loren Lomasky, *Persons, Rights and the Moral Community*, Oxford: Oxford University Press, 1987.
9 David Gauthier, *Morals by Agreement*, Oxford: Clarendon Press, 1986.
10 Joel Feinberg, *The Moral Limits of the Criminal Law*, 4 vols, Oxford: Oxford University Press, 1984–8.
11 Michael Sandel, *Liberalism and the Limits of Justice*, Cambridge: Cambridge University Press, 1982.
12 Alasdair MacIntyre, *After Virtue*, London: Duckworth, 1981.

13 Alasdair MacIntyre, *Whose Justice? Which Rationality?*, Notre Dame, Ind.: University of Notre Dame Press, 1988.

14 Michael Walzer, *Spheres of Justice*, New York: Basic Books, 1983.

15 Joseph Raz, *The Morality of Freedom*, Oxford: Clarendon Press, 1986.

16 Isaiah Berlin, *The Crooked Timber of Humanity*, London: John Murray, 1990.

17 *London Review of Books*, 14 May 1992.

2 NOTES TOWARD A DEFINITION OF THE POLITICAL THOUGHT OF TLÖN

1 R. Goodin and P. Pettit (eds) *A Companion to Contemporary Political Philosophy*, Oxford: Basil Blackwell, 1993.

2 Ibid., p. 176.

3 TOLERATION: A POST-LIBERAL PERSPECTIVE

1 F. A. Hayek, *The Constitution of Liberty*, Chicago: Henry Regnery, 1960, p. 64.

2 I have examined Berlin's idea of value-pluralism in my *Isaiah Berlin*, London: HarperCollins, Fontana Modern Master, 1994. A good summary explanation of his view is given by Berlin in 'The Pursuit of the Ideal' in his *The Crooked Timber of Humanity*, London: John Murray, 1990.

3 George Santayana, *Dominations and Powers: Reflections on Liberty, Society and Government*, New York: Charles Scribner's Sons, 1951, p. 238.

4 ENLIGHTENMENT, ILLUSION AND THE FALL OF THE SOVIET STATE

1 I refer, of course, to Francis Fukuyama's 'The End of History', *National Interest*, Summer 1989.

5 THE POST-COMMUNIST SOCIETIES IN TRANSITION

1 See my 'Harsh Birth Pangs of the New Order', *The Times*, London, 28 December 1989.

2 George Soros, *Nationalist Dictatorships versus Open Society*, New York: The Soros Foundations, 1993, p. 1.

3 George Soros, *Prospects for European Disintegration*, New York: The Soros Foundations, 1993, pp. 12–13.

4 I forecast the likely meltdown of the principal Western models in my 'From Post-Communism to Civil Society: The Reemergence of History and the Decline of the Western Model', *Social Philosophy and*

Policy, Liberalism and Economic Order, vol. 10, no. 2, Summer 1993, pp. 26–50.

5 As late as June 1991, James Baker, President George Bush's Secretary of State, stated in Belgrade that the United States intended to support Yugoslavia to maintain its 'unity and territorial integrity'. By that time the fact that the Yugoslav state was doomed was clear to many observers – including Mr Milosevic, who used the maintenance of Yugoslav integrity as a pretext to use the Yugoslav Army to attack Slovenia, Croatia and then Bosnia as they declared independence.

6 Francis Fukuyama, 'The End of History', *National Interest*, Summer 1989, and *The End of History and the Last Man*, New York, 1992. I have criticized Fukuyama's views in my *Post-liberalism: Studies in Political Thought*, London and New York: Routledge, 1993, pp. 245–50.

7 For this historical debate, see Alan Macfarlane, *The Origins of English Individualism*, Cambridge: Cambridge University Press, 1978.

8 I am thinking especially of the grand theory of cultural evolution that Hayek advances in his *The Fatal Conceit*, Chicago: University of Chicago Press, 1988; but Hayek's treatment of the emergence of market institutions in England as paradigmatic is evidenced in many of his earlier works.

9 I am indebted to conversations with Dr Stephen Davies on this point; but my use of it in the course of my argument is my responsibility alone.

10 See my 'The Risks of Collapse into Chaos', *Financial Times*, London, 13 September 1989.

11 For these data, I am indebted to Peter Stein, 'From Capitalist Success to Welfare-State Sclerosis', *Policy Analysis*, no. 160, 10 September 1991.

12 The quote is from Walter Eucken. See T. W. Hutchison, *The Politics and Philosophy of Economics: Marxists, Austrians and Keynesians*, Oxford: Basil Blackwell, 1981, p. 17.

13 I am indebted to Lord Dahrendorf for conversation on this topic.

14 Hutchison, *The Politics and Philosophy of Economics*, p. 160.

15 John Gray, 'The Delusion of Glasnost', *Times Literary Supplement*, 27 July 1989; reprinted in my *Post-liberalism*, ch. 8, p. 88.

16 Another possible exception is Hungary. For an excellent overview of Hungarian transition policy, see Janos Kornai, *The Road to a Free Economy: Shifting from a Socialist System: The Example of Hungary*, New York and London: W. W. Norton, 1990. I am not convinced of

the stability of the post-communist political settlement in Hungary, however, or even of that of its present borders.

17 For B. Lagowski's views, see A. Walicki, 'Liberalism in Poland', *Critical Review*, vol. 2, no. 1, pp. 3–38.

18 For Alksnis's views, see his interviews in *Le Nouvel Observateur*, 21–27 March 1991, and *Der Morgen*, 6 May 1991, where he advocates 'the introduction by force' of a market economy in Russia. For the Soyuz group, see E. Teague, 'The "Soyuz" Group', *Radio Liberty Research Bulletin*, 17 May 1991; and A. Kiva, *Isvestiya*, May 1991. The extent of involvement of such figures and groups in the failed coup of August 1991 remains unclear. For an early attempt at assessment, see my *The Strange Death of Perestroika: Causes and Consequences of the Soviet Coup*, London: Institute for European Defence and Security Studies, European Security Study 13, September 1991.

19 On this, see my 'Totalitarianism, Reform and Civil Society', in my *Post-liberalism*, ch. 12, pp. 164–8; and M. Heller and A. Nekrich, *Utopia in Power: The History of the Soviet Union from 1917 to the Present*, New York: Summit Books, 1986, ch. 1.

20 For Hayek's rationalistic critique of the idea of social justice, see his *Law, Legislation and Liberty: A New Statement of the Liberal Principles of Justice and Political Economy*, vol. 2: *The Mirage of Social Justice*, London: Routledge & Kegan Paul, 1976.

21 I have explained the idea of a choice-worthy public environment, using Joseph Raz's conception of an inherently public good, in my *Beyond the New Right: Markets, Government and the Common Environment*, London and New York: Routledge, 1993, ch. 3, pp. 111–14.

22 Sir Alan Walters and Steve H. Hanke, 'The High Cost of Jeffrey Sachs', *Forbes*, 21 June 1993, p. 52.

23 For an account of the Soviet and post-Soviet mafias in Russia, see Arkady Vaksberg, *The Soviet Mafia*, New York: St Martin's Press, 1992.

24 George Soros, 'Hard Currency for a Social Safety Net in Russia', *International Herald Tribune*, 5 January 1993.

25 See my *Beyond the New Right*, pp. 130–3.

26 The assessment comes from Professor J. P. Cole of the University of Nottingham and appeared in *The Independent*, 16 February 1993. The same article also reported that in both Dagestan and the Kalmyk Republic near the Caspian Sea, sand desert covered 15,000 hectares of pasture in 1954 but 1 million hectares in 1990; in the Arctic tundra, mining, prospecting and overgrazing of reindeer herds have caused the disappearance of 40 million hectares of pasture – an area larger

than Germany; and, in addition to the well-known death of the Aral Sea and the near-destruction of the world's largest fresh water lake, Lake Baikal, Europe's largest lake, Lake Ladoga near St Petersburg, is now poisoned by industrial pollution to the point at which St Petersburg's water supply is in jeopardy.

27   This assessment comes from David Roche, Director of Global Strategy at Morgan Stanley International, as cited in the *Financial Times*, 6 April 1992. I owe this reference to Robert Skidelsky and Liam Halligan's article 'Another Great Depression? Historical Lessons for the Nineties', *Social Market Foundation Report*, no. 2, London, 1992, p. 25.

28   According to the *New York Times*, 16 August 1993, there were 704 murders in Moscow in the first seven months of 1993, as compared with 462 in the comparable period of 1992. It is perhaps noteworthy that, despite this unprecedented crimewave in Russia, the murder rate in Moscow remains far lower than that in New York, a city of similar size. Such figures do not occasion in the United States the public comment that lower figures evoke in post-communist Russia.

29   I owe the expression 'chaos of nations' to Pierre Lellouche's excellent book, *Le Nouveau Monde de l'ordre de Yalta au chaos des nations*, Paris: Gasset, 1992.

30   In October 1989 I wrote: 'If it comes to pass, the fall of Soviet totalitarianism is most likely to occur as an incident in the decline of the occidental cultures that gave it birth, as they are shaken by the Malthusian, ethnic and fundamentalist conflicts which – far more than any European ideology – seem set to dominate the coming century' (*Post-liberalism*, p. 195).

6 AGONISTIC LIBERALISM

1   Stuart Hampshire, 'Justice is Strife', Presidential Address, American Philosophical Association, 1991 Pacific Division Meeting, *Proceedings and Addresses of the American Philosophical Association*, vol. 65, no. 3, November 1991, pp. 24–5.

2   There have, of course, been positivist exponents of the Enlightenment project who were in no sense liberals; it was against the greatest of these that John Stuart Mill directed his brilliant and unjustly neglected polemic, *Auguste Comte and Positivism*, Ann Arbor, Mich.: Michigan University Press, 1973. I ignore these positivist followers of the Enlightenment project because their form of thought is atavistic and is politically irrelevant. For the same reason I pass over Marxist versions of the Enlightenment project.

3   See my *Liberalisms: Essays in Political Philosophy*, London and New York: Routledge, 1989, pp. 231–3. Rawls summarizes his later views in his *Political Liberalism*, New York: Columbia University Press, 1993.

4   I refer, of course, to the thought of Michael Oakeshott. For a provisional assessment of Oakeshott's thought, in which its debts to a formalist and legalist tradition of liberalism are judged to be its principal weaknesses, see my *Post-liberalism: Studies in Political Thought*, London and New York: Routledge, 1993, ch. 4.

5   See my 'Berlin's agonistic liberalism', in my *Post-liberalism*, ch. 6; and my *Berlin*, London: HarperCollins, Fontana Modern Master, 1994, ch. 6.

6   Joseph Raz, 'Multi-culturalism: A Liberal Perspective' in his *Ethics in the Public Domain: Essays in the Morality of Law and Politics*, Oxford: Clarendon Press, 1994, ch. 6.

7   J. Raz, *The Morality of Freedom*, Oxford: Clarendon Press, 1986, ch. 13. I have considered the idea myself in my *Post-liberalism*, ch. 20.

8   Raz, *The Morality of Freedom*, p. 325.

9   Ibid., p. 327.

10 Bernard Williams, 'Conflicts of Values', in his *Moral Luck*, Cambridge: Cambridge University Press, 1981, ch. 5.

11 Raz, *The Morality of Freedom*, chs 7 and 8.

12 Isaiah Berlin, *Four Essays on Liberty*, Oxford: Oxford University Press, 1991, p. 130, footnote.

13 Rawls, *Political Liberalism*, Lecture VII. I have criticized this view in 'Liberalism and the Choice of Liberties', in my *Liberalisms*, ch. 9.

14 Stuart Hampshire, 'Liberalism: The New Twist', in *New York Review of Books*, vol. XL, no. 14, 12 August 1993, p. 46.

15 I have given an interpretation of Mill's comprehensive moral theory, and of its relations with his liberalism, to which I still hold, in my *Mill on Liberty: A Defence*, 2nd edn, London: Routledge, 1983.

16 It should go without saying that common cultural forms need not, and for anyone of liberal disposition should not, be integralist, in seeking to force on cultural minorities the choice of assimilation or ostracism; but I have spelt this out in my *Isaiah Berlin*, ch. 4.

17 The liberalism of Joseph Raz is akin to agonistic liberalism in having this communitarian dimension. On this, see my *Berlin*, ch. 4.

18 I have in mind, of course, Michael Sandel's *Liberalism and the Limits of Justice*, Cambridge: Cambridge University Press, 1982.

19 Isaiah Berlin, *The Crooked Timber of Humanity*, London: John Murray, 1990, p. 80.

20 Ibid., p. 85.

21 H. L. A. Hart, *The Concept of Law*, Oxford and New York: Oxford University Press, 1961, pp. 189–95.

22 Stuart Hampshire, *Innocence and Experience*, London: Allen Lane The Penguin Press, 1989.

23 On the absurdist aspects of Fukuyama's analysis, see my *Post-liberalism*, ch. 17. For Fukuyama's view, see his *The End of History and the Last Man*, New York: The Free Press, 1992.

24 L. Wittgenstein, *Remarks on the Foundations of Mathematics*, Oxford: Basil Blackwell, 1956.

25 See Richard Rorty, *Contingency, Irony and Solidarity*, Cambridge: Cambridge University Press, 1989, pt. 1.

26 Raz, *The Morality of Freedom*, pp. 198–200.

27 I have discussed the relevance of the East Asian models, and the irrelevance of the Western model to the transitional post-communist states, in 'From Post-Communism to Civil Society: The Reemergence of History and the Decline of the Western Model', *Social Philosophy and Policy*, vol. 10, no. 2, Summer 1993, pp. 26–50.

28 I have discussed the self-defeating effects of Western liberal individualism in *Beyond the New Right: Markets, Government and the Common Environment*, London and New York: Routledge, 1993.

29 Isaiah Berlin, 'Herzen and Bakunin on Liberty', in his *Russian Thinkers*, Harmondsworth: Penguin Books, 1978, p. 94.

30 Isaiah Berlin, 'The Originality of Machiavelli', in his *Against the Current*, Oxford: Clarendon Press, 1991, pp. 74–5.

7 THE UNDOING OF CONSERVATISM

1 F. A. Hayek, *The Constitution of Liberty*, Chicago: Chicago University Press, 1960, p. 41.

2 I have discussed some aspects of commercial expression in *Advertising Bans: Administrative Decisions or Matters of Principle?*, London: Social Affairs Unit, 1991.

3 For a good statement of the contemporary New Left position, see Hilary Wainright, *Arguments for a New Left: Answering the Free Market Right*, Oxford and Cambridge, Mass.: Blackwell, 1994.

4 I refer, of course, to Michael Oakeshott, and in particular to his essay, 'On Being Conservative', in his *Rationalism in Politics and Other Essays*, Indianapolis, Ind.: Liberty Press, 1991.

5 Edward Luttwak, 'Why Fascism is the Wave of the Future', *London Review of Books*, 7 April 1994, pp. 3, 6.

6 Adam Smith, *Lectures on Jurisprudence*, Indianapolis, Ind.: Liberty Classics, 1982, pp. 539–40.

7 Ibid., p. 541.

8 This is a point, made in regard primarily to British working-class communities, by Jeremy Seabrook in T. Blackwell and J. Seabrook, *The Revolt against Change: Towards a Conserving Radicalism*, London: Vintage, 1993.

9 The claim that it is the disappearance of authority that is the defining feature of the modern age is made by Hannah Arendt, and echoed by Alasdair MacIntyre, who adds the important rider that in a world without authority technical and managerial expertise will serve as its surrogate. See H. Arendt, *Between Past and Present*, Harmondsworth: Penguin, 1996, and Alasdair MacIntyre, *After Virtue*, London: Duckworth, 1981. He might have further noted that medical and therapeutic discourse tends to displace moral judgement and practice.

10 In the subtlest versions of this approach, of which that of James Buchanan is pre-eminent, the drastic simplification involved in the adoption of the *homo economicus* model of political behaviour is candidly acknowledged. The epistemology underlying this view is clearly instrumentalist or pragmatist. On Buchanan's work, see my 'Buchanan on Liberty', in my *Post-liberalism: Studies in Political Thought*, London and New York: Routledge, 1993, ch. 5.

11 See Sir James Goldsmith, *The Trap*, London: Macmillan, 1994, ch. 2, for a masterly demolition of the usual arguments for global free trade, and an authoritative warning of its dangers.

12 Herman E. Daly, 'From Adjustment to Sustainable Development: The Obstacle of Free Trade', in *The Case Against Free Trade: GATT, NAFTA, and the Globalization of Corporate Power*, San Francisco, Calif.: Earth Island Press, 1993, pp. 126–7.

13 On Oakeshott and Santayana, see my *Post-liberalism*, chs 2 and 6.

14 That the disposition to constitute for themselves particular local identities is universal among human beings was maintained by J. G. Herder and other thinkers of what Isaiah Berlin terms the Counter-Enlightenment. For an exposition and assessment of such views in the context of an exploration of Berlin's contemporary attempt to reconcile them with liberalism, see my *Berlin*, London: HarperCollins, Fontana Modern Master, 1994.

15 Oakeshott, *Rationalism in Politics and Other Essays*, p. 410.

16 On this remarkable case, see my *Post-liberalism*, p. 83.

17 Edward Goldsmith, *The Way: An Ecological World-view*, London: Rider, 1992, ch. 8.

18 George Santayana, *Dominations and Powers: Reflections on Liberty, Society and Government*, New York: Charles Scribner's Sons, 1951, p. 340.

19 On Mill's idea of the stationary state, see my 'An Agenda for Green Conservatism', in my *Beyond the New Right*, ch. 4.

20 For an exception, see Fred Ikle, *National Review*, February 1994.

21 I owe my understanding of the embeddedness of economic institutions in cultural traditions to conversations with Edward Goldsmith.

22 See my 'The Moral Foundations of Market Institutions', in my *Beyond the New Right*, ch. 3.

23 I refer to the liberal political philosophy of Joseph Raz, which I have discussed in my *Beyond the New Right*.

24 I have discussed the untransparency of value, and its implications for liberal theory, in my *Post-liberalism*, 'What is Dead and What is Living in Liberalism', ch. 20.

25 For a statement of this criticism of Raz, see B. Parekh, 'Superior People: The Narrowness of Liberalism from Mills to Rawls', *Times Literary Supplement*, 25 February 1994.

26 For a statement of this communitarian view, see Michael Sandel, *Liberalism and the Limits of Justice*, Cambridge: Cambridge University Press, 1982.

27 The best contemporary exposition of this reactionary view is probably Roger Scruton's *The Meaning of Conservatism*, Harmondsworth: Penguin, 1980.

28 David Willets, *Civic Conservatism*, London: Social Market Foundation, 1994.

29 I have discussed the idea of a negative capital tax in *Beyond the New Right*, p. 153, and I have criticized neo-liberal proposals for a negative income tax in chs 1 and 3 of the same book.

30 David Ricardo, *Principles of Political Economy and Taxation*, London: J. M. Dent, 1911, pp. 266–7. Ricardo's conclusions about the deleterious impact of machinery on the interests of labourers have been supported by Paul Samuelson in his 'Mathematical Vindication of Ricardo on Machinery' in *Journal of Political Economy*, vol. 96, 1988, pp. 274–82, and 'Ricardo was Right!', *Scandinavian Journal of Economics*, vol. 91, 1989, pp. 47–62. An excellent critique of the conventional arguments for free trade is to be found in the papers collected in *The Case Against Free Trade: GATT, NAFTA, and the*

Globalization of Corporate Power. I am indebted to Edward Goldsmith for drawing this invaluable book to my attention.

31 Sir James Goldsmith, The Trap.

32 I attempt such a tour d'horizon in, 'An Agenda for Green Conservatism' in my Beyond the New Right, ch. 4. I hold still to most of the views on policy defended there, without wishing to defend them mainly in conservative terms.

33 See my Beyond the New Right, ch. 3.

34 I have developed a case for voucher schemes for schools, drawing not on neo-liberal thought but on the work of Ivan Illich, in 'Agenda for Green Conservatism' in my book, Beyond the New Right, ch. 4.

8 AFTER THE NEW LIBERALISM

1 See my 'Against the New Liberalism', Times Literary Supplement, 3 July 1992.

2 I have discussed the unchosen character of cultural identity, with particular reference to Zionism, in my study of the thought of Isaiah Berlin, Berlin, London: HarperCollins, Fontana Modern Master, 1994.

3 For an assessment of Oakeshott's political thought, see my 'Oakeshott as a Liberal' in my book, Post-liberalism: Studies in Political Thought, London and New York: Routledge, 1993, pp. 40–6.

4 For a canonical statement of Roger Scruton's view, see his 'In Defence of the Nation-State', in J. C. D. Clark (ed.) Ideas and Politics in Modern Britain, London: Macmillan, 1990.

5 I have criticized the project of a global free market, in the context of recent proposals for global free trade, in 'An Agenda for Green Conservatism', in my Beyond the New Right: Markets, Government and the Common Environment, London and New York: Routledge, 1993, ch. 4.

9 FROM POST-LIBERALISM TO PLURALISM

1 J. S. Mill, On Liberty, in John Stuart Mill, On Liberty and Other Essays, ed. John Gray, Oxford and New York: Oxford University Press, World's Classics, 1991, pp. 13–14.

2 I have offered a critical assessment of Feinberg's restatement of Millian liberalism in my book, Post-liberalism: Studies in Political Thought, London and New York: Routledge, 1993, ch. 16.

3 See 'What is Dead and What is Living in Liberalism', in my Post-liberalism, ch. 20. An earlier version of some of these arguments is developed in 'After Liberalism', in my Liberalisms: Essays in Political Philosophy, London and New York: Routledge, 1989, ch. 12.

4   I have discussed Berlin's version of agonistic liberalism more comprehensively in my *Berlin*, London: HarperCollins, Fontana Modern Master, 1994.

5   I develop an extended argument for this view of mine in the last chapter of my *Berlin*.

6   I argue this in 'What is Dead and What is Living in Liberalism'.

7   See my *Post-liberalism*, pp. 286–7.

8   Ibid., pp. 319–20.

9   Ibid., pp. 314–15.

10 Ibid., p. 318.

11 Joseph Raz, *The Morality of Freedom*, Oxford: Clarendon Press, 1986.

12 I discuss the contrastive relations between civil society and totalitarianism in 'Totalitarianism, Reform and Civil Society', in my *Post-liberalism*, pp. 156–95.

13 For a good statement of his criticism of liberalism, see Roger Scruton, 'In Defence of the Nation-State', in J. C. D. Clark (ed.) *Ideas and Politics in Modern Britain*, London: Macmillan, 1990.

14 I develop an extended critique of the political thought of the New Right in my *Beyond the New Right: Markets, Government and the Common Environment*, London and New York: Routledge, 1993.

15 On this, see B. Parekh, 'Superior People: The Narrowness of Liberalism from Mill to Rawls', *Times Literary Supplement*, 25 February 1994.

16 See Raz, *The Morality of Freedom*.

17 In his reply to his critics. See Joseph Raz, 'Facing Up: A Reply', *University of Southern California Law Review*, vol. 62, March–May 1989, nos 3 and 4, pp. 1227 *et seq.*

18 I refer in particular to Raz's 'Multiculturalism: a Liberal Perspective', in his *Ethics in the Public Domain*, Oxford: Clarendon Press, 1994, ch. 7, in which the strongly assimilationist position he had adopted in respect of illiberal cultural enclaves within a broader liberal society is tempered and qualified.

10   ENLIGHTENMENT'S WAKE

1   M. Heidegger, *Discourse on Thinking: A Translation of Gelassenheit*, New York: Harper & Row, 1966, p. 60.

2   Alasdair MacIntyre, *After Virtue*, London: Duckworth, 1981, p. 38.

3   Ibid., pp. 49–50.

4   Ibid., p. 60.

5   Ibid., p. 107.

6   Ibid., p. 108.

7   Ibid., p. 111.

8   Alasdair MacIntyre, *Whose Justice? Which Rationality?*, Notre Dame, Ind.: University of Notre Dame Press, 1988, p. 335.

9   Ibid., p. 145.

10 Alasdair MacIntyre, *Three Rival Versions of Moral Inquiry: Encyclopaedia, Genealogy and Tradition*, London: Duckworth, 1990, pp. 172–3.

11 The most damning evidence for the deep and uncontingent character of Heidegger's engagement with Nazism of which I am aware is in the memoir of his pupil, Kurt Lowith, as reprinted in *The Heidegger Controversy*, ed. Richard Wolin, Cambridge, Mass.: MIT Press, 1993, as 'My Last Meeting with Heidegger for Rome', pp. 140 *et seq.*

12 For a very perceptive account of Nazism and Fascism, their many differences and their uniquely Western roots, see Edmund Stillman and William Pfaff, *The Politics of Hysteria*, London: Victor Gollancz, 1964.

13 Isaiah Berlin, *Against the Current*, Oxford: Clarendon Press, 1991.

14 See Richard Rorty, *Essays on Heidegger and Others, Philosophical Papers*, vol. 2, Cambridge: Cambridge University Press, 1991.

15 See my *Post-liberalism: Studies in Political Thought*, London and New York: Routledge, 1993, p. 271.

16 M. Heidegger, *What is Called Thinking?*, New York: Harper & Row, 1968, p. 160.

17 John Lukacs, *The Passing of the Modern Age*, New York: Harper & Row, 1970, p. 13: 'Centuries ago the Middle Ages were passing, without people noticing what was passing. The very term "Middle Ages" and the division of history into Classic-Middle-Modern Age did not become accepted notions until at least two hundred years after the waning of the Middle Ages. To us, the passing of the Modern Age and the recognition of its passing are much closer, at times so close as to be almost simultaneous.'

18 For an interesting study of Bacon in his relations with Nietzsche, see Laurence Lampert, *Nietzsche and Modern Times*, New Haven, Conn. and London: Yale University Press, 1993.

19 Charles Taylor, 'Engaged Agency and Background', in Charles B. Guignon (ed.) *The Cambridge Companion to Heidegger*, Cambridge: Cambridge University Press, 1993, p. 319.

20 Alexander Nehamas, *Nietzsche: Life as Literature*, Cambridge, Mass. and London: Harvard University Press, 1985, p. 210.

21 A different but somewhat parallel argument against the Kantian-Christian conception of morality is advanced by Bernard Williams in his *Ethics and the Limits of Philosophy*, London: Fontana, 1985.

22 Nietzsche's best statement of his critique of morality is probably that in his book *The Genealogy of Morals*.

23 Max Horkheimer and Theodor Adorno, *Dialectic of Enlightenment*, New York: Seabury Press, 1972, p. 23.

24 E. M. Cioran, 'Joseph de Maistre: An Essay on Reactionary Thought', in Cioran, *Anathemas and Admirations*, London: Quartet Books, 1992, pp. 28–9.

25 Max Horkheimer, 'Schopenhauer Today', in his *Critique of Instrumental Reason*, New York: Seabury Press, 1974, p. 72.

26 For an illuminating account of Hume's influence upon Hamman and Kierkegaard, see Isaiah Berlin's marvellous essay, 'Hume and the Sources of German Anti-Rationalism', in his *Against the Current*.

27 M. Heidegger, 'The Word of Nietzsche', in his *The Question Concerning Technology and Other Essays*, New York: Garland, 1977, pp. 62–3.

28 Ibid., p. 100. Heidegger's often idiosyncratic interpretation of Nietzsche is set out in his book, *Nietzsche*, 4 vols, New York: Harper & Row, 1979–82. Vol. 3, *The Will to Power as Knowledge and as Metaphysics*, and vol. 4, *Nihilism*, are particularly relevant to my present inquiry.

29 M. Heidegger, 'A Letter to a Young Student', in his *Poetry, Language and Thought*, New York: Harper & Row, p. 185.

30 The phrase comes from Stillman and Pfaff, *The Politics of Hysteria*, p. 78.

31 Ernest Gellner, *Conditions of Liberty: Civil Society and its Rivals*, London: Hamish Hamilton, 1994, chs 3 and 6.

32 Richard Rorty, *Contingency, Irony and Solidarity*, Cambridge: Cambridge University Press, 1989, pp. 44–5.

33 Ibid., p. 60.

34 Richard Rorty, *Objectivity, Relativism and Truth: Philosophical Papers*, vol. 1, Cambridge: Cambridge University Press, 1991, pp. 198–9.

35 Ibid., p. 194.

36 Rorty, *Essays on Heidegger and Others*, p. 48.

37 Rorty, *Objectivity, Relativism and Truth*, p. 209.

38 Ibid., p. 213.

39 Michael Billig, 'Nationalism and Richard Rorty: The Text as a Flag for *Pax Americana*', in *New Left Review*, no. 202, November–December 1993, p. 78. Another relevant criticism of Rorty's liberalism is that of Ronald Beiner in his 'Richard Rorty's Liberalism', *Critical Review*, vol. 7, no. 1, Winter 1993. A tough-minded but ultimately uncompelling critique of Rorty's pragmatism is found in Bernard Williams's

'Auto-da-Fe: Consequences of Pragmatism', in Alan Malachowski (ed.) *Reading Rorty*, Oxford: Basil Blackwell, 1990.

40 Rorty, *Essays on Heidegger and Others*, p. 159.

41 Ibid., p. 159.

42 Ibid., p. 161.

43 Rorty, 'Freud and Moral Reflection', in *Essays on Heidegger and Others*, especially pp. 157–8.

44 See Rorty's 'Wittgenstein, Heidegger and the Reification of Language', in his *Essays on Heidegger and Others*.

45 For an illuminating study of some of Heidegger's later views on language, see Charles Taylor, 'Heidegger, Language and Ecology', in Hubert L. Dreyfus and Harrison Hall (eds) *Heidegger: A Critical Reader*, Oxford: Basil Blackwell, 1991.

46 MacIntyre, *Whose Justice? Which Rationality?*, p. 345.

47 Heidegger, *Discourse on Thinking*, p. 55.

48 I owe the phrase 'world revolution of Westernization' to Theodore H. von Laue's interesting book of that title: T. H. von Laue, *The World Revolution of Westernization: The Twentieth Century in Global Perspective*, Oxford and New York: Oxford University Press, 1987.

49 I do not claim that this way of speaking or thinking is Heidegger's. If anything it inverts Heidegger's account of the relations between ontological and ecological concerns.

50 There are excellent critiques of Heidegger's anthropocentrism in John D. Caputo's *Demythologising Heidegger*, Bloomington, Ind.: Indiana University Press, 1993, especially pp. 122–3; in David Farrell Krell's *Daimon Life: Heidegger and Life-Philosophy*, Bloomington, Ind.: Indiana University Press, 1992, especially pp. 119–26; and, from the standpoint of the Kyoto School, in Masao Abe's *A Study of Dogen*, ed. Steven Heine, Albany, NY: State University of New York Press, 1992, especially pp. 125–41.

51 On Heidegger's debt to German mysticism, see John Caputo's excellent book, *The Mystical Element in Heidegger's Thought*, New York: Fordham University Press, 1986.

52 I have benefited from Hubert L. Dreyfus's paper, 'Heidegger on the Connection between Nihilism, Art Technology and Politics', in Guignon (ed.) *The Cambridge Companion to Heidegger*.

53 Heidegger, *What is Called Thinking?*, p. 119. On some interpretations of Heidegger, the view I defend in this paragraph is akin to that which Heidegger advanced in his last writings: see Caputo, *The Mystical*

Element in Heidegger's Thought; but I do not claim Heidegger's authority for my view.

54 I have discussed the Gaia conception in 'An Agenda for Green Conservatism', in my *Beyond the New Right*, ch. 4.

55 For the attempt to link Heidegger's thought with the a-theist and non-humanist spirituality of certain Buddhist and Taoist traditions, see Graham Parkes (ed.) *Heidegger and Asian Thought*, Honolulu: University of Hawaii Press, 1987. For more detailed studies of the affinities, and differences, between Heidegger's thought and Japanese Buddhist thinking, see Steven Heine, *Existential and Ontological Dimensions of Time in Heidegger and Dogen*, Albany, NY: State University of New York Press, 1985; Joan Stambaugh, *Impermanence is Buddha-Nature*, Honolulu: University of Hawaii Press, 1990; and, especially, Keiji Nishitani, *Religion and Nothingness*, Berkeley, Calif.: University of California Press, 1982. For a study of contrasts and affinities between the thought of the later Wittgenstein and Tibetan philosophy, see Robert A. F. Thurman, *The Central Philosophy of Tibet: A Study and Translation of Jey Tsong Khapa's 'Essence of True Eloquence'*, Princeton, NJ: Princeton University Press, 1991, especially pp. 90–111.

INDEX